NOT FOR LONG

NOT FOR LONG

THE LIFE AND CAREER
OF THE NFL ATHLETE

ROBERT W.
TURNER II

OXFORD
UNIVERSITY PRESS

Oxford University Press is a department of the University of Oxford. It furthers
the University's objective of excellence in research, scholarship, and education
by publishing worldwide. Oxford is a registered trade mark of Oxford University
Press in the UK and certain other countries.

Published in the United States of America by Oxford University Press
198 Madison Avenue, New York, NY 10016, United States of America.

Library of Congress Cataloging-in-Publication Data
Names: Turner, Robert W., II, 1962– author.
Title: Not for long : the life and career of the NFL athlete / Robert W. Turner, II.
Description: New York, NY, United States of America : Oxford University
Press, [2018] | Includes bibliographical references and index.
Identifiers: LCCN 2017052760 | ISBN 9780199892907 (bb : alk. paper) |
ISBN 9780199892914 (updf) | ISBN 9780190872854 (epub)
Subjects: LCSH: Football—United States—Social aspects. | Football
players—United States—Social conditions. | Football players—Health and
hygiene—United States. | National Football League. | Football injuries.
Classification: LCC GV951.T87 2018 | DDC 796.332/64—dc23
LC record available at https://lccn.loc.gov/2017052760

1 3 5 7 9 8 6 4 2

Printed by Sheridan Books, Inc, United States of America

FOR ROBERT AND DOLORES

Words cannot express the love I feel for you.

God bless you, always.

I owe a debt of gratitude to:

Coach Tom Higgins Sr., Piscataway High School

Coach Challace Joe McMillan, James Madison University

Coach Joe Carico, James Madison University

Dr. Richard Southall

Intellectual giants:

Dr. Stanley Aronowitz

Dr. Carol Stack

Dr. Keith E. Whitfield

Dr. James S. Jackson

Dr. Tamera Coyne-Beasley

Former teammates

and

To all the athletes who participated in this study

Peace, Love, and much Respect

CONTENTS

PROLOGUE: NFL MEANS *NOT FOR LONG*

INJURY, INDISCRETION, OR ILLNESS—any one of these can instantly end a lifetime of work for the professional American football player. Fail to be in the right place at the right time or demonstrate a propensity to be in the wrong place at the wrong time and you're out. Get distracted by social, familial, or personal obligations and you're out. A single misstep can leave you benched, block your hopes of a better contract or free agency, or take you out of the league all together. Your time on the field isn't the most brutal part of a life lived for and in the National Football League (NFL); it's the constant, gnawing uncertainty of what comes next. Every player knows that "NFL" really stands for "Not For Long."

To be a typical NFL athlete is to know that no matter how tired or horrible you feel, you must play better than everyone else in your position. If you can't deliver what the coach, the general manager, and the owner want, you're utterly replaceable. Thousands of eager athletes are waiting to suit up in your place—including some who would happily betray you to advance their own fleeting careers. Because each athlete is highly skilled and cultivated but always disposable, the pressure resting on those shoulder pads is immense and the surveillance is extreme. Every cab ride, workout, and social interaction is observed and recorded, and any bad behavior can be swiftly and harshly punished. By day, you will spend 12 to 16 hours absorbed in football-related activities: training, practice, game films, team meetings, position-specific training, and playbook memorization, but "blowing off some steam" is verboten. Day by day, your body will be pounded, crushed, bruised, and strained; your pain will likely be long term and debilitating; and you will face life-threatening, even deadly injuries over and over and over. Then you'll get up and do it again because it's what you've worked for—what your family, friends, mentors, and coaches have worked for—your whole life, and yet your grasp on this career, this persona of "pro football player," is so tenuous.

NFL athletes exert all of this effort and make great sacrifices along a career path that often starts in childhood but pays off, on average, for only 3.1 years, if at all.[1] By the time players reach the age of 27 or 28, their careers, even the most incredibly accomplished professional football players, are often finished. Then what?

To be an NFL athlete is to know all of this and to want to play anyway because being a professional football player means that you are the toughest, strongest, and fastest. You are the most agile, aggressive, and sleekest *badd azz* out there.

I know, because this is my story.

This text draws from my personal narrative as well as interviews and shared experiences with over 140 high school, college, current, and former NFL athletes. Now a sociologist, I'm well positioned to offer an insider's view of the complex, tournament-style competition required to get into the league, the institution that requires this development process and policies that shape football player's career, and the after-effects of the game, lingering long and looming large in the often truncated lives of participant-athletes after the NFL.

My own tenure in the Big Show was relatively brief. When the general manager of the San Francisco 49ers called me into his office, it was an abrupt dismissal. He said, as if it was a normal, everyday conversation for him, "We will give you a one-way airplane ticket anywhere. So where do you want to go?"

A lifetime of dreams, of preparations, routines, discipline, and work came crashing down around me, and I had no answer for his question. Where did I want to go? I didn't know. What was I going to do? I didn't know. How could I carry on? I didn't know. How would I make money? I didn't know. How would I face my friends and family as a failure? I couldn't.

From age 10 until my late 20s, my life revolved around football. I spent five years of my adult life chasing and living my dream of playing professionally: first in the United States Football League (USFL), then in the Canadian Football League (CFL), and finally, with a brief stint in the National Football League (NFL). Four seasons of jumping across leagues and living in different cities had already taken their toll by the time I got that hardest hit. I called my agent and told him I was done.

After the NFL, I experienced a crisis in my very soul. I felt depressed, hopeless, and upended. I avoided my friends and family. I drifted around towns and cycled through jobs, searching for something that would give me the excitement and meaning I found playing football. Nothing worked.

People lose jobs or change careers frequently. It happens all the time. So why were men like me—the toughest, fastest, most aggressive, masculine athletes—so fragile when faced with the quotidian tasks of life outside the league? As I found my path, training in sociology and studying the contours of a professional athlete's training and labor, the commodification of human bodies in a violent spectacle, and the institutions that cultivate and corral ideal players (but leave them almost wholly unprepared for their exit), I began to think of my "reentry" to civilian life as a peculiar and makeshift project. What social conditions make some football players more vulnerable than others when facing an unceremonious dismissal? What does it take to survive and succeed in life after football? And if these skills and coping mechanisms are taught earlier in the lives of football players—right alongside routes and plays—can that intervention help them to lead happy and productive lives when their playing time is up? Not only did I need to answer these questions for myself but I felt I owed it to those who came before and who would come after me to learn what happens and what *should* happen when your not-for-long career comes to a screeching halt.

PREFACE: THE ATHLETES' JOURNEY THROUGH THE NATIONAL FOOTBALL LEAGUE

IN HIS SEMINAL BOOK, *The Power Elite*, sociologist C. Wright Mills presents the concept of the military-industrial complex, a profit-driven alliance of business and governmental interests that connects seemingly independent profit-seeking parties around the business of war.[1] The term was quickly adopted as a paradigm for the dominant elements of a capitalist power structure, whether applied to the construction of big white weddings or the mounting specter of mass incarceration. Since the merger between the American Football League (AFL) and the National Football League (NFL) in 1970, the NFL has evolved from a loose confederation of teams in pursuit of the thrill of victory to an entity so popular, vast, and profitable that it is known as the crown jewel of the American "sports-industrial complex." The wheel of the football enterprise spins constantly these days. When a player steps onto the wheel, he embraces a system that benefits from the eventual obsolescence of his body. For this modern-day gladiator, the rules are simple—if you win, you continue; if you lose, you're finished. In fact, sorting individuals into groups of winners and losers using the outcome of sport tournaments so significantly threatens and controls the livelihood and ambition of players that the governing system of football essentially functions as a *totalizing institution*. Based on sociologist Erving Goffman's description of places such as prisons and the military as *total institutions* because they contain and entirely control such a wide array of human activities, my use of "totalizing" reflects a change to the individual himself.[2] Obviously, unlike prisoners and enlisted soldiers, a football player may exit his situation at will. However, the mental conditioning and indoctrinating processes of those athletes aggressively set on a career in professional football are incompatible with quitting.

In this book, I explore how the sports-industrial complex in its operation as a totalizing institution contributes to athletes' socialization and to Black male marginalization by presenting data collected from ongoing, situated, micro-level interactions with current and former players. I identify a number of structural and racial inequalities that an elite group of mostly White wealthy men use to exert almost total control over the bodies and social fortunes of professional football players—approximately 70% of whom are Black.[3]

Ultimately, the immense profit and control accrued by a few powerful individuals, combined with the willingness of players to suppress their desires and identities in order to share in the bounty, create such momentum that, as the wheel spins, it regularly jettisons players, sending them spinning off into the ether. Some fall early, some fall late; very few manage to hang on to the game long enough to achieve transformative success through football.

Social prestige and economic gain are just two of the many promises used to lure individuals into pinning their hopes and dreams on a career in the NFL. An athlete might want to play football because of a desire to receive recognition and establish a legacy in the folklore of our nation. After all, the American public loves a good success story. One of the most popular of these is *The Blind Side*, Michael Lewis's 2007 biography of Michael Oher, who was born into abject poverty in 1986 and through grit, gumption, and the help of a caring White family, was drafted in the first round of the 2009 NFL draft by the Baltimore Ravens.[4] Oher's up-by-the-bootstraps, rags-to-riches story became an Oscar-nominated film, and audiences wept and cheered every step along his path toward glory.[5] Similarly, Oliver Stone's 1999 movie *Any Given Sunday* demonstrates the aphrodisiac allure of fame and elite social status.[6] Add 24-hour sports programming into the cultural mix, and readers will understand how easily the celebrity a professional athlete enjoys can influence the career dreams of so many young people.

The seductive success myth of NFL athletes created by the dream-weavers at the NFL and perpetuated by the media leads most Americans to believe that all football players are paid gargantuan salaries just to *play* a game that they love. The NFL's press releases announcing multiyear deals with athletes for tens of millions of dollars, repeated media portrayals of sports professionals "making it rain" money at strip clubs, and reports of NFL athletes spending money on luxury automobiles, mansions, jewelry, fancy clothes, and other consumables lend credence to the perception that an NFL athlete has vast wealth. For the majority of players, the opposite is true.[7]

Rarely does one hear about how the game can and does leave bodies broken, identities in flux, and athletes vulnerable to exploitation. I address this deficit by sharing stories and insights from current and former players, especially around what I call "involuntary role exit"—or the social condition caused by a sudden or forced departure from a highly coveted social role. By sharing these insights, this work adds to the sociological understanding of the role exit process by shifting the focus to the involuntary exit from a desirable social position.

Do football players contribute to their own vulnerabilities? Michel Foucault contends, "The body is the surface on which the social is inscribed."[8] Likewise, Loïc Wacquant reminds us that a sociological investigation of the body is well suited to uncover the varied ways in which "specific social worlds, invest, shape, and deploy human bodies to the concrete incorporating practices whereby their social structures are effectively embodied by the agents who partake in them."[9] How does one investigate "the social inscription" of a person who obfuscates discovery by unwittingly adhering to the unwritten precepts of masculinity and the verbal veil of pride in order to advance in the sport tournament?

I had to gain the trust of the participants in order to see the social vulnerabilities behind athletes' prideful masculine façades and glimpse this "inscription" process on individual athletes. I re-immersed myself in the world of football. I worked out with the athletes, coached them from the sidelines, and accompanied them in their daily activities, all while understanding the importance of the investigator's own—that is, my own—organism, senses, and embodied intellect. To conduct a thorough, ethnographic, sociological investigation, I employed "various participation-like methods, of the structures of the life-world, meaning the forms, structures or features that people take as objectively existing in the world as they shape their conduct upon the presumption of their prior independent existence."[10] Years after ending my own football career, I jumped back in so that I might learn from the athletes as they worked their way into, through, and eventually out of the league. I learned that football players have a tremendous amount to teach us—about athletics no doubt, but perhaps even more so about our world and ourselves.

My scholarly mentor and personal friend Dr. Stanley Aronowitz reminded me often as I undertook this study that the key to understanding how and why athletes struggle in adjusting to life after football could be found in their personal life histories. Just as one cannot truly understand a game without first examining how the rules impact strategy, one cannot interpret the struggles and challenges of exiting football—at least for those athletes who view sports as a means for upward mobility or social status—without scrutinizing the personal histories, the social and symbolic relations of athletes' lives, and the structural and hidden cultural engine of American sports. As one of the central characters in this manuscript, OD, a former wide receiver for the New York Giants, offers a window into how athletes' lives are forever changed the moment a coach, a parent, an uncle, an older sibling, or a mentor identifies them as a *special talent*. As much as OD's story validated my choice to blend two sociological approaches (the life history and what is called a symbolic interactionist perspective), his testimony also served as a reminder of the myriad minefields athletes encounter as they transition through pivotal stages in their careers.

Michael Messner, in *White Men Misbehaving: Feminism, Afrocentrism, and the Promise of a Critical Standpoint,* and Michael Kimmel, in his 2005 book of essays *The Gender of Desire,* have documented how the rewards of masculinity inspire boys and young men to make tremendous sacrifices in the name of sports.[11] I investigate these rewards and follow their keen focus on the consequences of masculinity—including men's self-censorship and loss of voice in the larger social conversation and their common unwillingness to report vulnerability or hardship.[12] Perhaps, I thought, football players' voices are muted because they are thought to be strong and capable, but not too bright. Or, perhaps instead of speaking out, players are encouraged to focus solely on entertaining the masses rather than worrying about the risks they take on by playing the game. Former NFL player Darnell Dinkins said as much during the 2010–2011 NFL owner's lockout, proclaiming that players are seen as commodities, not people.[13] I argue that the ever-increasing supply of new recruits makes it possible for owners to see players not only as commodities to be bought, sold, and traded, but also as *expendable* entities, easily replaced when broken. The impact of that attitude on the psyches of current and former players is palpable. It gives rise to a great deal of bitterness and conflicted masculinity.

Wacquant asserts that before initiating a study, the essential first step is for the sociologist to immerse himself in and acclimate himself to the organizational field of his subject; through intensive training, the researcher might then come to comprehend the cerebral, artistic, principled habits, and day-to-day behaviors of his subjects.[14] Given my experience playing football, from the Pop Warner Leagues, through high school, college, and into the professional leagues, I had already inhabited the world of football. I shared a common vocabulary and understood the attitudes and vulnerabilities that develop from players' on- and off-field experiences (Figure P.1). This common ground helped me gain access to the more intimate aspects of my subjects' lives and stories, while my sociological skills allowed to me convert my understanding of the game's personal and social impact into an understanding of its meaningful essence. My insider status dramatically helped my entry into the field and allowed me to adequately dissect and communicate its processes without destroying its distinguishable characteristics, as I knew them. It also meant this study was a personal one.

FIGURE P.1: ROBERT "PACKY" TURNER AND FORMER PISCATAWAY HIGH SCHOOL ASSISTANT FOOTBALL COACH JOHN MAMMON.

When I traveled to preseason training camp for the Calgary Stampeders of the Canadian Football League (CFL) in Calgary, Alberta—the team for which I had played for two seasons many years earlier—I experienced both a shock and an odd reassurance kindled by excessive familiarity. I intended to merely reacclimate to my old surroundings and collect some preliminary data, particularly about how the world of professional football had changed since my career had ended 15 years earlier, and I was met with surprising warmth and support from my former high school football coach's son, Tom Higgins Jr., now head coach of the Stampeders and, hereafter, simply Coach Higgins. He greeted me as though no time had passed at all. He granted me unrestricted access to the team's training facilities, locker room, team management, and coaching staff, requiring only that in order to avoid an appearance of bias or endorsement of my project, I schedule interviews with athletes who volunteered to participate in my study through the team's marketing director. Then, Coach Higgins invited me to a private team barbeque cookout at a local amusement park so that I might meet the athletes and their families.

Within a week, something wonderful began to happen. As I shared my experiences, the athletes began to open up with their own stories. This initial set of semi-formal interviews proved so promising that I extended my trip. I remained in Calgary for six weeks conducting additional interviews and immersing myself in the daily lives of the athletes as a participant observer. Athletes began inviting me to their homes for dinner. They let me join in with them to play video games, attend private gatherings, bar hop, and hang out in VIP rooms at night clubs. I had encouraged my informants to choose the location of the interview, either for the sake of convenience or their privacy, and they invited me into their lives.

Overall, I conducted 35 initial and follow-up interviews in Calgary. I recorded audio and took handwritten notes, checking field notes against recordings so that I could ensure consistency and add nuance to mere words. Coding my notes and audio transcripts helped me find recurring themes and develop follow-up questions. One of my most prominent early findings was that I needed to learn more about athletes' personal life histories; that led to accumulating some 300 hours of documentation in Calgary, along with face-to-face interactions and field observations in California, Texas, New York, New Jersey, Florida, Connecticut, North Carolina, Wisconsin, and Maryland.

I had soon gathered some additional 50 hours of recorded phone calls (all recordings were made with the explicit consent of the interview subject, whether by phone or in person), dozens of unrecorded phone conversations (documented through field notes), nearly 1,000 hours of interviews, over 200 email exchanges, and countless hours of observations.

I conducted the majority of these interviews and observations with athletes, family members, coaches, sports agents, personal trainers, combine training facility owners, and other individuals involved in the world of amateur and professional football from January 2006 through the spring of 2015. I lived with athletes and their families, traveled with former NFL athletes to watch their sons play college football, and attended Super Bowl games. Each of these experiences developed my sensitivity to the subtle nuances of athletes' search for respect. Each encouraged me to reflect upon and analyze my own experiences, even as my sociological training forced skepticism and curiosity. I continued to log and review my written notes regularly—as I had in Calgary—after each interaction, using emerging findings to guide my next steps.

Throughout the study, I drew upon my sociological training and years of football experience to situate the subjects' words and actions within their cultural context. Observations of athletes' everyday lives allowed me to develop more reliable inferences than if I had depended solely on questionnaires. That is, the process of fieldwork allowed me to look beyond the narratives and perceptions presented by the athletes and to search for other factors influencing their behavior.[15] I researched details of each athlete's NFL background, gathered information for compiling his life history, and culled the data to find any apparent inconsistencies.

An important academic goal of my research is to reintroduce sport as a primary location for critical investigation. Since the 1990s, it has been pushed to the fringes of sociology; of the nearly 55 sections within the American Sociological Association, not one concentrates on sport as a subfield. Harry Edwards's assessment is an excellent summation of my own perspective: "American's traditional relegation of sports to the 'toy department' of human affairs neglects both its significance as an institution and the seriousness of its impact upon social relations and development."[16] As scholars and lay readers alike consider the empirical evidence presented in this book, I hope they will agree that sport can serve as a microcosm of the larger society.

By approaching sport as a site for social interaction, I believe anyone can explore racial and gender inequality, the roles and functions of institutions and organizations in individual lives, health and injury, aging, and people's experiences of work and labor. Through the prism of sport—alone and together—these topics can help any interested person gain a deeper understanding of our country and our world.

Professional football players are members of an elite club. Membership promises an increase in social capital, maybe even a status upgrade. I learned that the bonds between players and the lengths to which we athletes will go to impress, support, and make sacrifices for one another are two football themes that are both understudied and misunderstood.[17] For me, former NFL athletes Big Al and OD embodied the spirit of football brotherhood.

Over our 20-plus-year relationship, Big Al shared countless stories about the challenges of adjusting to life after the NFL. Reuniting with my old friend reminded me of the special bond I share with those few men who have dedicated their lives and bodies to a sport that is both unforgiving and nurturing, rigid yet artful, violent yet rewarding. Watching Big Al come face-to-face with the highs and lows that define the experience of life after an early exit from football helped me realize that few are equipped to successfully navigate the many obstacles that litter the road ahead of them. Though in the throes of financial uncertainty and personal upheaval, Big Al earned my undying love and admiration for generously sharing his kindness, ideas, and assistance with me and, in many ways, with the readers of this book.

OD, too, figured prominently in the creation of this book. OD's willingness to share his vulnerabilities deeply enriched this study, and, in turn, my life. He taught me to cope with and make sense of the challenging and often difficult life courses of athletes.

Finally, UC Berkeley Emeritus Professor Carol Stack, author of the ground-breaking works *All Our Kin* and *Call to Home*, figured prominently in guiding this project.[18] For two years, I sat across Carol's dining room table, breaking bread and discussing strategies for making my research accessible to the social scientific community, the football fan, and the general reader alike. Carol impressed upon me the central mission of ethnography—that those who use ethnography as a tool of discovery must seek to uncover the underlying patterns and processes that show how people live their lives. Through our weekly interactions, Carol challenged me to move beyond the typical methods of qualitative research, in which quotes and anecdotes are used to put human faces to the numbers of quantitative studies or to represent macro-level discoveries. Countless conversations with Carol resulted in months of reexamining, reviewing, and immersing myself in my dialogues with athletes, coaches, wives, parents, athletic trainers, agents, and others. She pushed me to find patterns that reveal personal and group vulnerability in social life. In the same way that her books underline the importance of reflexivity in conducting research on the rural poor, Carol impressed upon me that I must continuously challenge my own assumptions about sports in America. The shape and tenor of this manuscript were molded time and again through Carol's encouragement, support, and crucial insistence that I dig deeper, that I seek the motivations and reasons behind the stories my subjects shared.

A career in the NFL is, in many ways, a privilege. Still, where we often expect meritocracy, ruled by the best athletes and coaches, race and class permeate the experiences of Black NFL athletes. The perceptions of minority and White participation in sports differ, specifically because of the historical meanings and codes attached to race. In this book, I construct a historical analysis of the Black NFL athlete that maps out the social conditions that make the game irresistible to legions of African American male youth who may view playing in the NFL as one of the few remaining viable paths toward upward economic mobility and social relevance.

Fortunate enough to have a career in football, these athletes may be unprepared to handle the conflicting demands of the social world they enter. By and large, they will be uniquely unprepared for life after the game. Many athletes left the sport before they were ready or willing. Their early retirement caused these individuals tremendous stress and consternation. Playing was their primary or "master status." What came next had, in some ways, never occurred to them. Having already made that rocky exit myself, I scoured my own memory and my data to try to determine an ideal path for those players experiencing involuntary role exit. How could social context be deployed to scaffold a player's journey through and out of the system? What concessions can be made, what instruction can be offered, what training can be given to facilitate success after an early exit from the game? In the end of this book, I offer a discussion focused on what can be done to protect boys and young men against the exploitation, manipulation, and objectification that fuel the world of football alongside the many joys of a career, no matter how short, at the upper echelons of sport.

Social scientists have long sought to understand the lived experiences of individuals and groups. When I initiated this project as my doctoral dissertation, I wanted to help give a voice to the boys and men who play a challenging, fascinating, frequently dangerous sport. This book, a transformed and enlivened extension of that dissertation, is my attempt to educate sports enthusiasts and the curious bystander, but also, and perhaps more important, to arm parents, mentors, and coaches with knowledge to guide young athletes through the emotional and physical minefield known as American football.

Academic Progress Rate (APR)
American Football Conference (AFC)
American Football League (AFL)
Arena Football (AFL)
Canadian Football League (CFL)
Canadian Total Sports Network (TSN)
Chronic Traumatic Encephalopathy (CTE)
Collective Bargaining Agreement (CBA)
Defined Gross Revenues (DGR)
Entertainment and Sports Programming Network (ESPN)
Football Bowl Series (FBS)
Gross Domestic Product (GDP)
Group Licensing Authorization (GLA)
James Madison University (JMU)
Louisiana State University (LSU)
Major League Baseball (MLB)
Major League Baseball Players Association (MLBPA)
Mild Traumatic Brain Injury (mTBI)
National Collegiate Athletic Association (NCAA)
National Football Conference (NFC)
National Football League (NFL)
National Hockey League (NHL)
National Labor Relations Board (NLRB)
NFL Management Council (NFLMC)
NFL Players Association (NFLPA)
Olympic Project for Human Rights (OPHR)

Optional Training Activities (OTAs)
Organized Team Practice Activities (OTAs)
Personal Conduct Policy (PCP)
Predominantly White Institution (PWI)
Southeastern Conference (SEC)
Sports Broadcasting Act (SBA)
Sports-Industrial Complex (SIC)
United States Football League (USFL)
US Football League (USFL)

NOT FOR LONG

1

BROKE AND BROKEN

I WAS CHATTING with my buddy Steve K at a cocktail lounge in New York City's East Village—the kind of place young Wall Street types gather to enjoy overpriced martinis after a long day of trading—when I felt a tap on my shoulder. Suddenly I was engulfed in a bear hug that nearly lifted me off my barstool. "Robert Turner! Where you been, man?"

It was Big Al, a former tight end who played eight seasons in the National Football League (NFL). Fifteen years earlier, Big Al had encouraged the San Francisco 49ers to sign me to a free agent contract. He had served as my personal mentor and trainer for off-season workouts. Now, having released his bear hug around my back, Big Al explained that these days, to make ends meet, he was working as a bouncer at night and selling vitamins for a multi-level marketing company during the day. Four nights a week he would clock in at the bar around 10:00 PM to check IDs, bus beer bottles, and ensure young Wall Street hustlers remained orderly as they imbibed overpriced craft beers; at 4:00 AM, he would dash from the lower eastside of Manhattan to Penn Station and catch a train back to New Jersey. Since he was on duty when we ran into each other, we agreed to have lunch later in the week.

Though he was born in Drew, Mississippi, Big Al grew up just across the river from Ferguson, Missouri, in the hardscrabble world of East St. Louis, Illinois,[1] where the per capita income in 2013 was $11,618.[2] Big Al is no stranger to hard times. He is the kind of guy who looks for positive solutions to problems instead of dwelling on the negative. It seems like he's always busy organizing for this or that good cause, gathering other former athletes to help draw a crowd for charity and hopefully earn a little pocket change in the process.

Big Al was the Kansas City Chiefs' team representative for the NFL Players Association (NFLPA) during the season leading up to the 1982 strike. His was the deciding vote as to whether the team would enter the field on that Sunday afternoon in mid-September. In the weeks leading up to that game, Big Al received threats from across the league: if he decided to support the strike various league officials promised it would be the end of his NFL career.[3] Ultimately, he elected to support the strike because he believed all players needed severance pay, insurance, a pension, and a wage scale.[4] He was released by the Chiefs at the end of the season and then signed by the Philadelphia Eagles, where he played 10 games in 1983. He started the 1984 season (his last) for the San Diego Chargers, and then moved over to Bill Walsh's San Francisco 49ers. They won the Super Bowl that year, and then it was over. Just like that.

In 2009, *Sports Illustrated*[5] reported that within two years of retirement, 78% of all NFL athletes are bankrupt or in financial distress as a result of joblessness or divorce; a working paper released by the National Bureau of Economic Research reports that nearly 16% of NFL players drafted between 1996 and 2003 declared bankruptcy within 12 years of retirement.[6] Often while presenting these and other findings from my research at conferences and on university campuses, people ask two questions: How can sports professionals who earn so much money during their careers "go broke?" Why isn't the NFL doing more to help these former athletes? These questions raise important concerns that are addressed throughout this book.

Watching Big Al come face-to-face with the highs and lows that define life after football helped me realize that the road traveled by current and former athletes isn't optional or, for anyone other than the athlete himself, unexpected. But it is one for which players, released from the game that has occupied their bodies and minds since grade school or early adolescence, are often wholly unprepared. No wonder it seemed so many were faltering and failing along that same, well-traveled road.

At lunch after that fateful reunion, Big Al filled me in on the years since we'd last met. There had been personal challenges: his wife struggled with health issues that prevented her from working, his youngest daughter dropped out of college and moved back home to raise her baby, and each of his four other children was having trouble making ends meet. As the proud African American patriarch, Big Al wouldn't say that he was struggling financially and would never let on that life after the NFL had not turned out as expected. After all, it goes against the grain of the NFL's hyper-masculine culture and seemingly against the nature of many NFL athletes to show stress, ask for help, or admit vulnerability. In fact, in spite of the challenges of his present situation, Big Al insisted on picking up the tab for lunch that day. He said that he had gotten a good tip the night before. I accepted his generosity, then offered him a position as a marketing rep at the sports marketing firm I directed.

Financial pressure from immediate and extended family members or friends often plagues NFL athletes. OD, a former wide receiver for the New York Giants (Figure 1.1), said while he was playing relatives would constantly hit him up for money. It was like "I was the family's fucking ATM, because I was in the NFL."

In addition to financial difficulties, the NFL Players Association reports that 65% of 870 former NFL athletes reported having experienced a major on-the-field injury that required surgery or forced them to miss at least eight games.[7] According to Ken Ruettgers, former Green Bay Packer and founder of gamesover.org, 65% of former athletes endure chronic pain from permanent injury within one year of retirement.

FIGURE 1.1: ODESSA TURNER WITH THE NEW YORK GIANTS.

Athletes know that as employees of the NFL, they are well compensated to play a collision sport that places them at a high risk for injury. What a lot of people don't know is the extent to which injury leads to their early exit from the league. If the injury is severe enough, the player may not be able to work again in *any* capacity. That means that at the age of 27 or 28, when most NFL athletes exit from the game, severely injured athletes are cut off from their source of income. Many have yet to figure out what transferable skills they possess or realize they are frequently unqualified to do other kinds of jobs, and they usually haven't been in the league long enough to qualify for benefits. So are the NFL and the NFL Players Association under any obligation to ensure the well-being of these athletes? What level of responsibility rests on the league and the Player's Union for the health and financial concerns of former NFL athletes?

One day, when I met with OD, he was holding a large manila envelope containing X-ray film and MRI images that he wanted to show me. The menisci (the rubbery cartilage discs that cushion the knee joint) in both of his knees had completely degenerated. His doctors said that the only remedy for his pain would be full joint replacement on each leg—even while every surgeon he visited refused. He was "too young" to have both knee joints replaced. Each day that his femur and tibia grind together, his osteoarthritis worsens. He held an MRI film up to the light: "You can't tell by looking at it, but I have three ruptured discs in my lower back, too." And ever since his second concussion, OD experiences searing migraine headaches.

OD declared, "Rob, living like this is embarrassing. I feel like a fucking old man. Here I am in my forties, and I can't do shit 'cause my body is all fucked up. I used to be able to do anything I wanted to do on the football field, and now I can't even take a shit without it hurting sometimes." For each NFL franchise he'd played under, he saw another team of doctors. After all their tests, he felt injured again. It was an emotional blow to see how badly his body was broken.

OD was a married 21-year-old father when the New York Giants drafted him in 1987. Since the Giants were fresh off a Super Bowl victory, OD wasn't called on to be a starter as a rookie; instead, he was expected to be a main contributor on a star-studded team. In his fourth season, OD helped the Giants secure their second Super Bowl victory. Although a knee injury required surgery and prevented him from playing in "the Big Game," OD was a starter in the wide receiver slot and a top special teams performer that season.[8]

In the late 1980s, athletes ruled the New York City club scene. New York Mets stars Darrell Strawberry and Dwight Gooden, alongside OD's Giants teammate Lawrence Taylor, fueled headlines with rumors of illicit drug use and wild partying. OD enjoyed hanging out with Taylor and his other teammates at the strip clubs, bars, and discos, but the bright lights of Broadway really weren't his speed. One time, he recalled, he and Taylor (now a Hall of Fame linebacker) went to a strip club. Taylor confessed that sometimes it would be nice to be just another guy on the team: "OD you got it good. You don't know what it's like to have people constantly recognizing you everywhere." Still, even though OD wasn't the biggest star on the team, just playing in New York meant there were plenty of distractions to go around. OD says he stayed away from serious drugs like cocaine or heroin, for the most part, because he had two young boys at home. But to handle the pressure and pain, he joined many of his teammates and other athletes in the league in smoking marijuana daily.

A second serious knee injury came in the 1991 season. The NY Giants opted to omit OD from the 37-man protected roster, leaving him without Plan-B free agency protection.[9] Eventually, the San Francisco 49ers claimed his rights—and good thing, too. The 49ers were Super Bowl contenders with Joe Montana at quarterback, and they signed OD to a more lucrative contract than he had with the Giants. In two successful years with the 49ers, OD's injuries continued to mount. He suffered another knee injury and two concussions. Injuries meant missed games, and missed games meant boredom. OD said he started smoking excessive amounts of marijuana in San Francisco, where he was bored and living in a hotel while his wife and kids remained in New Jersey. OD said he and a fellow teammate were placed on the injured reserves list, traveling with the team for away games but spending most of their time blazing up a bong or smoking joints in their hotel rooms. Female groupies would visit and party with them "since they had nothing better to do." A little oddly, OD looks back fondly on that time in his career: he was "getting paid and having the time of his life." He had no idea that years later, he would be suing the NFL for disability and early retirement benefits.

After eight years in the league, OD was cut by the 49ers. Before calling it quits, though, he attended camp with the Minnesota Vikings, and then moved to the Canadian Football League to play for the Ottawa Roughriders. When OD learned that I had played in Calgary, he told me he preferred the CFL to the NFL because football in the United States is "really only about big business."

Now, my experience conducting research with athletes has taught me that like so many other entertainers, they can be prone to embellish their careers. I know I have (partly because it was difficult to accept that I could no longer play the game I loved). Talking to OD spurred me to fact check his story. In that search, I uncovered the following interview, originally published as a reporter's recollection in August 1995:[10]

Q: Why would you play for Ottawa, and why the CFL?

OD: Well, I was retired after being released from Minnesota. I had accomplished what I wanted. I had received a phone call from Ottawa, you know, to show me around the city and see the team, but I turned them down. Later, my wife said why not give it a try? So I did.

Q: Do you not have any more interest in playing in the NFL?

OD: No, the NFL has become too strict, its all business and all the fun has been taken out of the game. For the CFL . . . This is football. It's a wide receiver's dream. It's more relaxed.

Q: What is your greatest highlight memory . . . winning the Super Bowl with New York?

OD: No, it was scoring a touchdown with the 49ers on my first reception. Jerry Rice had been hurt and I was on the bench, my number came up and I went in to score on the next play. I am certain that I will have a lot more highlight memories in the CFL.

Records confirmed that OD had a terrific season for Ottawa (1,054 yards receiving and 8 touchdowns), but he quit after one year. I asked why he decided to walk away after just one season in the CFL. OD explained his decision to end his career this way, "The season ended and I was just kind of driving along this long road in Canada not really heading anywhere in particular. I got out to the country with nothing to see but countryside for miles. I just kind of looked down the road and something told me it was time to quit so just like that I just decided that I didn't want to play no more."[11]

Little did he know then that his on-the-field injuries would take such a toll on his body and eventually qualify him for full disability status. As with many other things involving the NFL, he had to work hard to get what he felt he was due from the league. Shortly after our initial meeting I discovered that OD was in the middle of a protracted legal battle with the NFL over a disability claim for injuries sustained over the course of his career. His legal proceedings extended well beyond the four years of my field research; however, one of the benefits of our long-time relationship was that I was able to track the trial's outcome while witnessing how those injuries continue to affect him.

During his disability trial OD testified that he struggled with depression when the pain in his knees, back, or hips became unbearable. OD told NFL doctors that standing upright for a prolonged period of time or sitting for too long caused so much pain that he had to quit his job as the recreation director at a state youth correctional facility. Perhaps the most salient moment of OD's testimony involved the confession that he sometimes sits alone in a dark basement for days on end, smoking marijuana because it helps him forget about the pain.

In addition to dealing with the long-term effects of chronic pain from injury and poor money management, legal issues remain a persistent problem for OD and many other current and former NFL athletes. After two years, the NFL settled OD's disability legal claim with a large one-time payout, plus a monthly income of five-figures for the remainder of his life. Immediately after the case was resolved in his favor, OD ran into trouble with his lawyer, Atlanta-based attorney Kurt Ward, who produced a document allegedly signed by OD and demanded that OD surrender 40% of the total monies awarded to him by the NFL. OD adamantly claims that his signature was forged on the document. OD never disputed that Ward's services were retained, but he denies ever agreeing to compensate the attorney with proceeds from his settlement. He does acknowledge that Ward is entitled to out-of-pocket expenses for a battery of medical tests in Atlanta, Florida, and New York, plus fees for legal services. After OD refused to meet the lawyer's demands, Ward filed a lawsuit to have the outstanding balance paid directly from OD's NFLPA pension account. After months of attempting to resolve the matter, OD turned to the NFL and the NFL Players Association to fight the case. The league filed a motion claiming that it is unlawful to collect legal fees from the NFL pension and disability plan. It took another two years for this second case to wind through the court system before the judge ultimately ruled in favor of OD and a second plaintiff listed in the case. OD finally won his settlement in June

2011.[12] As soon as his case was settled, OD was taken to court for an increase in alimony and child support.

OD's and Big Al's life histories serve as a precursor to the salient themes examined in greater detail throughout the remainder of this book. Injury is perhaps the most obvious issue that impacts NFL athletes' lives well beyond their final days on the gridiron. An extensive legal battle for disability and retirement benefits is but one example of the struggle for dignity and respect some NFL athletes endure as their legacy fades from the public's collective consciousness. In addition to the lingering effects of concussions, chronic pain, bouts of depression, severe osteoarthritis, and joint replacement surgery, NFL athletes are often plagued with the emotional and mental strain associated with the loss of a desired social status and athletic identity. OD's story also offers insight into the ways in which race, social class, family background, education, historical events, and other sociological constructs intersect to influence athletes' attempts to adjust to life after the NFL.

AS THE NATION'S most popular sports league, the NFL functions as a powerful business cartel that wields political and cultural influence well beyond its $9 billion annual revenues.[13] Rather than thinking of the NFL as a single entity comprising 32 teams with 2,000 athletes and 10,000 alumni, for the purposes of this study I view football as an organizational field[14] comprised of youth football leagues, high school and college football teams, the NFL, the NFL Players Association (NFLPA), and NFL alumni. With the proliferation of television coverage, sports programs, websites, blogs, video games, and Fantasy Football, the game of football fuels the hopes and dreams of millions of young athletes across the country and thus, further contributing to its own popularity.

In this book, it is my goal to build on the work of famed sociologist Harry Edwards as I explore questions around the effect that the popularity of professional sports has on communities and individuals nationwide. In a well-documented television interview, Edwards explained that at Cornell University his dissertation committee was skeptical about the merits of a sociological analysis of sport as a social institution. According to Edwards, in the mid- to late 1960s sport was relegated to the study of physical education, since sociologists did not feel that it was "up to their standard as an area of career focus or analysis." To combat this prejudice, Edwards recounts that he presented the committee with a simple question, "How can we believe as soci-ologists, that a dyad—a two person relationship or a triad—a three person relationship—is worthy of analysis that includes volumes and hundreds of dissertations, but 100 million people watching the Super Bowl is not worthy of investigation from a sociological perspective? It seems to me that seems to be a bit upside down." Edwards claims the committee had no response to that other than "Okay, go ahead."[15] Today Harry Edwards is widely considered the founder of sport sociology in America and credited with orchestrating the Olympic Project for Human Rights, which led to the now famous Black Power Salute protest by US track athletes Tommie Smith and John Carlos at the 1968 Olympics.

During summer training camp with the San Francisco 49ers I vaguely recall seeing Edwards with his shaved bald head and distinctive goatee on the sidelines observing practice. But, at the time, my attention was so consumed with trying to make the final roster that I could barely focus on anyone other than defensive back coach Ray Rhodes and veteran free-safety Ronnie Lott. I didn't give it much thought until I came across his photograph in the book *The Sociology of Sport* when I was immersed in my graduate studies in sociology. More than most sociologists, Edwards's unique brand of academic research and advocacy has generated a broad impact among sociologists and a legacy as an activist and mentor to Black athletes.

While driving to watch his son play in a game against West Virginia University, OD recounted a story to me about Harry Edwards helping him overcome a rough time in his life. OD explained that one day when he was playing for San Francisco during his fifth season in the league, he was struggling to make it through practice. Edwards, who was frequently observing from the sidelines, pulled him aside and asked what was going on. OD said at that moment, he broke into tears and started crying so hard he could hardly speak the words that his mother had died. Edwards told OD he would explain the situation to the coaches and the team would handle all the travel and funeral arrangements. He then told OD to take as much time as needed with his family back home in Louisiana. As OD shared this story it became clear that he held Dr. Edwards in high esteem. Not only did OD educate me about the value of Dr. Edwards's work with Black athletes and his investigation of sport as a social institution, his words pushed me to revisit Edwards's scholarship as I attempted to understand why certain athletes struggle with transition to life after the NFL.

It is my hope that sports enthusiasts, athletes, coaches, educators, parents, and other interested parties discover something in the remaining pages that helps explain how the ills of society persist in sports, shows how enmeshed football has become in American culture, and helps readers understand that what is broken needn't stay that way.

2

THE STAR, THE JOURNEYMAN, AND
THE DEDICATED SPECTATOR

I SAT IN my rental car in Martinsville, New Jersey, scratching out interview questions on a new yellow legal pad. Prepping to interview Skip Fuller, the performance director at TEST Sports, about NFL Combine Training techniques, I was uneasy. My eyes traced along the TEST Sports facility's forest green tin roof overhang. Its colonial-style architecture was a nod to the town's history as an encampment site for the Continental Army during the Revolutionary War, but its enormous swath of windows, French doors, and rich walnut paneling was more reminiscent of a country club. It wasn't at all like the places I had trained to play football. I pressed the buzzer, then held the door as spandex-clad matrons passed through with yoga mats tucked under their arms.

The receptionist pointed me to a comfortable chair. While Skip finished a meeting, my mind cycled through the importance of each stage of an NFL athlete's development. The high school years represent the first milestone on the path to an NFL career. Typically, the seeds of a player's eventual demise can be spotted at this stage. Football evolves from a fun game to a serious pursuit, especially in an athlete's senior year of high school, when the competition and stress deepen. The foundation is laid for the *football habitus*—the athlete learns how to discipline himself in order to continue in the sport tournament, adopting and internalizing the norms of a progression to the pros. At the end of high school, some 95% of athletes will be cut from the game.

Of the things that are the most critical for an outsider to understand about the American football athlete's experience, the most enduring is the sport tournament; it underpins all the difficulties football players encounter when entering, maintaining, and ending a professional football career. I find Rosenbaum's[1] corporate tournament mobility model a useful concept in considering the world of organized football.[2] As this concept is applied, an athlete's career is a series of competitions, from the junior football leagues to professional ranks. Winners and losers are separated at each selection point. Winners move on to compete in higher-level tournaments but are never assured that they'll move beyond any given competition; losers are relegated to lower-level contests or wholly denied the opportunity to compete any further. When any given contest ends, the victor must turn to preparations for the next contest. What most people don't understand is that no matter how many times he wins, a player must *always* be ready to fight hard in the next round. A winner will not remain a winner forever.

Each fall about 2.8 million boys (and some girls) play Pop Warner–style football in junior leagues all across America.[3] Some are just there for fun, enjoying glazed doughnuts after the games and a participation trophy at the end of the season. Others—and perhaps their parents and mentors—entertain powerful NFL dreams. The sport tournament begins from that point of entry, sorting from a cohort of similarly aged children: Who can run the fastest? Who is better at catching or throwing the ball? Who is more determined to win? Who is the strongest? The winners of these small competitions play in the game; the losers sit on the bench or try a different position on the team. Eventually, this weeding out process forces many young athletes out of football. Some lose the desire to compete; some switch to other sports, are injured, or are no longer allowed to play because the activity requires too much time, money, or parent involvement and interaction.

Those who stay in the game through middle school experience physical changes that impact their ability to hang on. Football favors the taller, faster, stronger, and heavier athletes. Athletes with deficits in any of these areas are forced out of play while many survivors will try out for high school teams. Of the 2.8 million who play in junior leagues, only 1 million will advance to play football in high school, where the competition deepens. Now the game requires greater dedication, sacrifice, and obedience. It selects for larger size, faster speed, and better technique. Most players never make it past this level. According to NCAA statistics, 6.4% of high school football players will move on to play NCAA football (Division I, II, & III) in college. Of those players who make it to college football, only 1.6% will play football professionally.[4]

This is a brutal winnowing, but even among that supremely small subset of athletes who keep going, the "winners," there is a division based on skill, size, and natural talent: stars versus journeymen. The star athlete, like a thoroughbred racehorse, possesses obvious talent and expresses it through his unique physicality. He makes something incredibly difficult look effortless. A star is the kind of highly ranked athlete major college football programs pursue. Gatekeepers who cultivate young talent will invest their time in him, hoping that he will someday shine on the biggest stage in professional football. His success will reflect validation on those who discovered and nurtured him. Journeymen are more nondescript. These athletes will appear in few headlines as they bolster teams' stars and lay the foundation for success, game after game. Their route to the pros is often through the low end of the college draft or through a rookie free agent contract. Though stars and journeymen travel separate paths into the NFL, their exits from the league will be more similar: unceremonious, unprepared. Retirement ends the tournament as virtually every player is forced out before he is prepared to say goodbye.

SKIP FULLER BURST into the lobby. As I stood to shake his hand, Skip's warmth and friendly disposition put me at ease. Skip had played football for Somerville High School in New Jersey. I asked if he had been in school around the same time as my younger brother Kelly, who went on to play tight end for Purdue University. A wide grin spread across his face. "Kelly is your brother? Yeah I remember him." Later, a colleague told me that Skip was one of the best defensive tackles to ever play at Somerville, where he was a member of the 1983 undefeated state champion football team. He had gone on to play for a national championship as a West Virginia University Mountaineer before signing a free agent contract with the Miami Dolphins.

Skip apologized for keeping me waiting. "I want you to meet someone," he said, leading me past a yoga class, elliptical machines and treadmills, and all the way back to the weight room.

"This is my star pupil," he said, indicating Cody Bohler. Cody was an imposing Teutonic presence at 6'7" and 275 pounds. He stood and flipped his long blond hair behind his shoulders (Figure 2.1). He had just completed his junior season as a starter for Immaculata High School, a nearby Catholic prep school. While other students headed off to afterschool jobs or to hang out with their friends, Cody religiously committed two to three hours, five times

FIGURE 2.1: CODY AND SKIP WORK OUT AT TEST SPORTS CLUBS.

a week, to his workout regimen. On school days, he arrived at TEST around 3:30 PM in his blue Catholic school sweater vest, gray pants, and white shirt, a tie dangling around his thick neck. As Cody and his buddy Mike dove into their workout, I witnessed true dedication to the sport. I had the sense that if Skip told Cody to jump, this kid would not bother asking how high or for how long—he would jump. According to Skip, Cody needed to combine an intensive weight-lifting regime with a speed and agility workout four days a week in order to reach his goals. "Basically we got to get him stronger, but first we need to get all that soreness out from the season and get his body adjusted to lifting again."

"I'm real proud of how far he's come." A puzzled look must have crossed my face, because Skip quickly pointed to a photograph on his corkboard, which showed Cody as a 6'2", 265-pound freshman. Though just three years younger and 10 pounds lighter, Cody looked like a different person. Back then, a distinctly pudgy Cody played on the offensive line for Immaculata. He had been knocked around a lot as he struggled to make his presence felt on the field.

I asked Cody why he started working out with Skip. He told me, "I just saw how big [the other players] were, and I knew I had to get in shape to compete with those guys." This realization propelled Cody into a workout odyssey. After his freshman season ended, he spent the next two years changing his diet and ramping up cardiovascular conditioning and weight training. His body went from soft and doughy to strong and muscular. I was shocked at the difference between his freshman physique and the body of the young man in front of me. It was clear that he had dedicated himself to the pursuit of a career in football.

I watched as Cody, his hair matted with sweat, bench-pressed 225 pounds. Skip told him to adjust his grip. I followed Skip back to his desk where we could see Cody through a window. I asked about the money that parents spend to get their kids into football-ready shape. As a fitness professional and former athlete, I was curious to hear Skip's opinion on whether these new training methods and focusing on a single sport at a young age makes a difference on the football field. "When you and I played," I said to Skip, "we didn't have the benefit of all this stuff. We just went out there and started hitting each other. So, I'm curious: do these drills and new training methods really help a kid become a better athlete than a kid from a poor, inner-city school in Miami that's hungry to play college ball?" Skip's response confirmed my apprehension:

> If a kid ain't an athlete, there ain't much anybody can do. It really doesn't matter how much time he puts in at the gym. All I can do is take what's there and make it better. Bottom line is, he's already got to have what it takes. If he can't bounce back after getting knocked on his butt, then he ain't no football player.

Following his freshman season, Cody had announced to his parents that he needed to lose 40 pounds and get stronger. His father Tom, the owner of a small heating, ventilation, and air conditioning company, purchased a TEST Sports Club membership. Over the next two and a half years, Tom and his wife spent thousands of dollars in cash and barter for various goods and services for their son and his football dreams. This total included personal training, nutritional supplements and protein shakes, consultations with a nutritionist, and summer camp and football academy registration fees. Some families are willing to pay more than $75 per hour for a trainer to run their kids through fast feet ladder drills, 40-yard sprint mechanics, 3-cone drills, and 20-yard shuttle technique drills, but it doesn't take long before these prices can become overwhelming. After working with Cody for a while, Skip encouraged his family to save money by having Cody go unsupervised for this phase of his training. Skip said he told them, "He's been with me long enough to know what I expect from him. If he doesn't put the work in it will eventually come out. I'll run him every once in awhile just to see where he's at."

Not surprisingly, athletes and their families are always on the hunt for competitive advantages in the recruiting game. The Bohlers, like so many football parents, have committed precious resources and time to support their son in his journey to the NFL, but their financial outlay pales in comparison to all the training and hours of preparation Cody has invested to remain competitive in the sports tournament. Two or three times a week, Cody and his workout-obsessed high school buddy Mike will spend hours and hours repeating speed and agility drills.

"Skip is like a second father to Cody," his dad Tom confirmed late one afternoon. "People recognize how much this kid gives of himself, so they're willing to spend time on him. Cody wants it bad. He's not afraid of working for it."

How did such a change occur in Cody's body? And more important, why? For two years, Cody inhaled two 5,000-calorie shakes per day, over three times the total daily recommended caloric intake for an active 14- to 18-year-old male.[5] His goal was to reach 300 pounds as a high school senior because that's the size the college recruiters are looking for in an offensive tackle. For every athlete with multiple scholarship offers, thousands of less fortunate prospects agonize over what more they need to do to earn a higher ranking on recruiting coverage websites like rivals.com and attract the attention of major college scouts. So Cody was determined to control his vital football statistics (weight, strength, speed, and agility). By the end of his senior season, Cody did build himself up to a 300-pound giant. Knowing that coaches want big guys on the offensive line, Cody was perfectly willing to put his long-term health at risk for Type 2 diabetes, high blood pressure, and heart disease, all to give the college recruiters and coaches what they wanted.[6]

NCAA Division I football programs only offer 18 to 25 scholarships to incoming freshmen each season, and hundreds of thousands of football players nationwide are willing to do whatever it takes to catch the attention of a single college recruiter.[7] Each year, high school seniors from coast to coast enter their final football season with visions of a college scholarship. They want to be the next Tom Brady or the next Heisman Trophy–winning quarterback Cam Newton.[8] To that end, they eat, sleep, sweat, and breathe football.

At this point, any discussion about teenage athletes feeling pressured to resculpt or ramp up their physiques would be incomplete without mentioning performance enhancing drugs (PEDs). I do not believe Cody ever used PEDs, and they were not the focus of my study. However, some young players who don't have caring, involved parents might fall into the trap of anabolic steroid use. An article published by the Mayo Clinic shows that one in 20 American teenagers reports using steroids to increase muscle mass.[9] Forbes.com reports that Biogenesis of America, the clinic at the center of the latest PED scandal, counted high school athletes among its customers.[10] And another article states that 13% of high school football players are believed to be taking the drugs.[11] PED use seems to be escalating. Could this trend be construed as part of the "what it takes" mentality of gridiron culture? Or could illegal PED use be yet another thing that kids copy from the pros?

Like the consumption of huge numbers of calories through body mass shakes, PEDs leave a trail of unwanted side effects. The numbers of high school PED users is not exact, nor is there any available, long-term data. However, the list of side effects holds across sources: PEDs are known to shorten or inhibit the growth of the body's long bones (particularly the upper leg and upper arm bones, the femur and humerus), shrink the testicles, and cause hair loss, liver disease (including cancer), and aggressive behavior, irritability, depression, and moodiness.[12] Recruiters do not, at least openly, encourage taking PEDs, and the biggest and the fastest athletes may never touch steroids. It's difficult to know, as few will admit to using PEDs. Are prospective college athletes tested for anabolic steroids? Not necessarily. We know that colleges want their football players massively big and fast. But do they want them clean?

Cody might be an anomaly, an overzealous teenager obsessed with getting the attention and acclaim of college football scouts. Still, high school athletes in general seem compelled to drastically resculpt their bodies—in essence, to go against nature—for a shot at college ball. In fact, much of the game seems ruled by a "whatever it takes" culture. Major college programs are always on the hunt for the prototypical 6'6",

340-pound offensive tackle with long arms, a specimen who is quick as a cat and can bench press an elephant. Some 15 of the top 39 linemen in the high school class of 2006 (ranked by rivals.com) tipped the scale at 300+ pounds. According to the *Tulsa World*,[13] the average Oklahoma high school offensive lineman was 183 pounds in 1930; by 2006, he was almost 273 pounds. Even more shocking, high school offensive linemen have gained almost 50 pounds since 1982. If the trend continues, the newspaper predicts that these young men will weigh an average of 300 pounds by 2021. American children, as a whole, have gotten heavier, but offensive linemen have grown at a significantly faster rate than the general population.[14] High school football has evolved to the point that young men like Cody are willing to spend time, money, and concerted effort in transforming their bodies for a chance to play in college.

Motivated by the pressure to gain an edge over the competition, Cody headed back into the gym each off-season. Once in full swing, Skip led Cody through a rigorous workout and conditioning program targeted to strengthen specific muscle groups. His routine closely resembled that used by many major college football programs. During the winter and spring months, Cody worked out four days a week to master advanced power lifting exercises. By the time March rolled around Skip began to add heavier weights to most of Cody's base exercises. In January, for example, his bench press routine started at three sets of five repetitions at 225 pounds. Every two weeks, Skip added 10–20 pounds until Cody was able to power through four sets of 5–8 reps at 275 to 300 pounds without any visible signs of fatigue.

Another game Skip played with Cody is called Fourth Quarter. He begins the workout session by handing Cody his list of exercises and then proceeds to push him until sweat soaks his workout gear. Just when Cody thinks he has reached the end of the workout, Skip yells out "fourth quarter!" This signals another 5 to 15 minutes of fast-paced lifting. "I push him this way to build mental toughness and help him with his endurance. Anybody can play hard when he's fresh. It's what you do when you're tired that counts." Cody's drive and determination is indicative of the unwavering sacrifices that young men believe are necessary to keep their dreams of playing football alive.

To unlock the mystery of why a teenager would push himself to such physical extremes, one need only examine Cody's recap of Mike Farrell's[15] assessment of his talent: "I'm competitive right now at this level," Cody said,

"But if I want to move up to the major college level, I have to gain another 30–35 pounds and increase my footwork."

The rapid rise of high school recruiting websites such as rivals.com, max prep sports, scout.com, and 247sports.com has also contributed to the expansion of the American sports-industrial complex. Each of these websites uses a slightly different evaluation metric to rank players. The rivals.com website calculates scores by ranking athletes based on game film evaluations, personal observations, and input from professional, college, and high school coaches. This results in a numerical star ranking system that ranks athletes on their expected impact in college and by position. A five-star prospect is considered one of the nation's top 25 to 30 players, four-star is a top 250 to 300 player, three-star is a top 750 player, two-star is a mid-major prospect, and one-star is, essentially, unranked.[16] Since 2007, when rivals.com was purchased by Yahoo! Sports, the star-ranking system has become the coveted marker of success in the high school football war. Today, athletes, parents, scouts, and coaches rely so heavily on this recruiting information that the utility of these websites has evolved tremendously. They are now unofficial college recruiting gatekeepers. Most young athletes will never grow large enough or run fast enough to earn a website ranking; as a result, they will never be seen as legitimate Division I college prospects. Once high school athletes fail to impress the rivals.com staff, their chances of earning a major college football scholarship are severely diminished.

Had Cody ever met Mike Farrell, a rivals.com analyst who is regarded as one of the nation's foremost recruiting analysts covering high school and collegiate recruiting? No. Imagine the devastation of being overlooked because something about you is inadequate and you have no way to control it. Had Mike Farrell ever talked to Cody to determine his level of commitment to play the game? No. Does commitment matter? Yes, but only as one among many factors. Cody took Farrell's assessment as gospel. The analyst represented yet another hurdle in the run-up to the NFL career he had always wanted. But to Farrell, Cody was just another set of statistics: Bohler, Cody. 6'7", 275. OL. Immaculata H.S. Somerville, NJ.

It is difficult for Cody and other high school athletes to trust a system that segregates them by physical stature and ability but does not take into account their passion and desire to succeed. It's difficult to be judged as a statistic or number by someone you've never met, to be measured against competition you cannot see, to always wonder if there's something other guys are doing that you don't even know about.

As a moderately recruited offensive lineman from Somerville, New Jersey, Cody Bohler is one end of the spectrum. On the other end is Nyshier ("Naz") Oliver, a highly touted athlete from a football powerhouse high school in Jersey City, New Jersey. Scholarship offers from Notre Dame, Tennessee, Rutgers, Boston College, Pittsburgh, West Virginia, and Cincinnati came pouring in during Naz's junior season. Not so for Cody.

Besides the obvious physical differences, Cody's and Nyshier's high school football careers help to contrast the different paths athletes travel to remain in the football sport tournament. While Cody is a tall lineman with a long frame and flowing blond hair, Nyshier is a 5'11" 175-pound slender athlete with a chestnut complexion. Cody is a suburban White kid from a working-class town in central New Jersey; Nyshier is an African American raised in the densely populated urban enclave of Newark. One fights for the attention of scouts and college recruiters while the other is considered an elite, blue chip athlete and high school star the recruiters try to charm. The common thread is a shared, all-consuming passion. Both young men yearn to move on to their college "apprenticeship," then perform on the biggest stage in football, the NFL.

Naz benefited directly from the recruiting website star-rating system and was overwhelmed with college program suitors. He initially burst on the high school athletic scene as a track star, setting a state record for freshman sprinters with a time of 10.38 in the 100-meter dash. Based on the strength of this performance, he was named First Team All Hudson County for the 100-meter and Honorable Mention for the 200-meter in his freshman season. His list of accomplishments over the first three years of high school is impressive: First Team New Jersey All-State Group 4 Non-public High School Football Team, 2007 Hudson Reporter All Area Football, 2007 Hudson Reporter Offensive Player of the Year, and Associated Press 2007 Second Team All-State football. He performed well academically, too. The oldest of five children, Naz told me he was proud of his 3.10 grade point average and the example he set for his siblings.

Newspaper articles and high school scouting reports often referred to Naz as a rare athlete with unlimited potential.[17] In fact, he landed on my radar during a training session at TEST. I had heard a lot about a young athlete named Will "The Thrill" Hill, who, as the number one rated high school prospect in the state of New Jersey, had dozens of colleges bidding for his services. A buzz circulated around TEST: Hill planned to attend its 2008 Winter Football Academy. As a former defensive player, I was eager to check out Hill's performance in position drills conducted by J. B. Brown, a 12-year NFL veteran defensive back. But while many of the fathers in the crowd were awed by Hill's performance, my attention was drawn to Naz. Speed and agility were, without question, two of his greatest assets; I was compelled, however, by his desire to compete.

Theodore, Nyshier's father, walked up and said by way of introduction, "I see you're telling him some of the same stuff I've been pointing out."

"He's pretty good," I said. "His stance is a little narrow. But once he begins to trust himself, he'll really be special."

Theodore told me that Naz had only played three games as a defensive back. "He really plays running back. He ran over 1,200 yards and had 20-something touchdowns this season." I was struck by how quickly Naz had distinguished himself as a defensive back—but why had he given up running back when he was so good at it?

I went home determined to find as much information as I could about this impressive young athlete. I soon discovered that Naz had accomplished more in one season than most kids could dream of in an entire high school career. Like many star athletes, Naz excelled in sports at a young age. As a kid, he was said to be bigger than most others his age, which allowed him to shine in Pop Warner. By the time he was 12 years old, coaches from top area prep schools began attending his games to coax him into playing for their programs. And once he settled into high school, Naz's career really began to take off. Although he was not able to start on his freshman team due to a problem with some school registration documents, by season's end, Naz still managed to become the featured running back and score the bulk of the squad's touchdowns. The fathers who attended the TEST Football Academy often spoke of Naz as a great competitor with tremendous athletic ability. I began to wonder why he was working out with the defensive backs instead of focusing on the nuances of running the football.

The following week I asked Naz's dad, Theodore, why Naz wasn't training with the running backs. Theodore coyly responded,

> That's not even Naz. He's not big headed or nothing. Running back ain't a challenge no more. So he's focusing on being a defensive back. Schools that want him say he can play either position, so he's focusing on DB.

Naz's decision to challenge himself at a different position was arresting. Of all my years in and around football, I couldn't recall ever meeting *anyone* who rejected the spotlight of being an offensive starter simply because it was too easy.

Even natural athletes are tested by the game. Naz was witnessing firsthand that even the great ones must work harder to make it on the next level. No matter how many accolades or awards are listed after Will Hill's name, Naz's high school teammate continued to show up at the TEST Football Academy and work diligently. Why? Because, as OD, the wide receiver position coach on the sidelines, shouted while watching Hill practice, "He better step up his game, 'cause them boys down in Florida got something for his ass. They DO NOT PLAY down there at the University of Florida."[18]

OD laid out the situation. To him, it was a simple question: Who's hungrier? By making an example of Will Hill, OD let all the athletes in attendance know that on the football field, somebody is always ready to fight you for that piece of steak. The farther an athlete advances in the sport tournament, the tougher the competition gets. So OD warned them all, "You'd better be ready." Even a star can burn out.

COACH KNOWS BEST

The first commandment of football is the same today as it was in the leather helmet days: listen to your coach. Do everything he says. Follow the rules. If you please the coach, you will play. The system around the coach will support your dreams of advancing to the next level. My teammates and I knew the deal: we had to be willing to work hard, to train, to refine techniques, and to play in extreme weather. After all, we knew that a real athlete's focus had to be ironclad, forged by determination, sweat, and certitude. As Tennyson writes, "Theirs not to reason why, Theirs but to do and die."[19]

A week after we met, I noticed Cody was kind of going through the motions during a set on the bench press. Cody seemed to have lost his excitement. He hadn't been sleeping well, and he was obviously troubled. Skip, mildly agitated by this lack of effort, started in: "Cody, I don't see why you let all that stuff bother you." He had noticed Cody was distracted by another player's performance.

"He's such a suck up," Cody complained. "I mean, the guy ain't even that good, and he throws out his card to everyone he meets."

"I know he's not that good," Skip agreed. "But what's that got to do with anything? Next year is your year. You'll show 'em what you're made of."

"I know, but... After all that hard work I put in last year, I still can't get any recognition," Cody said as he tied his shoes. "I know my coach tells all the recruiters I need to work on my footwork. He thinks my feet are slow. I move better than any other lineman on the team. Then he turns around and just praises Jordan."

"I don't see it. I watched [Jordan] a couple of times last year. He's just a big blob," Skip replied, jotting a note on his clipboard. "He's not that strong, and he doesn't move his feet. I'm not trying to be biased or anything. You know me; I'd be honest and tell you if I felt otherwise, but you're way better than him."

Cody stared down at his feet. "I know, but damn. It just bothers me 'cause it feels like I'm not even getting looked at. It's like the coach is directing all the attention to Jordan, and I don't even matter."

Cody felt underappreciated by his high school coach and betrayed by one of his teammates. Cody could work out and sculpt his body. He could gain weight. He could build endurance and mental toughness. But he could not control how an important gatekeeper evaluated his talent.

COHORT TENSION

Here's what is *not* in the NFL Career Path brochure: most of the time, there's generally only one Top Dog on a high school team. With everyone looking to advance in the sport tournament, competition intensifies, especially as the time nears for colleges to select the players who will receive their football scholarship offers. Cody was distressed because he did not feel as though he had his coach's favor. For a high school athlete, the power wielded by his head coach can be a blessing or a curse.[20] In fact, the absence of their coach's favor was a frequently mentioned frustration among the younger players I interviewed. In reality, the odds are against most high school coaches ever coaching an athlete talented enough to earn a Division I scholarship. It's the rare coach who has a track record for spotting talent and sending them to the next level. The result is that cohort tension between athletes starts in high school, but because of the structural inequalities in the institution of football, it never dissipates—not even during life after football.

College recruiters are generally responsible for scouting certain geographic regions, which means that building relationships with high school head coaches is vital for identifying major college Division I talent. There is a perception among high school coaches that the recruiting scouts look to them to cull the field of potential recruits. The coach doesn't want to waste the recruiter's time or lose credibility with the scouts because he wants to be seen as a reliable evaluator of talent. As a result, some coaches may promote only one player to the recruiters, even when there are several good players on his team (frequently the case on championship teams).

Several minutes into our conversation, I began to sense that my own years of football experience might help Cody with his anxiety. As Cody slumped down in a blue plastic chair that could barely contain his large frame, he slowly explained the reasons behind his frustration with his teammate's shameless self-promotion. I asked, "What does Jordan's deal have to do with you? Why does he even matter? What if you just went out and did your thing, regardless of how much he sucks up? Help me understand where you're coming from."

Through the fragmented dialogue, the message Cody delivered was loud and clear: the recruiting process was taking an emotional toll. With only slightly more than 5% of all high school athletes advancing to play college football, it's no wonder he struggled with feelings of inadequacy. If Cody could not win over the coach's favor, he suspected he couldn't win recruiters' attention, either.

It is imperative for college recruiters to trust the judgment of high school head coaches, and for head coaches to know which recruiters to trust. Not every high school athlete is Division I material, and recruiters must discern which players can compete on the next level. According to *USA Today*,[21] Ray McCartney, former recruiting coordinator for the Wake Forest University football program, believes that high school coaches often feel obligated to help any young man who gave his heart and soul to his program to get into any college on the next level. It is left up to the university recruiters to see if they agree or disagree whether the kid is a good fit for a higher or lower level program.

During our first conversation, Cody confessed he dreamed of playing for Notre Dame. After a quick ribbing about the "Fighting Irish's" horrible 2007 season, I asked, "Why Notre Dame? They haven't been winning much lately." His face beamed. "I don't know. I've just kind of liked them ever since I was a kid. I think it would be kind of neat to run out of the locker room wearing those colors and being on TV." Cody's response took me back to my days as a high school athlete. I dreamed of winning a national championship as a member of the University of Southern California Trojans. The USC Trojans and the Notre Dame Fighting Irish enjoy an enduring perception as traditionally excellent, well-regarded programs— regardless of their present win/loss record. As such, these colleges serve a critical role in helping college football retain its position as an important American cultural institution.

For all but the star athlete, though, the recruiting process spurs feelings of hopelessness and despair. Some players hang on the sidelines, desperately hoping the coach will give them a chance to shine. Others hang onto their positions, their regimens, their discipline and determination. Because they work so hard doing everything they think they should be doing, it disheartens many when the college recruiters don't call.

The situation becomes all the more stressful since Division I programs like Wake Forest typically begin the recruiting process with more than 1,000 prospects on their early recruiting board. Over the next 24-month period, recruiters whittle that group down to 100. The school actively recruits 40– 50 prospects, knowing they will sign only 18–25 athletes to scholarships each year.[22]

It is incredibly difficult for high school athletes to manage their anxiety regarding the scouting and recruiting process. One day, a young man is flying high because he lifted a new maximum weight. The next, his world comes crashing down amid rumors that a high school rival was offered a college scholarship. For instance, knowing that each college needs only a few players in each position, Cody experienced a mini crisis when he heard that the Fighting Irish had already signed several offensive linemen to their

2008 freshman recruiting class. Here's an exchange during an off-season workout:

> Cody blurted, "Notre Dame signed like four or five offensive linemen (already) this year!"
>
> Skip responded with the slightest affect of sternness. "SO?" He asked.
>
> Cody replied, "I know . . . It's just that . . . man!"

Cody understood that NCAA rules permit schools to carry only 85 scholarship athletes on the roster each season and 10 or 12 of those players are already in his position, so Notre Dame was unlikely to sign any more offensive linemen this year. Rumors alone seem to have closed the door for Cody, and with it, his dream of running out of the locker room in a navy, green, and gold uniform.

This brief yet poignant interaction speaks to a young athlete's emotional vulnerability. Skip was trying to get Cody to focus on his game and to let go of everything else. But for Cody, it felt like his football dreams were collapsing around him. Even at this early stage in his career, Cody was frustrated to have worked so hard to control his football destiny, only to find that he has limited control over the recruiting process. Coincidentally, less than a month later, Cody received a letter from Charlie Weis, the Notre Dame head coach, who requested a copy of his game film and high school transcripts. Immediately, and even though Cody had committed to Temple University by then, his mood lifted with Notre Dame's hint of interest.

Meanwhile, Naz and his family struggled to decide among scholarship offers from Notre Dame, Clemson, Cincinnati, Boston College, Tennessee, Rutgers, and Pittsburgh. The demands of fame, education, and athletics do not, on the surface, seem to present a problem for Naz. He comes across as a well-adjusted young man who takes things in stride. Naz is not sliding two 20-gallon storage boxes full of recruiting materials out of his closet like the quarterback in the *Frontline* special *Marketing Kiehl Frazier*,[23] but he is highly recruited. He does not struggle for attention or wonder if he will play in college. No. For Naz, college is just a matter of where, not if. Up to this point, the efforts Naz has made to advance his football career have been well rewarded.

Behind the scenes, though, a recruiting battle was stirring up. Like many star athletes, Naz and his family experienced a mounting barrage of attention in the winter months of his senior year. Their mobile phones were under constant attack with text messages from recruiters, coaches, news reporters, and friends seeking the inside tip on where Naz planned to attend college. Recruiters visited his high school and pulled him out of class to remind him of the greatness of their programs. College head coaches visited Naz's mom seeking to earn her approval in hopes of persuading him to sign with their school.

Deciding which college football program to attend is perhaps the single most important choice a star prospect like Naz faces because, when it comes to the NFL, where you play in college matters. But nothing really prepares an athlete or his family for this onslaught. If the athlete chooses well, the program may cultivate his talent so that when his college career is complete, he can sign a multimillion dollar NFL contract. Otherwise, his chance at remaining in the sport tournament may be to sign a free agent rookie NFL contract and hope for the best.

This is why National Signing Day is one of the most highly anticipated events in college football. Since 1981, the first Wednesday in February has been generally recognized as the first official day high school seniors can sign a National Letter of Intent to play for the college of their choice. College football coaches begin making overtures to these adolescents as early as eighth grade, but the recruiting war hits full stride in the athlete's junior and senior football seasons. There are limousine rides, promises of the newest Nike gear, dinners at fancy restaurants, phone calls from famous alumni, and the company of beautiful coeds who want to talk about what a great school they attend.

For over a decade, ESPNU's *SportCenter* has contributed to the hype by promoting a 10-hour special with live look-ins, simulcast on ESPN3 for viewing on computers and mobile devices.[24] Not to be outdone, CBS Sports Network and CBSSports.com provide an additional eight hours of coverage with on-air commentary from recruiting experts and former college head coaches. These programs typically dispatch television crews to cover top athletes across the country. They interview each top prospect's friends and former coaches about his athleticism, dedication, and school records. Their cameras tour the school hallways and gymnasium, pausing at the trophy case.

The college recruiting process is not equal for all athletes or coaches, though. As National Signing Day approaches, determining which college to attend is another source of anxiety for highly rated recruits. Worrying about whether *any* college will recruit them is a crushing concern to the journeymen and most other athletes. The numbers, after all, are against them.

New rules adopted by the NCAA Division-I Board of Directors[25] and the current climate in football has made recruiting more challenging than ever. Brian Polian, a former assistant coach at Texas A&M, Stanford, and Notre Dame and former head coach at the University of Nevada, offers insight into the challenges faced by top prospects, "The recruiting process is hard enough to deal with, and now the guys at the highest level enter a media spotlight that very few people are prepared for, certainly not a 17- or 18-year-old."[26] The players and their families have to understand what the recruiting process is all about. Perhaps most crucially, they should know if the program and the staff they are considering to play for is stable and well regarded in the coaching community. The inherent problem is that coaches are paid handsomely to win, so who really knows if a coach will leave for a better opportunity? How can an outsider tell if a program is on stable footing?[27]

College coaches are under immense pressure, too. They must compile the best recruiting class possible, and every year, there are those who know that their jobs are on the line if they don't convince talented athletes to play for them.[28] College coaches in the major conferences are expected to deliver— for administrators, fans, players, and alumni-winning programs. At North Carolina State, Athletic Director Debbie Yow fired head football coach Tom O'Brien. Even though O'Brien had led the Wolfpack to three straight bowl games and had beat in-state rival UNC five times in a row, the current mediocre season—split into seven wins and five losses—did not impress his boss. Yow said that she and O'Brien had "different ideas" about how to become a top-25 program. Coach O'Brien felt the program had a bright future and was proud of his team's academic accomplishments, "Wolfpack football is as sound, academically, as it's ever been with a (single year) APR of 990."[29] Apparently academics weren't as important as winning football games.

Compared to when I played, the competition for top talent among colleges today is practically an arms race. Coaches and recruiting staffers have an abundant amount of information about each athlete, but as is so often the case, that information does not flow both ways. It is extraordinarily difficult for a young recruit to find out about program issues, staff changes, and the strengths and weaknesses of the programs they are considering. Without proper guidance from parents, high school coaches, or mentors, fast-talking recruiters who promise a future in the NFL can easily seduce young athletes.[30]

After learning about my football background and the research I was conducting, Naz's dad Theodore solicited a little advice. He walked with me to the sidelines and confided, "Right now, Naz is thinking about Clemson, 'cause he attended a camp down there and kind of liked the way it felt. What do you think about Clemson?"

"If I had a kid who was a top prospect and could write his own ticket, I would consider something else," I said frankly. "I've learned through Derrick Mayes, one of the guys I'm following in my study, that alumni networks go a long way in helping you once football is over. Mayes went to Notre Dame, played five years in the NFL, and now he calls on alumni to help with his business ventures."

"Well Boston College is coming at him hard, too," Theodore added.

"It's interesting that you should mention BC. There's a guy working out with the elite athletes who just graduated from BC and played defensive back," I remembered. "He tells me it's a great school with a lot to offer, but not a lot of guys from there go on to make it big in the NFL. According to this guy, they didn't really have a secondary coach last season, and BC plays a lot of zone scheme, which could hurt his chances of getting drafted. Let me make a call, 'cause I'm sure he would be cool to talk with you."

"Yeah, do that. We are going for a visit to BC this weekend and it would be good to get the inside scoop." He took a deep breath. "So . . . what other schools do you like?"

I paused to be sure he knew that I was only giving advice, "Well, please don't take this as I'm saying that these are the only schools to consider 'cause everyone has to find a perfect fit for himself." I continued, "Of the guys I've interviewed, the ones who played at Stanford and Notre Dame have done real well after football. You can get a solid education at these schools, plus you're playing football at the highest level. These are real solid brothers who look after one another, played in the NFL, and are doing big things now."

Theodore pulled over a buddy and enthusiastically recounted my assessment. The fathers talked about how stressful the whole recruiting process has become. It seems that a family must either draw from the experiences of others who have already been through the recruiting wars or they must develop their own method of evaluating the rush of scholarship offers. The stakes for the high school stars are really high.

The process is more straightforward for the Bohler family. Cody's father Tom explained that the most important thing is that Cody gets a top-notch education. So *if given a choice*, they will encourage Cody to go to the school that offers him the best education.

Like many fathers I encountered while conducting this research, Tom was proud of both his boys, but there seemed to be a slight tinge of regret when he talked about his older son Ryan's decision to quit playing competitive sports. Football, baseball, and other sports offer many fathers the chance to bond with their children. Knowing the days of supporting Ryan's baseball dream had come to an end, Tom was eagerly anticipating the next chapter of Cody's football career. That meant, along with steering Cody toward a good education, Tom wanted him to get the highest level of training, nutritional guidance, and personal instruction. These would enhance Cody's chances of reaching the next level. He recounted, "Cody's surrounded by good people. He's got Skip, Billy Ard [former New York Giants offensive lineman and Super Bowl Champ], Brian from TEST here, and yourself. . . . You know, there's a lot of people that are for him. . . . We'll do anything we can to keep him going."

For all of the physical instruction, hours of personal training, and insider tips parents pay for, nothing prepares most athletes for the emotional roller coaster ride of college recruiting. As I mentioned, slightly over 5% of all football athletes will have the chance to play beyond high school. The vast majority of kids know that their final game is coming and begin preparing for it after their senior season. For thousands of others, the dream comes crashing down when National Signing Day passes quietly.

One of football's hardest lessons was revealed in a conversation I had with Cody. He had been restless and withdrawn; when I asked what was going on, Cody said, "The whole recruiting process is very stressful. It makes you feel kind of like a dog going after a piece of meat. I feel really bad because it makes you selfish, but you know that if you don't go for it then somebody else will."

"What's the matter with being selfish?" I asked.

"Well, it's not really in my nature. The whole thing makes you kind of become somebody you're really not. But that's the only way to get what you really want."

"It's 'not in your nature' because of your family upbringing and being raised Catholic?" I asked. "Is that because you've been taught to put others first and to serve your brother?"

"Exactly, that's what I mean about it being stressful," Cody replied. "You start to understand that you got to put yourself first no matter what. You get this burning passion deep inside you that won't go away. You just have to fight like a dog or else somebody else is going to take it away. I know that sounds bad but . . ."

"Is there anytime that you don't think about this fight and the stress it produces?"

"Well, I don't think about it all the time, but it's pretty much always there. I mean, I try not to think about it when I'm with my girlfriend," he smiled shyly. "Or when I'm at the movies and stuff, but otherwise it's always there. It's really stressful."

In the winter of 2008, it was too early to know how things would work out for Cody, but he did have advantages in the form of a supportive family and a personal trainer who understood the recruiting game. Cody's dad, Tom, described the family's commitment, saying Cody "really has aspirations of going to the highest levels. If that's what he wants to do, I'll obviously support him in any way I can."

Naz's father Theodore was just as unconditional in supporting his son in the pursuit of a football career. Theodore had graduated from Weequahic High School in Newark in 1990 and shortly thereafter became a single father. Committed to avoiding the mistakes his father made, Theodore began working a series of odd jobs at Newark International Airport, in retail or anything else he could get his hands on to take care of his responsibilities. "Even though things didn't work out between me and his mother, she's never had to worry about me. I've always been there. [Naz] lived with me for three years when his mom had a rough time in her life. I know what it's like to grow up without a father, and I made sure that wasn't happening to my son."

Theodore shepherded Naz through the streets of Newark, where a high murder rate and rough social conditions mean comparisons to HBO's *The Wire*.[31] Gang and drug-related crime, boarded-up doorways, steel bars on store windows, domestic violence, a shrinking tax base, a down economy—all these things contribute to tough times in New Jersey's biggest city. So getting Naz into sports was more than a way to support natural talents; it could keep

Naz safe. Theodore enrolled Naz in a terrific parochial school, nurturing and developing his athletic prowess. Theodore told me, "I was what you might call a 'social student.' I just didn't take school too seriously. My older sister got a basketball scholarship to Howard [University], and everybody was giving her all the attention, so I just kind of went the other way. I've seen what an education did for her, and I want that for my son." Theodore is an African American father trying to keep his son out of the reaches of the gangs, out of harm's way. He wants Naz to stay on the straight and narrow, to become a productive citizen. He is committed to doing what's best for Naz.

Theodore asked if I would talk to Naz about college. Naz said he wasn't interested in sociology too much, but he planned to study psychology. We cracked a few jokes about differences between the two disciplines before I asked what qualities he was looking for in a school. He responded, "I just want to go to a good school, play ball, and get a good education." I nodded and asked, "What do you consider to be a 'good school'? I mean, what should a school offer in order for you to consider it to be a good school?" Naz paused, then responded in a barely audible voice, "I never really thought about that before."

Though Theodore credits his son with an innate ability to persevere, he has clearly had a hand in cultivating Naz's tenacity. Their powerful bond was evident. Theodore told me that since Naz was just an adolescent, they'd gone to Weequahic Park track three times a week. Naz runs 2.2 miles around the Weequahic Park track, then does 20 sprints up and down "Dead Man's Hill" while wearing a 20-pound weight vest. Although the training was originally a way of instilling structure and discipline in his son's life, Theodore later confessed that it was also a way of ensuring that the two spent time together. Theodore's voice broke up ever so slightly as he spoke of Naz beginning to exercise his independence as a young man. "From the time Naz started playing ball at St. Peter's, I never missed a minute of practice or any of his games during the first two years," Theodore said. "Then, one day last season, his coach came over and said that he's never had a parent spend this much time watching his kid. I guess he wasn't used to a Black parent being around that much, but later Naz told me that I didn't need to show up as much. He said that he trusted what the coaches were telling him and that everything was fine. I have to admit, that kind of hurt me, but I understand what he was trying to say. Honestly, Naz is my best friend."

Naz played it a little cooler: "My Pops is cool. He's always there for me and all my brothers and sisters. My younger brother is an even better athlete than me, and my father will do everything for him too. That's just the way he is."

At Naz's last home game of the season for St. Peter's, Theodore caused quite a stir when he arrived sporting a navy blue Notre Dame varsity jacket stitched with gold lettering. Theodore beamed with pride as other parents crowded around, slapping hands and giving congratulatory hugs for steering his son to such a great school. As a single father of an African American son, Theodore can be proud. First of all, his son made it to his senior year of high school, still alive, not in jail, and doing well in an excellent private school. Second, Naz is an elite athlete with choices as to which college to attend. Theodore couldn't be prouder to wear that Notre Dame jacket. He's been a fan of the Fighting Irish all of his life, and a scholarship to Notre Dame validates all the sacrifices Naz and his family made to get him there. Theodore might tell me he never wanted to influence Naz's school choice, but he confessed that he was thrilled with Notre Dame. It was a fine program.

MY INTERACTIONS WITH Cody, Naz, Theodore, Tom, and Skip helped me identify common experiences shared by young athletes trying to succeed in the football sport tournament. As with many institutions, the NFL fraternity is a heterogeneous group of individuals, yet the journeyman and the star are two of the most common types of athletes who persist in the league. In observing these two young prospects, I began to sense that neither travels an easy path. The game requires all athletes to submit to a strict code of conduct. Today there are so many young athletes working with personal trainers and receiving individual coaching that standing apart from the crowd is a challenge. Just as Cody had to learn how to balance self-interest with family values while pursuing his dream, retired NFL athletes like J. B. Brown and OD forbid Naz or Will Hill to rest on their laurels. At TEST Football Academy, the older generation mentors young NFL hopefuls on how to remain focused, stay hungry, and be prepared when challenges arise. The journeyman, Cody, struggles to earn his coaches' respect and catch the attention of a big-time recruiter. Naz, the star, has to keep his head out of the clouds and focus, even as recruiters and others hover ever closer.

When I think about my introduction to the series of football tournaments that would become the central focus of my teenage life and young adulthood, my first recollections are from the summer just before my freshman year of high school. After four successful years of Pop Warner football, and with great expectations, I arrived in the high school gym to register for the freshman football team. I could not believe my eyes when D-Hunt, a teammate from across town, showed up for his physical examination. We were buddies with similar backgrounds: our parents had fled the accelerating urban decay of Newark for the suburbs. But while I had been swimming and horseback riding at YMCA summer camp, D-Hunt had spent the summer in the weight room with his older brother, Mark.

The freshman coach was noticeably impressed with D-Hunt's muscular adolescent physique. On the first day of practice, D-Hunt was handed the starting quarterback position and anointed team captain. My friend's immediate "success" was a real blow to my ego. I had been a star in Pop Warner, and D-Hunt had never even played organized football. I was indignant. As a 14-year-old athlete whose talent had been institutionally affirmed, it had never occurred to me that I would have to compete for the coach's attention against someone who had not even been trained by Pee Wee League coaches. In the end, D-Hunt's real passion turned out to be baseball. My football talents began to shine, perhaps because I was determined to work harder and harder, to never be overlooked or underestimated again. In sports, competition lurks around every corner—even in your own locker room.

Another pivotal moment came in my sophomore year in high school. Coach Mammon pulled me aside during a tackling drill. "Son, if you keep working like that, it will be a real pleasure coaching you." I wanted that kind of affirmation daily, and I became determined to please Coach Mammon. His words boosted my confidence and inspired me to dedicate every ounce of my being to the sport. My sophomore season was probably the most enjoyable one of my entire football career, as I played not only for my sophomore team, but for the Junior Varsity and Varsity teams. As a 15-year-old, I suited up to play three football games at three different levels each week.

New Jersey has long been a hotbed of college football recruiting, so there was no lack of attention. My Middlesex County rivals Jonathan Williams and Kenny Jackson were two of the brightest stars. At the end of my junior year, Jackson and Williams were awarded First Team All-State and All-Conference honors. Williams was touted as one of the finest running backs in the nation. By the end of our senior year, both Williams and Jackson (who attended

Somerville High School, and South River High School) had been awarded All-American honors and signed national Letters of Intent to play for Joe Paterno at Penn State. Earning a football scholarship to play for a national powerhouse is huge: it virtually guarantees that an athlete will be seen on national television and land on the radar of NFL scouts. At the time, there was hardly a bigger coup than to land a place on the Penn State team.

I was initially bypassed for these kinds of national awards but was honored to play alongside Jonathan and Kenny in the New Jersey All-State North-South football game at Rutgers Stadium. I relished that opportunity and was determined to grab a bit of the spotlight. As the time approached for us to report for a weeklong training camp, I could hardly wait to graduate from high school and start practice for the all-star game.

Along with my new teammates, I checked into Rutgers' dorms and finally headed for our first practice. By the time the South squad coaches called my group of defensive backs to the line for wind sprints, it had become obvious that the roster was loaded with terrific football players. I had never heard of Irving Fryar,[32] but clearly he was a superior athlete, perhaps the best on the field that week. I grimaced as Fryar beat me at wind sprints and every other football drill. No matter how hard I tried, it was impossible to outshine him. I'd never played with such a gifted athlete, and I learned from the moment we met. There is a difference between star athletes like Fryar and journeymen, like me.

Because colleges were not heavily recruiting me, the state all-star game was an important tournament marker. It gave me the confidence I would need to excel on the collegiate level, where the skill differences among most players is much more narrow. During the game, I returned the second-half kickoff up the middle and broke for the South sidelines for a seventy-five-yard return. My father told me that he overheard Dick Anderson, the offensive coordinator for Penn State, ask an assistant coach what school I would attend. My father told him that I had accepted a scholarship to James Madison University in Harrisonburg, Virginia—because Penn State never recruited me. Though Coach Anderson would produce his business card and explain there was a place for me at Penn State if I decided to transfer anytime before my junior year, I ultimately stayed at JMU, figuring I would receive more playing time. The paradox of my decision, of course, was that athletes from smaller schools are often overlooked in the NFL draft because scouts question the talent and level of competition they have faced. NFL teams are apprehensive about drafting players from the NCAA Football Championship Series (FCS) division in early rounds without being certain those athletes can compete against NFL-level talent. So while I was a four-year starter at JMU, there was still no guarantee I would have gained significant playing time at Penn State.

For the star and journeyman alike, high school football is just the first milestone in the obstacle-laden sports tournament. None of the accolades, rivals.com rankings, or high school media clippings means much once an athlete arrives at college. Every member of his new team entered school with the same NFL dreams. Once mom and dad entrust their son to a college coach's care, it's time for him to turn the page and prove his worth on the next level.

WHERE THERE ARE stars and journeymen on the football field, there are dedicated spectators in the stands and listening at home. Growing up in Newark, New Jersey, my fascination with "Broadway" Joe Namath, who masterfully guided the New York Jets to victory in Super Bowl III, fueled my passion for football. I can still remember gathering around the television set with my father and uncles to scream for the "Green Machine" or around the radio to listen to broadcasts of Mets' games with my Nana and Pop-pop, who raised five children together though they were both blind. My love for football was sealed when Jets running back Emerson Boozer spoke at our Pop Warner football banquet. From the moment I laid eyes on Boozer's Super Bowl ring, I vowed to play professional football. For the next sixteen years, I poured every ounce of my energy into fulfilling that dream. And like most athletes, when I left the game, my love of it turned me back into a dedicated fan.

In order for football to remain a relevant aspect of the sports-industrial complex, it actually needs that abundant supply of dedicated fans. According to published reports, nearly half of American sports fans identify college or professional football as their favorite sport. To capitalize on this interest, Mark Waller, the NFL's chief marketing officer, invited millions of fans to share stories in a sleek promotional marketing campaign titled "Together We Make Football." Among the fans featured in the promotion was Lee Krost, a 75-year-old quarterback who still plays in a flag football league.[33] The spot makes it clear that dedicated spectators play the most valuable position in American football.[34]

Unbeknownst to me, I was first recruited to adore and then to participate in the sport tournament while sitting in my Nana's living room and watching as the men in my family shout excitedly at the television for the NY Giants, and Jets, Yankees, and Mets, or whoever else was playing on any given day. Not surprisingly, like millions of other boys, teenagers, and men across America (and worldwide), I have remained a dedicated spectator long after my days on the playing field ended. Perhaps one could even say that my participation within and my exit experience from the sport tournament are the very things that compelled me to write a book about how football impacts the men who have dedicated their lives to the game.

3

THE FIELD OF GOALS AND DREAMS

"YOU WANNA GO?"

Normally I'm unscathed when I hear a threat like that. I played football for sixteen years; I'm confident in my ability to "man up." But the aggressive tone was out of place on the sidelines of a TEST Sports NFL Combine Training session.

I turned to face my challenger. He was tall, solid. Based on his muscular form, I guessed he was a former pro football player.

"If that's what you wanna do," I said. I told him that I played pro ball, and that I could handle myself.

"I see you're talking to one of my guys," he growled.

It occurred to me that I was infringing on his territory by giving pointers to Naz. In the never-ending sport tournament, each interaction is a contest. It doesn't matter how many contests you win, backing down is not an option. Even if you're no longer playing the game, it's instinct. The idea that the next contest is always around the corner has been drilled into you. By interacting with this man's pupil, I was a threat, and he couldn't just let that be.

"I'm writing a book about the struggles of players after they leave the game," I told him. I explained that I was in graduate school studying for my PhD in sociology. The deep lines on his face softened. "Then you're gonna want to talk to me. My name is Odessa Turner, but people call me OD" (Figure 3.1).

EARLY IN THE 20th century, the boll weevil decimated cotton crops all across the Mississippi Delta, sending thousands of working-age African American men and women to the northern states looking for jobs, a diaspora known as the Great Migration. Communities were torn apart. Those who stayed behind suffered from poverty and a lack of job opportunities. Parents left

FIGURE 3.1: ODESSA TURNER AT AUTOGRAPH SIGNING.

children with other family members and sent home what money they could spare on payday, but the people they left behind hung on by working odd jobs and bartering for food and services. Each year, they sweated through entire summers of 90-degree days, the humidity so high that they'd perspire through their shirts before breakfast and remain wet until suppertime. They endured.

OD was born into this milieu in 1964. He spent his first 10 years in a run-down shack in an unincorporated section of Ouachita Parish, just outside of Monroe, Louisiana, about an hour and a half east of Shreveport, Louisiana. OD remembers his early childhood as poor but happy. His parents worked odd jobs, and he and his brothers would drop their bait for catfish and skip stones from the silty banks of a nearby creek. He and his brothers played a game that was like football. Because they couldn't afford to buy a ball, they made one out of some rags and string. When they chased small animals, OD could outrun the rabbits.

When he was 10, the family moved to Monroe so his daddy could be closer to his job. Like many towns in the South, Monroe was racially segregated, and OD's family moved to the "Black" part of town. His high school, in the early 1980s, was overwhelmingly Black—segregation that endures today.[1]

By his own admission, OD had little interest in education or sports. His decision to play football happened by accident, basically a result of following in his older brother's footsteps. As a freshman, OD played alongside his brother on the offensive and defensive line. He was tall and skinny, but still faster than most others on the team.

In the summer before his sophomore year, OD caught a glimpse of wide receivers Sammy White (Minnesota Vikings 1976–85) and Charles Smith (Philadelphia Eagles 1974–81), both locals, working out for their upcoming NFL season.[2] One of the players noticed OD and asked his name. The athletes thought he might make a good receiver because of his height. The position had never occurred to OD, but White and Smith told him to run out onto the field to catch a pass. They tossed the ball around for a while, and the receivers offered to help OD learn how to run pass routes over the course of the summer. OD confessed that before meeting these two athletes, he had never thought about attending college either. Playing wide receiver, earning an athletic scholarship to college, and playing in the NFL were way down on the list of priorities at that point in OD's life. But when high school football practice started later that summer, OD's high school coach switched his positions to wide receiver and defensive safety. As the season progressed, OD gained a reputation as a star athlete.

OD credits those older guys for helping him get excited about football, for turning his life around, and teaching him to enjoy coaching young players so much. He likes the thrill of watching a kid receive the lessons and make a positive change for himself. And he's great at it: in all my years involved with football, I have never seen anyone as dynamic as OD teach young athletes to play the wide receiver position. His enthusiasm and energy are truly infectious. His genuine concern for the young people he coaches coils him into a tight spring, ready to unfurl at any moment. At TEST, high school kids anxiously stood in line for a chance to run routes for OD's discerning eyes. He enjoyed the respect.

I was initially drawn to OD because of his no-nonsense approach to coaching. I saw him dressing down Will Hill, the All-America high school safety from northern New Jersey as he was preparing for his first season at the University of Florida on a football scholarship (long before he signed a free agent contract to play for the New York Giants, was released, then picked up on waivers by the Baltimore Ravens). Will let a receiver fake him out during a one-on-one drill, and OD read him the riot act. OD barked at this five-star athlete like a Marine drill instructor dressing down a recruit at basic training. He told Hill, "Those Florida boys will eat you alive if you plan on playing like that down there."

OD is a study in contrasts. He struggles to understand families who "pay all that money" to give their children private athletic coaching sessions and send them to skills-development camps, but he reaps the benefits (in paychecks and coaching experience) of those indulgences. He disapproves of the fact that guys like TEST co-owner Brian Martin, who had zero NFL experience, were making so much money from what OD and other African American former NFL players did for those kids. But OD hasn't figured out how to turn his coaching skills and football experience into a lucrative business of his own. Even though he couldn't give a specific example, OD resents the idea of entrepreneurs such as Brian Martin taking care of White former NFL players while the African American guys got the scraps. African American former NFL players made these sports-training businesses commercially viable, but in OD's assessment, they reaped damn little of the financial rewards.

As I listened to OD's story, I realized that I never heard him mention that he took a money management class in college. OD never said anything about what his parents taught him about calculating interest payments, making solid real estate investments, deciphering the stock market, or any of that. His parents, who "raised him up right," couldn't have known what struggles he would eventually face as a professional football player—not in making money but in keeping it. His parents couldn't teach him what they didn't know. They couldn't prepare him for success in a college classroom, because they had no institutional knowledge of college. OD's indifference to his education could have been a reflection of his parents' attitudes. Or perhaps it was a result of a larger common attitude reflected in the lower per pupil spending ratios common in predominantly poor and Black communities. Maybe it was the tacit understanding that a career in football would give much more to the player and his family than an education ever could. Sociologist Harry Edwards asserts that this permission to forgo all else in the interest of succeeding in a sport pursuit disproportionately damages the social and financial resiliency of African American athletes and robs their communities of young African American men who might otherwise have become doctors, lawyers, accountants, or teachers.

MEDIA AND MONEY

Dr. Edwards acknowledges that money was an essential element of sports even in 1968, but, especially after the turn of the century, the world witnessed exponential growth of American football into the multibillion dollar industry it is today. Several major factors contributed to the transformation of the NFL from a loose affiliation of a handful of teams to today's tightly controlled and unimaginably profitable sports enterprise.

The NFL's partnership with the media has yielded enormous profits for sports in general, and football in particular. Before the 1950s, when broadcast television began to change the shape of professional football, players, coaches, and owners comprised its organizational field. Local newspapers and regional magazines were the primary sources for college recruiting news, and athletes and coaches looked to *Street & Smith Yearbooks* magazine as the definitive college football guide. Before each season began, young athletes would devour its pages, comparing their statistics against the most highly sought-after recruits in the nation. At the end of each season, statewide newspapers selected All-State football teams, and everyone anticipated the announcement of the annual *Parade Magazine* All-America team.

Enter Brian Rasmussen, founder of the Entertainment and Sports Programming Network (ESPN). It took his visionary genius to recognize America's appetite for 24-hour sports television. In 1978, Rasmussen hosted a press conference in Plainville, Connecticut, to announce preliminary plans for his fledgling cable network.[3] Over time, ESPN methodically built a loyal following by landing contracts to broadcast National Collegiate Athletic Association (NCAA) football and basketball, major league baseball (MLB), and the National Hockey League (NHL). In 1980 ESPN began broadcasting round-the-clock coverage, including college football recruiting news on *Sports Center* and the station's first live broadcast of the NFL draft. In 1987, the NFL awarded ESPN its first cable television agreement, which featured 13 broadcasts and the Pro Bowl.[4] ESPN's crowning achievement in professional football came in 1998—it would remain NFL's exclusive cable carrier through 2005.[5] The two fates of football and ESPN have been permanently intertwined, as the growth of each business has fed off the other. These days, those "commitment announcements" from highly recruited high school football players declaring their college choices are broadcast live on ESPN's *Sports Center.*[6]

The NFL successfully pits the broadcast and cable television networks against one another in order to negotiate rich contracts for its broadcast rights. In 2006, the NFL secured the largest television contract in sports history when it sold packages for Sunday afternoon games to CBS and Fox for nearly $8 billion ($4.3 billion from Fox for National Football Conference [NFC][7] broadcasting rights and nearly $3.7 billion from CBS for the rights to American Football Conference [AFC] games). For the right to broadcast every game through the 2010 season, the NFL also entered into a five-year contract worth $3.5 billion with DirecTV. Throw in another eight-year ESPN contract for $8.8 billion dollars, and the NFL raked in $3.75 billion *per year* between 2006 and 2012 for the right to broadcast its games. The exposure offered by television broadcast and video-streaming outlets of NFL games attracts multinational corporations, such as Nike, and enables them to tap into the rapidly expanding cultural consumption of the American sports-industrial complex (SIC) by licensing the NFL brand and securing product endorsements from popular players.[8] With each technological advancement, new dot.com, and video game, the NFL licenses its brand to add even more dollars to its bottom line. These co-mingled corporations generate the gross domestic product (GDP) of a small country.

With money like that passing through handshakes at the upper echelons of the league, it's no wonder players want a larger slice of the pie. Indeed, a lengthy legal battle over decertification and years of antitrust labor litigation (discussed more thoroughly in Chapter 9) culminated in a January 1993 collective bargaining agreement (CBA) between the NFL and the union that represents its athletes, the NFL Players Association (NFLPA). Among other things, measures in the 1993 CBA tied the salary cap and payroll minimums to the contracted TV portion of the league's defined gross revenues (DGR). More broadcast money would mean higher pay for players. The median NFL salary rose from $628,000 to $1,687,000 between 1994 and 2006.[9] The combination of high salaries, television exposure, and heightened social status has helped make the NFL attractive not only to athletes and fans but also to legions of sports agents, coaches, trainers, and owners of facilities such as TEST Sports and ESPN Wide World of Sports in Orlando, Florida. The sports-industrial complex continues to churns on. The result is that the social timetable for NFL athletes is out of sync when they are compared to most men in their age cohort, which often leaves former football players emotionally and financially vulnerable in retirement.[10]

THE COMBINE

When the NFL adopted a plan for unrestricted free agency in 1993,[11] it meant a paradigm shift in the way prospects prepared for the draft. Free agency had offered rookies and young veterans the chance to cash in on big paydays early in their careers. Within a few years of the new rule, first-round draft choices were commanding multimillion-dollar contracts, which encouraged sports agents to take a more active role in raising athletes' draft status. Just as rising profits in US boxing between the world wars led to new deals in which promoters advanced money to fighters to cover training and living expenses in return for a cut of the prize money, sports agents were creating new ways to maximize their own profits as well as their clients'.

Jerry Palmieri stepped into the fray. A Boston College strength coach, Palmieri developed a method to prepare athletes for the grueling physical tests called the NFL Combine. The NFL Combine is an invitational four-day tryout for the top-rated former college athletes. Palmieri's training regimen, which "taught to the test," hit pay dirt when star pupil, linebacker/defensive end Mike Mamula, performed masterfully at the combine in 1995. In an interview with espn.com Mamula recalled,

> At the time, nobody knew what the hell Jerry [Palmieri] was doing because everybody else was more focused on football drills. But I went into the combine having done every test hundreds of times while other guys had never done some of those specific drills.[12]

After running the 40-yard dash in 4.6 seconds and acing the combine's strength and agility test, Mamula was drafted as the seventh pick in the first round by the Philadelphia Eagles. Mamula's meteoric rise earned him a four-year contract reportedly worth $6 million, which included a $2.6 million signing bonus. Mamula is now considered the poster boy for combine training and the millions of dollars agents, prospects, and wanna-be recruits invest in combine camps.

Former New York Giants general manager Ernie Accorsi explains how important combine training has become to an NFL draft prospect: "It's not that different than a high school kid preparing for the SAT. I'd be lying to you if I didn't tell you that a player can make or lose money at these things. It becomes your identity."[13]

When I played football in the mid- and late 1980s, preparation for professional tryouts mainly consisted of weight training, track workouts for speed and endurance, and position-specific drills to develop quickness and skill. In those days, athletes would grab a couple of workout partners and hit the weight room three to four hours a day, three to five times a week, and they'd run sprint intervals on the track four or five times a week, depending on the number of months remaining before the try-out. On late spring afternoons, a group of local current and prospective players from the US Football League (USFL) and the Canadian Football League (CFL) would gather at the Rutgers University football field with a quarterback to run offensive and defensive passing drills. If everything went according to plan, we would be in peak condition right before camp started. The only "science" we knew was hard work and luck. We practiced football drills until we could perform them asleep. If an athlete tweaked a hamstring or rolled an ankle, his only recourse was to rehab with a high school coach or to turn to his college athletic trainer for help.

I really had not given much thought to commercial training regimens and off-season workouts until Jamal, a four-year CFL veteran wide receiver, mentioned that he would spend a month at Cris Carter's Fast Camp[14] in Austin, Texas, before the start of every season. Jamal explained that Carter, a Hall of Fame receiver for the Eagles and the Vikings, had developed an off-season speed training workout program specifically designed for wide receivers. As Jamal offered more details, it began to dawn on me that athletes with financial resources could use Carter's program to gain a leg up on the competition. Jamal had just signed the largest free agent contract in the CFL during the previous off-season. Too much was at stake for him to leave his career up to chance because, like the NFL, the CFL does not guarantee employment contracts. To keep his position on the team secure, Jamal couldn't delay his training until preseason camp; he needed to report to work fleet-footed and ready to run like the wind.

TEACHING TO THE TEST

For this book, I set out to find a program similar to the Cris Carter camp where I could observe athletes going through the speed workout routine. A *New York Times* article led me to a Parisi facility in northern New Jersey,[15] but there were dozens of speed camps and NFL combine training programs across the country. My search for the best example of this new era of sports training brought me to the TEST Sports Club facility in Martinsville, New Jersey, where I met with founder and chief executive officer Brian Martin and performance director Skip Fuller.

TEST Sports Club has an impressive array of strength training, cardiovascular, and flexibility equipment. The two things that really set the 24,000-square-foot facility apart are its 70-yard indoor field house and its state-of-the-art sport rehabilitation and physical therapy program (Figure 3.2). Martin

FIGURE 3.2: TEST SPORTS INDOOR TRAINING FIELD.

explained that football agents value these features, which is why so many prospects choose to prepare for the NFL Combine at TEST. Athletes who suffer injuries near the end of their college careers can rely on the athletic trainers at TEST to help get them back on the field quickly. I knew from personal experience and wished that after I sustained a serious neck and shoulder injury at James Madison University (JMU), I'd had access to the daily ultrasound and electricalic stimulation treatments administered by sports medicine professionals at TEST. My options for physical therapy had, instead, been extremely limited. Once I graduated from college, I was no longer covered under my parent's health insurance and, without an agent to cover medical expenses, my only recourse was to apply ice and heat, rest, and pray.

In today's sports economy, college athletes have little chance of making an NFL roster unless they are from well-off families or are able to sign with agents who agree to advance cash for the best training facilities, coaches, and medical staff, like TEST. Players who are unfamiliar with successful money management strategies may learn too late that these cash advances are often tied to high percentage fees payable when the player signs his first contract. Sometimes, desperately cash-poor players know it's a bad deal, but they sign on anyway because they don't see another way to achieve their goals.

The most noteworthy piece of the new sports economy is that former college athletes who dream of playing in the NFL are not the only athletes who attend speed camps and combine training programs. Brian Martin has developed a business model with tremendous financial upside. The message to football players of all ages is that eventual success in the NFL comes from working hard like professional athletes do. But Martin adds another layer: he says that his programs are developed to focus on teaching youth proper movement patterns to get them trained as early as possible "before bad habits turn into career ending injuries." His goal is to ensure that kids will use these patterns every day, in life and in sports, as they accrue neuromuscular gains in speed, strength, and power. His subliminal message is that only an early and constant over-investment of time and resources can beat out the competition. As a result, the tentacles of the sports-industrial complex have reached all the way down to Pee Wee football. Training camps now regularly host kids as young as six. New Jersey residents can send 7- to 11-year-olds to a one-day summer skills camp at Parisi Speed School or to an eight-week Thursday Night Football camp throughout the school year. Parisi has also partnered with Martin to offer a two-day summer Football Skills Intensive Training Camp at TEST Sports Club.

The TEST HS/Youth Football Academy signifies an important shift in the manufacturing of sport as a cultural product. Unlike the European amateur sports model in which athletic clubs are separate from the educational system, Americans believe athletic participation encourages students to reach their highest potential on the field, in the classroom, and at home.[16] This attitude prevails in college as well.

During a guest lecture I delivered at the University of North Carolina at Chapel Hill, an overwhelming number of undergrads said they believed the best athletes eventually rise to the top. Some begrudgingly conceded that even talented athletes sometimes benefit from a little "extra help" in the form of favoritism by coaches or politics, but they basically believed sport was a meritocracy. I certainly thought the same during my playing career. I knew my parents moved our family from the inner city for better opportunities, but I was in graduate school before I was challenged to consider how privileges like access to proper coaching, safe equipment, and health insurance impact who gets the chance to step onto a playing field. These issues came to life as I spoke with Skip Fuller about my observations of the kids who attend sports camps and training academies. TEST Sports Club is located in an affluent unincorporated community with an average household income of $167,094. Most people would probably agree the kids who work out at TEST come from wealthy families. It's no Monroe, Louisiana.

The first day I attended the TEST HS/Youth Football Academy, I watched intently from the sidelines as a father solicited OD for advice about spending $3,000 on a DVD package to help market his kid directly to college scouts. As the conversation progressed, it was apparent he believed OD had contacts in the college coaching community who could open doors for his son. Eavesdropping, I saw clear parallels between parents enrolling their kids in after-school science and math camps and registering them for sports academies. Although hiring private tutors and paying for SAT preparation courses has been a common practice for years, investing in sports training programs to enhance their children's college applications is a relatively recent phenomenon among middle-class families. Sport entrepreneurs like Brian Martin look a lot like recruiters that hire Ivy League graduates to teach at elite SAT/ACT prep programs.

On that first day, I also saw a steady stream of middle and high school athletes enter the field house, lining up against the walls to study NFL hopefuls perform their combine workouts, not unlike OD watching players run drills back in Monroe, Louisiana, in the early 1980s. But by 7:00 PM, nearly 150 kids were eager to run high knee sprints and practice blocking drills. When I thought about TEST's program pricing, which included a six-week program to attend unlimited weekly classes for $299, or $22 per class for the older kids, not to mention the hundreds of youth athletes who are also invited to attend Martin's eight-week summer camp at a cost of $400 apiece, it was clear that TEST HS/Youth Football Academy was a moneymaking machine.

I see Brian Martin, and other like-minded sport entrepreneurs, as part of the ever-expanding sports-industrial complex. Facilities and programs such as TEST Sports, HS/Youth Football Academies, the NFL Combine training programs, and Cris Carter's Speed Camps have created a seismic shift in sports that now favors individuals with ample financial resources or sponsors. Today, sports agents invest millions of dollars to elevate the draft status of a pool of predominantly Black NFL prospects. Young athletes, with the support of their families, also have access to world-class training facilities and programs once reserved for only the most elite competitors. These changes occur as sport entrepreneurs seize on American's obsession with fame and fortune in a market-driven economy that perpetuates the expansion of the sports-industrial complex.

Many public and private high schools offer gyms where kids can lift weights and work out at no cost, so how does a small business owner like Brian Martin attract legions of kids to train at his facility? Former NFL athletes play an important role in the professionalization of youth football and in an entrepreneur's ability to market these new enterprises to an ever-broadening audience. Professional athletes lend credibility to facilities like TEST because of the skills, knowledge, and networks they possess. Endorsements from big name athletes are vital to the success of private facilities that offer elite-level training. Since the Northeast is an attractive location for former NFL and collegiate athletes, sport entrepreneurs like Martin can offer numerous camps and instructional clinics led by former professional athletes throughout the year. A four-hour drive on interstate I-95 in either direction provides access to an abundance of former New York Giants and Jets, Washington Redskins, Baltimore Ravens, Philadelphia Eagles, and New England Patriots interested in pocketing a couple hundred dollars for a few hours' work. The parents I observed seemed thrilled to watch a Super Bowl hero instruct their children in the proper way to pass, catch, and run through tackling dummies. The older high school students looked forward to these sessions because it gave them an opportunity to showcase their talents before the pros.

During my time rising through the football ranks it was nearly impossible to meet a professional athlete, let alone train with one. With the rapid growth of the sports-industrial complex, former NFL athletes have become more accessible to the public—for a fee, that is. Rather than relying solely on amateur coaches, young athletes from well-off families are now turning to former elite athletes and other specialists for expert training.

After talking to dozens of high school and college athletes I began to realize that middle- and upper-class families from California to Massachusetts pour millions of dollars into private high school football programs so their kids have a chance to attract the attention of college recruiters. Journalist Ben McGrath of the *New Yorker* magazine offers a detailed account of a new class of national touring high school football teams.[17] The subject of McGrath's article is Don Bosco Prep, a perennially ranked national powerhouse football program. Don Bosco is located in Ramsey, New Jersey, an affluent suburb of New York City. After a decade of mediocrity, the principal of Don Bosco Prep hired a new coach to take over the football program. In 1999, Coach Toal's first year at the helm, the Don Bosco Ironmen reached the state finals. Three seasons later, prep star and former Green Bay Packer running back, Ryan Grant, led the Ironmen to a state championship. McGrath reports that a habitual 50-point margin of victory has led to sponsorship deals with Reebok, New Balance, and Nike. As scouts from major college programs make frequent stops to campus, student applications for admission have increased by 60% from New York/New Jersey/Connecticut metro area junior high kids who hope to be the next highly sought after recruit. In addition to private lessons and summer football camps, super programs like Don Bosco's play an instrumental role in the professionalization of football youth sports.

I observed another fascinating pattern unfold with sport academy and training sessions: while lower- and working-class kids see sports as a chance for a better life, many middle-class and well-off Americans are now spending thousands of dollars to participate in privatized, professionalized youth sports.[18] Social scientists apply the term "cultural omnivore" to well-heeled families who seek to replace cultural highbrow snobbery as a status marker for cosmopolitan and eclectic tastes.[19] Most of the research in this area has focused on musical taste where fans of classical music and opera are reportedly more likely than others to also enjoy "middle-brow" and "low-brow" music genres.[20] A similar move is sweeping across the world of youth sports. I have witnessed parents drop their young daughters off at after-school volleyball and field hockey camps, then shuffle their boys to private football lessons.

Possibly the most striking example of sports cultural omnivorism that exists today is located in Bradenton, Florida. The IMG Academy[21] offers summer camps, weekend programs, and year-round sports academies to the young novice and to the professional athlete alike. What sets IMG Academy apart is the $60,000 annual fee that combines specialized sports instruction with a private school education for kids from elementary school all the way to post-graduate college students. Adolescents who attend IMG academy can enroll in the country club and Olympic sports training programs like tennis, golf, soccer, and lacrosse; or working-class competitive sports such as football, basketball, and baseball. IMG also offers a Performance Institute, which includes a College Planning and Placement Coaching Program designed to help high school athletes reach their goal of studying and playing sports on the collegiate level. Well-heeled families are rapidly redefining football from a low-brow grunt sport into a cultural event that endows their children with a specific brand of social capital.

As with colleges, private high schools can recruit, enroll, and support athletes in a way that most public schools cannot. With more financial resources, these programs can invest in building better facilities and better support networks for players. With better programs come better athletes. With better athletes come more victories. With more victories come better athletes. All of these positive developments attract media attention and more exposure. Media attention and better exposure beget increased admissions. The more kids who seek admission, the more selective the institution can be. Better begets better; richer begets richer. And so it goes.

Another development that perfectly aligned American's craving for sports and the adolescent boy's thirst for stardom was ESPN's decision to nationally televise high school football games. Traditionally, television high school football broadcasts were limited to local state championship or all-star games. In 2005, the Disney family of sports broadcasting networks (ESPN, ESPNU, and online broadcaster ESPN3) began airing regular season matchups between nationally ranked high school teams. That year ESPNU introduced the *Old Spice High School Showcase*, which featured eight nationally ranked high school teams. Network executives moved quickly to expand the schedule from four to thirteen games per season after the game between Nease High School (Florida) and Hoover High School (Alabama) attracted viewers in nearly 1 million households—the highest rated high school football game in television history. Coincidentally, that game also served as a national coming-out party for future Heisman Trophy winner and NFL quarterback Tim Tebow.

The demand for high school football broadcasting has since grown to the point that 31 national games were televised in 2011. The University of Texas Longhorn Network planned to televise up to 18 additional games before charges of unfair recruiting advantages from rival college football programs caused the Big 12 Conference to scrap the idea.[22] From the network's perspective, the appeal for more high school football programming is a simple matter of economics: low broadcast cost, advertising revenue, and filler programming during otherwise dead airspace.

Nationally televised games equate to exposure for high school athletes. Parents view these games as a once in a lifetime opportunity to showcase their children's talents to a national audience. For the high school coaches, television broadcasts bring attention and possibly better recruits to their programs as well as potential advertisers, sponsors, and product endorsements. Surely, young athletes across the country now dream of bursting onto the scene in a nationally televised ESPN game; however, that perk is only reserved for a few highly ranked football programs. The selectivity of these broadcasts has perhaps contributed to a sense of frustration and despair for lightly recruited athletes who hoped to earn a major college football scholarship.

Entrepreneurs like Brian Martin challenge the traditional model of coaching by convincing families of the benefits of after-school training. While financially stable parents have long provided their children with private piano lessons and academic tutors, entrepreneurs are tapping into America's obsession with sports by repackaging this concept and bringing it to the masses. Brian Martin and his contemporaries helped transform private training for professional athletes into a legitimate cultural product for mass consumption.

TOWARD THE END of the TEST Football Winter Academy, I had a long talk with OD. I mentioned that I thought he had a real gift for coaching. He thanked me for the compliment. I asked him what I thought was an obvious question. "Have you ever thought about running your own football camp for kids?" OD was about to turn and walk away when he stopped. He turned back, and with a mild stutter, he told me that he wanted to run his own camp. He just didn't know how to get started.

OD shared his vision for his summer camp. He wanted to host camps in wealthy northern New Jersey; Westchester County, New York; and southern Connecticut communities. He reasoned that families in these neighborhoods would pay enough that former NFL athletes like himself could earn what they are really worth. OD also wanted to host free or reduced price football clinics in poor and disadvantaged communities throughout the Northeast. I joked with OD that his strategy was the Robin Hood approach. He wanted to charge higher fees for hosting camps in wealthier communities and pay former athletes higher wages for working those jobs, and meanwhile offer disadvantaged athletes similar opportunities for a lower cost. OD believed that if he could secure enough high-paying work in the suburbs, the former NFL guys would agree to accept smaller fees for running camps in poorer communities. The final piece of OD's strategy was to use his status as a former NFL athlete to secure corporate sponsorships to help financially underwrite the camps in disadvantaged communities.

I agreed to help OD by contacting high school and Pop Warner coaches to see if we could drum up some support for the plan. Between February and June 2008 I sent out over 125 emails and followed up with nearly 200 calls.

OD's plan never took off in the wealthier sections of New York, New Jersey, or Connecticut since many coaches in those communities ran their own camps. Historically, head coaches from prominent Division I football programs have held a tight grip on the youth instructional football market. College coaches used their lofty positions to draw starry-eyed kids to campus. In addition to supplementing their income, iconic coaches such as Joe Paterno and Lou Holtz used these summer camps to identify and recruit top high school talent. These highly esteemed coaches not only hosted summer camps, but they also exercised their authority to teach and mentor young athletes granted by the mission of interscholastic and intercollegiate sports programs. By virtue of their position as educators, college coaches often side-stepped accusations of profiting off kids since summer camps represent a legitimate opportunity for athletes to acquire new skills. Through the 1960s, '70s, '80s, and '90s, middle- and working-class families would load up the station wagon and drop off their boys at Penn State, Ohio State, and other big-time college football campuses to learn the fundamentals of football.

Slowly, high school coaches who ran successful programs began to recognize they could cash in on their local fame as well. Retired head coach Dick Dullaghan of Ben Davis High School in Indianapolis was one of the first to start this trend when 22 youngsters attended his camp 40 years ago. Coach Dullaghan's "Bishop Dullaghan Football Camps" reflect the tremendous growth that has occurred in the youth football market over the years. His brochure boasts that over 2,500 athletes attended the Bishop Dullaghan Football Camp in 2011 from all across the nation.[23] Coach Dullaghan's Football Camp and the TEST Football Academy are two examples of the proliferation of football programs now aimed at young athletes from Pee Wee football to the professional level.

OD and I did have limited success with two public high schools in Connecticut. The head coaches and athletic directors at both schools knew OD from his playing days with the Giants and were eager to have NFL athletes host a camp on their campuses. The problem we encountered was that both schools are located in communities with higher than average unemployment rates. The technical school we worked with is located in a semi-rural area; the other school is situated in a blighted urban neighborhood overrun by gang activity. After receiving my initial email, Coach Vinnie called from Platt Tech high school to see if we would run a camp for his team. Coach Vinnie started off by telling me the school did not have money budgeted for a football camp and that most of the kids came from families that could barely rub two nickels together. It was obvious his team could benefit from our program; however, OD insisted on being paid. He was adamant that the NFL athletes he works with were tired of being asked to donate their time to a "good cause." Coach Vinnie offered to have his coaching staff serve as volunteers if that would help supplement the cost. Before we ended the phone call, Coach Vinnie said he just wanted me to know "this is only our second year playing varsity football. Some of my kids got knocked around pretty bad last year when we played against the rich schools." Coach Vinnie must have known that I am a sucker for a tough situation.

Within a few hours I had a similar conversation with Coach Petro from an inner-city school in Hartford, Connecticut. He got right to the point: "Listen Coach Turner, I'm not going to blow smoke up your ass," he said. "My kids got some real challenges. I know how to coach, so that's not really why I need your help. The starting quarterback from last year's squad was sitting home and got executed gangland style earlier this summer and the kids took it pretty hard. I'm an Old Italian guy who's about to retire. These kids need some positive Black male role models and I thought you could help." With those two short phone calls I was reminded how much race, social class, and family background really do matter. For months I had been observing kids whose parents paid $240 without hesitation for an after-school football academy in a state-of-the-art training facility. And suddenly, I had coaches telling me about these high school kids who could not afford a two-day football summer camp for $25.

Given the pressure resulting from the rapid rise of the sports-industrial complex combined with inadequate training facilities and other resources, it is impressive that kids from disadvantaged backgrounds ever find their way to the NFL. Plenty of young athletes can run fast and catch a football, but that talent often goes unnoticed without the proper guidance and training. Coach Vinnie and Coach Petro shed light on obstacles faced by urban and rural teenage athletes who believe that football is a pathway to a better life. After several long discussions with OD, we were able to bring both schools together for a two-day summer camp. I persuaded OD to accept $1,000 from each school since their coaching staffs agreed to assist with the coaching duties. OD was emphatic in his requirement to stay within a 10-to-1 NFL athlete to camper ratio. Unfortunately, the $2,000 budget only allowed us to hire four former NFL athletes, not seven. Even though the situation required a good deal more compromise than he wanted to make, OD's first summer camp was up and running.

A few days before camp started, Coach Vinnie called and asked OD to keep an eye out for Charles—a young man he felt had the potential to play wide receiver in college. Charles had the raw talent to qualify for the 200- and 400-meter state finals in track as a junior, but Coach Vinnie worried that his performance might suffer during the upcoming football season from playing on such an inexperienced team. Coach Vinnie confessed that as a second-year head coach he lacked the expertise and the networks to make sure Charles received the attention he deserved from college recruiters. Coach Vinnie's concerns were legitimate. Charles made nice strides over the two-day camp, but he needed someone like OD to help develop his talent to prepare him to play on the college level.

At 8:30 AM in late July 2008, 65 high school athletes paced the sidelines of Platt Tech's unmarked practice field, anxious to get started. OD was so pumped he almost forgot to put the car in park before jumping out the driver's side door. He grabbed a bag of footballs and began barking out instructions for the kids to loosen up by jogging around the field and forming lines to stretch out.

On the second day of camp, OD blew his whistle and called for both teams to "grab a knee" so I could talk to them about the importance of grades in the college recruiting process. About five minutes into my talk, OD cut me off and screamed at a kid from Coach Petro's program. "Hold on a minute, Coach Turner. I'm sorry for interrupting you, but we have a young man who wants to talk while you're talking. Apparently he knows more than you do about the importance of academics. My brother, why don't you step right on up front and take over for Coach Turner, since you know so much!" Rasheed tried to apologize and sink back into the crowd, but OD was not having it. "Oh no partner, you get right up there and speak your piece. See I deal with kids like you all the time. You think you so fuckin' hard, and don't have to listen to nobody. But you one of them hard headed motherfuckers. I've watched you since we got here and you don't want to listen to nobody. You think that just because you're a decent athlete, you can do whatever the fuck you want." The episode escalated when Rasheed took a defensive posture, "Nawh it ain't like that. But you know, I said I was sorry for talking. I just be trying to get my teammates to stop messin' up and do their jobs on the field."

OD cut off Rasheed right there, "See, that's your fuckin' problem little brother. You can't be a football player and worry about what your teammates is doing. Do your damn job and trust your teammates! Let your coaches worry about everybody else. I've seen too many young heads like you who think they tough; most of them end up coming to see me when I worked over at Spofford Detention Center before they get shipped upstate to do a bid."[24] Once OD finished giving Rasheed hell, he turned back to me, "I'm sorry Coach Turner, but y'all fellas got to understand that this man played pro ball then went back to school to become a doctor. He don't need nothing from you, but y'all trying to get where he is. So listen up and be serious about what he's sayin.'"

Before we packed our gear in OD's SUV, Coach Petro called Rasheed over and said his undersized star linebacker is a good kid who was trying to straighten up after a couple of run-ins with the law. I asked Rasheed about his grades and plans after high school. Rasheed said he hoped football would get him into junior college somewhere far away from Connecticut. I told Rasheed to talk with Coach Petro about his goals then meet with a guidance counselor or the school principal for help. We exchanged phone numbers and I agreed to check in with him after the season ended. After one brief phone call, I never heard from Rasheed again.

After the final camp session ended, I spent most of the ride back to New York City reflecting on the events of the past two days. Charles, Rasheed, and the other Connecticut high school athletes were a sharp contrast to the kids OD coached at TEST. Rasheed and the other athletes at OD's camp brought to mind the different social theories on race, masculinity, and sports I read in graduate school. Coach Vinnie told me his kids were mainly from working-class rural families and attended vocational school to learn a trade. Most of his kids had no illusions of playing football beyond high school. After a few conversations with kids on Coach Petro's teams, I began to understand how playing football could serve as a survival strategy for avoiding gangs and selling drugs as well as a gateway to college, which is consistent with much of the literature about Black males and sports.[25] The sole White athlete who played for Coach Petro decided to try out for the varsity team because he thought football could help get his family out of poverty, too. Rasheed, Charles, Coach Vinnie, Coach Petro, and others at that Connecticut camp are living examples of how race, social class, and masculinity operate simultaneously on multiple levels in the world of football. When OD screamed out, "Stand up and take your ass whipping like a man," those instructions can take on drastically different meaning for a high school athlete at Platt Tech or one of Coach Petro's football players, as compared to the suburban kids at TEST Sports in Martinsville, New Jersey.

While families in well-off communities enroll their kids in first-rate facilities and private schools, young athletes from less advantaged backgrounds travel a far different path to college athletic fields. It is tempting to view sports as a level playing field where the most talented athletes rise to the highest echelons of the game. However, it is a mistake to overlook how social factors such as quality coaching, access to top sport camps and training facilities, adequate medical care, and good visibility for recruiting affect who gets to compete in the sport tournament. Sure, Charles or any of the other high school athletes who attended OD's Connecticut camp could be the next Division I football star recruit, but the possibility of that happening is far slimmer without access to the inner workings of the sports-industrial complex.

4

COLLEGE FOOTBALL

THE TRANSITION FROM high school to college football is a major event in every athlete's life. After four years of careful guidance under the watchful eyes of parents and trusted coaches, the young man is ready for some freedom. National Signing Day comes with enormous anticipation all around as high school seniors sign binding letters of commitment to attend—and play for—a specific NCAA-affiliated college football program.

The phrase "student-athlete" is always carefully highlighted. It's part of the National Collegiate Athletic Association (NCAA) mission statement, there to help justify why athletes are unpaid but also to point out how their work is rewarded: often some combination of tuition, room and board, textbooks, and, of course, the all-important platform to show off their talents to adoring fans and NFL scouts alike. The NCAA is the governing body of college-level athletics, and the college athlete, parents, and his school must comply with its rules for the privilege of playing amateur, intercollegiate sports. Since its inception in 1906, this not-for-profit organization has done a great deal of good for the wide variety of athletes who comprise its membership, but for our purposes here, I will discuss it as the functional creator and enforcer of rules and regulations pertaining to college football athletes and programs. In that role, the NCAA aims to ensure that the college athlete has a pure and unfettered experience of playing amateur sports.

Examples of the regulations under the NCAA jurisdictional umbrella include rules that compel athletes to uphold certain academic standards—to ethically achieve and maintain a 2.0 grade-point average and to work toward graduation; rules that forbid athletes from earning money or receiving any kind of gifts or enrichment that may be construed as intended to secure influence over the outcome of games; and rules that restrict the number of hours a sports program can demand of the student-athlete's time. When the number and degree of infractions warrant, the NCAA enacts rules to address issues in specific sports groups, such as Division I football. In fact, as you might suspect, there are *quite* a few rules directed at college football programs and *quite* a few measures in place to sanction players, coaches, and programs.

If the NCAA discovers a breach of its rules, it launches an inquiry to determine whether the institution or university has done enough to control or enforce existing rules and school-specific policies and whether that school exhibits sufficient will to enforce future comprehensive compliance with the NCAA rules and policies. The investigations can, and frequently do, take years. If the NCAA sanctions a school for allowing an academic scandal or exhibiting a lack of institutional control,[1] for instance, all of the program's student-athletes suffer. Even if they have nothing to do with the violation, sanctions cast a pall on the whole program, and career dreams can be shattered.

More worrisome to the college or university is the NCAA's ability to penalize the errant institution by taking away participation rights, whether in regular or post-season play. Consider a June 2010 incident in which the University of Southern California was found, by the NCAA, to have failed in exercising institutional control (a system of monitoring and enforcement of NCAA rules) regarding student-athletes in multiple sports. The NCAA imposed a two-year post-season ban on USC, the school's football program lost 30 NCAA scholarships over a three-year period, and it was placed on four-year probation.[2]

THE AVERAGE COST to support a Big Ten football program is $19.5 million, but the average team revenue is approximately $43.4 million. Schools can make even more revenue if their teams make it into post-season play.[3] With that amount of money at stake, university presidents, football coaches, and athletic administrators have strong incentives to discipline student-athletes who step out of line. Sanctions like those meted out to USC in 2010 are crushing, so schools work to keep the athletes on the straight and narrow, with good grades to boot.

The good grades part can be especially tough. Many times, high school athletes are overly focused on sports, which deprive them of learning experiences. They can arrive on campuses unprepared for college-level academics. A review of admissions data by NCAA Division I Football

Bowl Series (FBS) in 2009 found that many schools had relaxed, "special" admissions standards for highly recruited athletes.[4] In fact, the practice was found to be so pervasive that athletes at 27 universities were reportedly 10 times more likely to have benefited from special admissions programs than the general student population.[5] Critics contend that as a result of these lower admissions standards, too many athletes are over-matched in the classroom, and that this situation makes cheating and other types of academic scandals inevitable.[6] For their part, many programs work to bring student-athletes up to par in the classroom. If they are unprepared for the rigors of coursework, student-athletes are provided remediation and extensive academic support to help maintain their eligibility to participate. As a result of pressure from the NCAA as well as scholarship losses at some Division I athletic programs, schools have increased their academic support budgets to between $20,000 and $40,000 per year per scholarship athlete. Additionally, according to the *New York Times*, in 2005 more than 100 major college athletic departments spent a combined $150 million on academic support programs. Institutions such as the University of Southern California, the University of Georgia, and the University of Maryland have poured millions into state-of-the-art educational and learning facilities for athletes, and some schools supply football players with a tutor for each class.[7] These "learning specialists" develop action plans, organize schedules, and help athletes plan for tests and papers. Mary Willingham,[8] a former instructor in the Education 399 (peer tutoring) program at the University of North Carolina at Chapel Hill, described the setup:

> Basically, they [athletes] just get a schedule and they just follow the schedule. Sort of like the military. They really don't have a choice in the classes they take because the advisor just puts them in classes. So, if one of the guys—and I saw it happen all the time—said, "I'm not coming to Psych 101 tutoring. I don't need it. It's not necessary. I'm fine in that class." Then they would get written up like they were a high school student or middle school student, and then that note would go somehow to their coach, and then they would have to do something or other. There was not a lot of negotiating. It was pretty much all mandated. So the athletes would get mad, for example, if they thought

they had a good grade on a test and felt like they didn't need tutoring, which seems OK with me. But they were still mandated to have to go to tutoring.

Many athletes I interviewed for this study confirmed that these practices have been common in Division I football for decades. Their attendance is checked throughout the semester. Their actions are observed. Absences and misbehaviors are reported to coaches, who dispense punishment. Athletes who want to play in the NFL learn to acquiesce.

Of course, the struggles for those athletes who are unprepared or under-prepared for college-level work can be overwhelming. Athletes are compelled to follow the dictates of their coaches and the NCAA rules, simultaneously absorbing the negative attitudes and stigma that come from needing extra help for coursework. On the surface, football athletes are treated far differently today than they were back in my day. However, the shame of remedial learning remains unchanged.[9]

When I arrived at James Madison University (JUM), I had to deal not only with being unprepared for the academic rigor of college but also with the awkwardness of life as a visible minority at a Predominantly White Institution (PWI). As an athlete, I had figured out how to skate through high school without developing strong study habits, but this came back to haunt me very quickly at JMU. The worst experience of my academic career took place early in my freshman English composition course. I wanted to sink under the desk when the young, blonde teaching assistant (TA) folded my first paper in half, turned it face down, and slid it underhand across the desk to me—not so subtly announcing to me in front of the entire class that I needed to go to the reading and writing lab for remedial help before turning in any more assignments. She could not have known that singling me out like that would evoke painful memories of junior high, when I was relegated to remedial education. Even as an 11-year-old city kid, recently arrived in a predominantly White suburban school district, I had noted that most of the students in remedial education classes were Black boys like me. (Since then, I have wondered if this was the administration's way of dealing with the influx of Black boys pouring into their schools from Newark, Harlem, Brooklyn, and other inner-city neighborhoods.) I was also fully aware that I was not stupid. None of that dampened the shame. Now, years later, I once again felt the sting of being thought of as intellectually inferior. After shedding a few bitter tears, I swallowed my pride, scheduled an appointment in the reading and writing lab, and vowed to master every skill I seemed to be lacking. I promised myself that I'd never let anyone belittle me that way again.

I was not surprised to learn that other athletes had similar shaming experiences. Roland, a young Black man from Washington, DC, offered a detailed account of a Virginia Tech University professor who repeatedly singled out football players for being late to her 8:00 AM class even though they had explained to her several times that their mandatory 6:30 AM team workouts prohibited them from arriving on time. What this professor may not have understood was that the totalizing institution of college football requires athletes to place football as the highest priority. Maybe she was chiding them for not taking a stand against the coaches or for not insisting that they leave practice early so they could arrive at class on time. Maybe she didn't understand that those athletes felt that leaving practice early to arrive at class on time would put their future football careers in jeopardy. Maybe she didn't understand, as Roland said, "I had no choice."

I want to return to OD's story as an example of how the system works to the detriment of the most vulnerable young men. From humble beginnings, OD established himself as a bona fide star football player and a top college-recruiting prospect in his junior year of high school. High profile schools such as Louisiana State University (LSU), Grambling University, and the University of Alabama offered him athletic scholarships; however, his mother wanted him to attend Northwestern Louisiana State (Northwestern State) because the coach there offered a package deal to his older brother, but *only* if OD promised to attend one year later.

OD's high school senior year turned out to be a real breakout season. His mother, who had not attended any of his games previously, did not know how well OD was doing until one day a grocery store clerk handed her a copy of a local newspaper article in which OD's gridiron accomplishments were featured prominently. After the season ended, OD was selected to play in the state all-star game, which was well attended by college recruiters who tried to persuade his mom to let him accept a scholarship to their schools. He remained true to his promise to his mother and chose to attend Northwestern State. Even though OD could have played for higher profile programs, he put the needs of his family first. This is a recurrent theme in the athletes' retellings of their struggles in life during and after their football careers.

OD describes his four years at Northwestern State as rocky. In his freshman year, OD's brother invited him to attend a sex party on campus. OD declined and told his brother "not to get involved with that mess." Not long afterward, OD's brother was implicated in a gang rape case when the victim placed OD's brother at the scene. Charges were later dropped against his brother, after testimony was given that proved he didn't participate in any of the sexual activities. However, OD's brother was promptly dismissed from the team. He lost his scholarship, which led to his early and involuntary exit from the game. OD honored his commitment to remain at Northwestern State instead of transferring to a bigger, wealthier program. Why? In part, he stayed on because the coaches allowed him to start as a wide receiver on offense and a free safety on defense. But more important, OD values loyalty. OD wanted to stay near his mom, but he also felt indebted to his head coach, who helped him financially after OD announced that he needed to drop out of school to support his pregnant girlfriend.

Although OD excelled on the gridiron, his performance in the classroom suffered that year. When his grades fell below a 2.0 GPA in the spring of his junior year, OD was declared academically ineligible and had to enroll for summer courses at a local community college. OD was told he would be reinstated if he repeated two courses and received passing grades in both. Without his financial aid, OD quickly became homeless and lacked money to pay for food. He described how he slept on friends' couches and in the dugout of a local baseball field during the summer. He felt the shame of not being able to take care of his most basic needs.

OD's story gives us a good example of how the current system can imperil individuals who are financially vulnerable. The truth is that OD would have gone straight to the NFL if that path had been open to him. Unlike many players, OD was able to hang on through these difficulties and had his scholarship reinstated that fall. The following football season, he was selected as an all-conference performer for the third straight season. NFL recruiters flocked to talk with OD about the upcoming draft and to interview his college coaches.

Even though OD played football professionally and did quite well for himself, he is still bitter about the way Northwestern State handled his situation. In 2010, OD declined an invitation to return to campus for his induction into the Northwestern State athletic "N" Club hall of fame. A posting on the athletic department's website declares that OD is regarded as one of the most skilled athletes in the football team's history.[10] According to OD, "The team and the school turned its back on me when I needed them most."

MATT HEWITT, A TALL, light-brown-skinned, recent college athlete I interviewed at the TEST Sports NFL Combine Training Program explained how running with the wrong crowd in Englewood, New Jersey, during his first two years of high school cost him dearly: "Had I kept on, I could have ended up in jail or on the streets. Too much bad stuff was happening so I started concentrating on football. After my junior year in high school my GPA was only 1.8. That summer I went to the University of Maryland's football camp for QBs and receivers.[11] When the coach asked about my grades and I told him [I had] a D average, he just walked away. Didn't even bother sayin' nuthin'. My senior year I pulled my grades up to a 2.3 and started learning how to study—too late though."

The NCAA rules required that Matt attend a junior college prior to accepting scholarship offers. His poor academic performance in high school also forced him to turn down numerous offers from schools that wanted him to enroll after his third semester in junior college. "There were a whole bunch of schools willing to sign me, but they wanted me to transfer in December. But, because my high school grades were so low, I had to pass up scholarships to some big-time schools. Syracuse was real close to signing me, then backed out at the last minute."

In an unusual set of circumstances, the University of Arkansas made a last-minute athletic scholarship offer. As a Razorback, Matt matured as a student and earned a place on the University of Arkansas' Lon Farrell Academic Honor Roll for the fall of 2006.[12] When asked why he did not receive that honor again, Matt simply stated, "It got too hard. Football started taking up more and more time. They demand a lot from you in football and it's pretty hard trying to juggle everything."

Matt's comments help to shed light on an equally important issue. While some college football players graduate at higher rates than some groups in the general student population, athletes from disadvantaged backgrounds who play for major college programs often struggle to remain on track academically.[13]

Many athletes spoke of being placed in academic majors with certain "athlete-friendly" classes. The practice of academic steering in university athletic programs forces athletes to suppress their own interests in favor of committing to a course of study that their academic handlers feel can keep them eligible. Phillip Bobo's insights below are particularly informative with regard to the extent of this practice.

Bobo, a former wide receiver at Washington State University, shared an extremely uncomfortable situation that he and many other college football players experience—a lack of control over their course of study. "If you don't have either parent who's experienced the process of going to college, you're automatically doomed to fail," he said. "I was the first person ever to experience college from my family. When I got to Washington State, the counselors were more interested in me playing football than in me learning a trade, so I became a social science major, whatever the fuck that means. They asked me, 'What are you interested in?' and I said, 'Movies and music,' and they said, 'Ah well you have to do xyz.' They asked me what I was interested in and what I wanted to do, but their thing was to make sure I played ball. They just lumped me into this shit, and at that point I was done with school."

"Remember in high school I had over a 3.1 GPA," Bobo continued. "But when I went to college I was like, I'm not interested in none of this shit. I want to do music and I want to do film. I was like, why are you teaching me this shit? [They said]—*'Because you have to graduate, and you have to stay eligible!'* My first year I got a 2.7 and I got it because I needed a 2.5 to pledge Omega [Omega Psi Phi fraternity]," he said. "That was my motivation to do well in school. After that I got a 2.0 the whole time. I wouldn't go to class at all; then I would do something at the end of the semester; and then the teachers would do something to change my shit so I could stay eligible. I didn't even earn that shit. I didn't do shit for four years, 'cause I redshirted. I just did enough to keep them off my back. I got one A my whole time in college, that was in Psych 101, sex education [laughing out loud], and that's it. I just felt not interested. None of my high school coaches or counselors mentored me about college at all, either."

Bobo attributed his academic underachievement to two factors: his parents' inability to help him appreciate the value of a college education due to their lack of institutional knowledge, and his academic counselors' commitment to maintaining his academic eligibility over supporting his intellectual curiosity. Instead of pursuing his passion for entertainment, which might have led him to become a radio/TV/film or theater major, Bobo simply chose to accept that he was destined to be a football player.

"Everybody's thing was like 'Man, look what you doing in football, why don't you stick with that?'" Bobo said. "My thing was that football is just where my life happened to be going so that's where it is."

Perhaps growing up homeless on the streets of East Pasadena had left Phillip Bobo feeling frustrated and powerless to stand up to his coach or to his academic advisors at WSU, or maybe it was just easier for him to abide by the unwritten code that big-time college football programs recruit athletes to play football, not to graduate as dean's list students. In either case, Bobo never received encouragement to be anything other than a football player. "I had nobody who would try and help me get there," Bobo said. "I never took it upon myself to say, 'What the fuck are you telling me? I want to do this, how do I do this?' The exploration of trying to attain goals outside of football was nonexistent. The way my life was built up, being an actor was never an option for me. My shit was football. But I was dying inside."

In an attempt to gain greater clarity on the academic steering situation described by former academic tutor Mary Willingham and others, I sat down with a group of 15 student-athletes at the University of North Carolina at Chapel Hill in the summer of 2013. The session included a mix of football players, wrestlers, a swimmer, track and field athletes, male basketball players, and a student manager for the women's basketball team. These students shared anecdotes about the challenges they faced playing sports at a high-profile major Division I program. Among the more notable comments that day, James, a White, male, long distance runner on the track team, reported that it was a common practice among athletic advisors to steer athletes toward easier classes or less demanding majors. This charge was not new to me, but it was the first time that I encountered a White athlete from a non-revenue-generating sport willing to confirm the practice. Malik, a defensive back for the Tar Heels, also described an episode when former head coach Butch Davis declared in a team meeting, "If you wanted an education, you should have gone to Harvard. You came to North Carolina to play football."[14]

STARTING IN THE mid-1980s, the NCAA implemented a series of rules designed to increase Division I athletes' graduation rates; under the latest provision, teams must earn a minimum score of 900 for their four-year academic progress rate (APR) or a 930 average over the two most recent years. Teams that fail to meet these standards cannot participate in post-season play, including all NCAA tournaments and football bowl games.[15] In spite of these NCAA initiatives to keep athletes in school and graduation rates high, nearly every athlete I met at TEST training for the NFL Combine withdrew from school after his final college football game. Of the 25 athletes I interviewed at the TEST NFL Combine Training Program, six players did graduate from college, while most others were 9 to 15 credits short of earning degrees. Two of the NFL prospects that did matriculate from the University of Minnesota joked about how crazy it was for Division I football players not to graduate if the university was providing a free education; yet the reality is that most of the athletes I interviewed were too preoccupied with making it to the NFL to focus on graduating. After completing a six- to nine-year high school and college apprenticeship, some athletes believe that they have a greater chance of obtaining upward mobility through professional football than by counting on a university degree. Some athletes do feel empowered to select majors and design their own course schedules. One such athlete is former Stanford University defensive back Vaughn Bryant,[16] who elected to complete his bachelor's degree in sociology before reporting to preseason training camp with the Detroit Lions. Unfortunately for Bryant, his delay put him behind the competition for a spot on the team. He was cut from the roster before the first game. Vaughn valued his education where others apparently did not. Athletes who acquiesce to the demands of their program—such as Bobo and several of the Tar Heel football players—are well aware of the possible costs of bucking the system.

In several instances, athletes admitted that attending college served an instrumental purpose. After one of the workout sessions at the TEST NFL Combine Training Program (Figure 4.1), several college players—all of whom left college early so they could prepare for the NFL draft—reminisced about their college days while downloading music online and playing video games in a budget hotel room paid for by an agent near Martinsville, New Jersey.

FIGURE 4.1: TEST SPORTS NFL COMBINE TRAINING WORKOUT.

"I can really honestly tell you that I have never read a book in college," claimed Moe, a former Nebraska Cornhusker wide receiver. Tierre, a fellow Cornhusker, choked back his laughter.

"What do you mean?" I asked incredulously.

"'Nuff said. You see I brought this Joe Montana book," Moe said as he lifted the book off the desk for everyone to see, "I bought this book at the airport on my way out here 'cause my girl said I should at least read something before going to the NFL. She made me think and I started feeling bad 'cause I never read a book in college."

Unsure of what to say next, I finally asked, "How could you go to college and never read a book. The university buys textbooks for you, don't they?"

Tierre, Moe's former teammate at the University of Nebraska, jumped in, "YOU DON'T HAVE ENOUGH TIME!"

Many factors may have an impact on a college student's academic progress, yet the athletes in that room believed the NCAA system makes it difficult for athletes to succeed. The conversation shifted to a question about the rules regarding maintaining academic eligibility, and within seconds the room was filled with rip-roaring laughter.

Moe then stated, "When I left for college my mom said 'C's get degrees.' And I heard some statistics that a 4.0 student ain't always just the smartest people out there. I heard that the B–C range are the smartest people 'cause they don't really study as much." Roland nodded in agreement, "Yeah, 'cause they don't have to study as much to get good grades." Before I could probe further, Tierre revisited his earlier comment by suggesting that the off-season demands on his time were even greater than during the season.

Roland, who was engrossed in an intense Madden NFL video game with Moe explained, "People have no idea how difficult it really is." Growing up in a poor section of the northeast quadrant of Washington, DC, Roland and his three siblings were raised in a small single-family home by his mom. For Roland, playing sports was a way for him to keep away from gangs and out of trouble. The pressure on Roland during his college years was to support his family and his little daughter, who was born when he was a college freshman.

I challenged Roland to defend his view by repeating what some might argue in response to the statement, "Hey, these athletes receive well over $100,000 in free education; what in the world are they complaining about? If all you're doing is going to college to play ball and focus on the NFL, then you are throwing away a valuable opportunity."

Roland replied, "It ain't that we only trying to get by. It's just that we don't have enough energy. We can't put our all into class, because when we put our all into class, we slackin' on the football field, which is our main focus for being there. Without football, a lot of people wouldn't have been in school." Each man in Moe's hotel room nodded in agreement, suggesting that Roland was offering a realistic view of big-time football at schools like Virginia Tech, the University of Nebraska, and the University of Arkansas.

Several of the athletes I interviewed for this book would have skipped the college experience if another viable path to the NFL existed. The vast majority of these athletes did not choose his college or university based on the school's academic profile. In sum, if the NFL had its own developmental league for professional football, similar to the minor leagues in major league baseball and the NBA's developmental league, then the challenge of academic integrity and eligibility in major college football would likely be insignificant.

5

THE TOTALIZING INSTITUTION

ONLY A CERTAIN kind of athlete can make it in the NFL. Gaining entry into this exclusive enclave is not solely a reflection of a player's level of commitment, physical talents, work ethic, or devotion to the sport. The winning ticket holder in the NFL lottery is a player who displays a combination of all of these characteristics as well as a complete adoption of a football *habitus*.[1]

In this book, I delve into the lives of current and former NFL athletes to learn how and why so many struggle after an early or involuntary exit from the game. The athletes I encountered demonstrate that the seeds of a general athletic *habitus*—a system of dispositions and a way of thinking about and acting in the world of sports—are generally planted in aspiring young Pop Warner and high school football players. Later in life, through education, training, and discipline within the organizational field of football, a specific *football habitus* is fully integrated in athletes.

Entering a major college football program means entering what Erving Goffman refers to as a *total institution*.[2] In his classic treatise, *Asylums: Essays on the Social Situation of Mental Patients and Other Inmates*,[3] Goffman emphasized that all institutions, to some extent, are designed to capture the time and interests of their members. For example, a central feature of the total institution is the deterioration of the kinds of boundaries that ordinarily separate where individuals sleep, play, and work. In total institutions, all aspects of life are conducted in the same location and under a single authority, and members' daily activities are carried out in the immediate company of others. All activities are tightly scheduled, and a body of officials imposes explicit formal rulings.[4] Examples of total institutions include mental institutions, prisons, and the military.

If a total institution commands control over every aspect of a subject's life, a *totalizing* institution coerces an individual into surrendering that control.

The casual observer may not classify NCAA Division I football programs as total institutions but consider that all aspects of elite college football players' lives are conducted under a single authority. Coaches and athletic support staff have significant influence over the players' schedules, where they sleep, their transportation, when to eat, what to eat, workout routines, class schedules, homework schedule, academic majors, and social circles. They set behavioral guidelines and team rules for players, and coaches and institutional enablers take the steps necessary to confirm that the athletes comply with the increasingly stringent rules included in the National Collegiate Athletic Association (NCAA) 2014–2015 Division I Manual.[5]

It takes time and a thorough indoctrination process for an athlete to fully integrate a football *habitus*, and that process is the domain of Division I college football programs.[6] In college, these dispositions and skills combine with the institutional logic of football. Ultimately, in the process of playing and growing in the game, young football players internalize that logic to the degree that they believe no sacrifice is too great.

Coach John Shoop, former offensive coordinator at Purdue University, said as much in the spring of 2013. I asked what attributes he seeks in recruits. Coach Shoop's recruiting philosophy (strikingly similar to the NFL's) starts with finding superior athletes who want to be winners in every aspect of life and who are *willing to sacrifice* and *to do whatever it takes* (his emphasis) to win a Big Ten title, to earn a college degree, and to play in the NFL. These attributes, he believes, are the keys to success. Instead of advocating the use of fear and intimidation to force college athletes into submission, as legendary Ohio State head coach Woody Hayes and coach Bear Bryant from the University of Alabama did "back in the day," coaches like Shoop now strive to instill self-discipline and internal motivation in each player. They develop and wield power over their players first by introducing clear and consistently enforced behavioral expectations. Compliance is monitored. Consequences are emphasized and reemphasized. Although each football program has a slightly different approach to indoctrinating athletes, there is at least one universal directive: players must follow team rules without exception and without question. Athletes often do not feel they have the power to challenge the system. After all, the coach has the vision. The coach knows best. It is this long-term psychological conditioning—not an NCAA rule—that is the first tool of domination.

Bill Walsh, former head coach at Stanford University and head coach and general manager of the San Francisco 49ers, discussed the importance of this first lesson in an article circulated in coaches' offices across the country: "How to Indoctrinate New Players into Your Program."[7] Walsh is quoted as saying, "Coaches must condition the minds of their athletes, and it's an ongoing process. You cannot read 8 to 10 rules before a team practice or include a typewritten page in the playbook and expect your responsibilities in this area to be complete. As coaches, we need to constantly teach and reiterate the necessary framework for the entire football program."

In service of the idea of year-round sacrifices, Walsh reminds his coaching brethren that conditioning athletes' minds is an ongoing process. He instructs coaches to develop a standard of performance or "behavior guide" for athletic and academic performance and to repeatedly emphasize that the point of self-sacrifice is to build the team. The player must automatically comply with the coach's wishes. In sociological terms, Walsh is describing a socialization process.

So what happens to athletes who don't obey the rules? I can only recall one time that I witnessed a college teammate challenge the system, and things deteriorated rapidly. Our starting free safety at JMU refused to heed the head coach's demands, even as the other defensive backs complied. A few days later, his locker was empty. The coach's only comment to the team was that he expected everyone to follow the rules or be replaced. As a 20-year-old athlete, I couldn't fathom how my teammate could throw away a promising career by challenging the coach's authority. Several of my teammates and I pleaded with him to suck it up and acquiesce to the coach's demands for the good of the team, but he ignored our pleas and refused to return to the team. And seeing the clear consequence of resisting authority further intimidated and indoctrinated all of the players who remained.

Even so, 20 years ago, coaches were more lenient regarding player behavior. For instance, in 1995, Lawrence Philips, a talented running back from the University of Nebraska, was arrested for domestic violence.[8] He was charged with assault for dragging his girlfriend out of a teammate's dorm room by her hair. He pleaded no contest to lesser charges. Tom Osborne, his coach at the time, received heavy criticism for doing nothing more than suspending Phillips from playing. Osborne argued that the best way to help Phillips was to keep him within the structured environment of the football program.

Today, Division I head coaches such as University of Alabama's Nick Saban and Charlie Strong at the University of South Florida quickly jettison athletes who break the law or violate team rules. There are too many other talented players waiting in the wings. Since the coach's goal is to win football games, rather than struggling with and cajoling an errant player, top programs simply send the player packing.

WITH GROSS ANNUAL revenues topping $3.4 billion in 2013,[9] it is clear that college football is big business. There is tremendous pressure to win—not solely for the bragging rights but also for the sake of making more money with increased ticket sales, securing bigger television contracts, and participating in post-season play. Winning teams are good for coaches who are rewarded with higher salaries and maybe greater exposure (if they're looking to make a jump to the NFL). Winning is good for the athletes, who gain reputation and scout attention that may bring them into the NFL. Winning teams bring greater television revenue and highly rated recruits to their school. Winning teams please alumni, who contribute to university endowment funds and help build new athletic facilities.[10] University budgets annually allocate millions of dollars to improve weight rooms, expand practice facilities, and provide generous academic scaffolding—all to attract and keep the best talent so they can win more ball games. Not surprisingly, coaches are paid more than ever, too. Between 2006 and 2012, the average salary for an NCAA FBS head coach increased by 70%—a rate that outpaced the much-maligned compensation of corporate executives.[11] Coach Saban receives over $7 million in annual salary at the University of Alabama.

If the primary goal of major college Division I football programs is winning games, the incentive for most Division I football players is to play in the NFL after their college apprenticeship ends. These goals are not always in perfect alignment. Matt Hewitt played football for the Arkansas Razorbacks in the NCAA's Southeastern Conference (SEC), long considered one of the best in college football. During the 2007 season, Hewitt's team beat the eventual national champions Louisiana State University (LSU). With his high-profile game appearances, it seemed certain that Hewitt would "get a look" for a spot in the NFL draft. But at the close of their college careers, eight players from the acclaimed team were asked to attend the 2008 NFL Pre-Draft Combine— Hewitt was not among them. I met Hewitt at the TEST Sports Club NFL

Combine Training Camp, where he was preparing for Razorback Pro-Day Combine, a chance for NFL recruiters to see players outside of the pre-draft NFL Combine context. Hewitt looked unapproachable as he stalked around TEST between workouts: he kept his sweatshirt hood up and a pair of trendy Beats headphones effectively sealed out distractions. "Are you sure you don't mind talking to me about your story?" I asked, "You seem like you don't want to be bothered." Hewitt answered, "Nawh, Rob, it's cool. Hell, somebody needs to write a book about my experiences in football. Ain't nothin' come easy for me. All I know about football is struggle. I'm quiet 'cause I'm just thinking about what I got to do to make it."

Hewitt was upset about being left out of the 2008 NFL Pre-Draft Combine. But as he sat balancing on an exercise ball in the TEST field house, Hewitt observed that his own willingness to put the team's needs above his own may have contributed to his Combine absence. He described arriving at the University of Arkansas after a two-year stint in a junior college. Early in his first year at Arkansas, he played well enough to become a starter on all special teams while serving as a backup free safety. After the third game, he was asked to switch positions when the starting strong-side linebacker suffered a season-ending shoulder injury. Though undersized at 6'3" and 205 pounds, Hewitt filled the slot quite well. The 2006 season ended with the Razorbacks at 10–4, playing against the University of Wisconsin in the Capital One Bowl. To please his coach and continue in the linebacker position, Hewitt bulked up to a solid 220 pounds by the following spring. But that summer, his position coach called and told him to lose weight—he had to move back to strong safety. Still, in his final season for the Razorbacks, Hewitt performed solidly. He recorded 118 tackles, 4 forced fumbles, 3 fumble recoveries, 2 pass interceptions, 1 sack, 9 quarterback hurries, and was a second-team Associated Press All-SEC selection.[12] When I asked how someone with such solid credentials could be overlooked, he replied, "Man, you tell me. The scouts must figure I was moved to linebacker 'cause I was too slow to play in the secondary. But that's ridiculous! I have never been timed in my life.[13] Nothin' in football ever came easy for me. But I'll show 'em. Just like before. All I need is a chance." Hewitt's willingness to change positions for the good of the team may have worked to his disadvantage as he tried to transition to the professional level.

Former Washington State University wide receiver Philip Bobo was asked to make a similar sacrifice for the Cougars. In the fall of his junior

year, Bobo was on track to have a spectacular season, and he was very
much looking forward to leaving school early to prepare for the NFL draft.
But midseason junior year, Bobo injured his hip. He said, "Against Oregon
I got hurt with a hip pointer or some shit, but I still played. The next game
they took me down to Stanford, and I really wasn't ready to play, but they
shot me with some shit then my whole leg went numb. The trainer hit a
nerve and my whole shit just went numb. I sat out the first half so the shit
could wear off. They put me in one play so I could catch one pass and keep
the [pass reception] streak going."

    With an opportunity to play in the NFL at stake, why would Bobo or any
other college athlete agree to be injected with an unidentified substance?
Without a parent or a mentor to intervene, athletes often acquiesce to the
coaches' and training staff's wishes so they can get back on the field quickly.
There is little choice but to trust that the doctors and coaches know what they
are doing and that they will do what is best for the athlete. In Bobo's case, the
coaching staff felt the long-term risk of further damage to Bobo's body was
worth taking to keep his short-term pass-catching record intact. The strategy
worked for the team but backfired for Bobo. By season's end, Bobo had recorded the lowest number of receptions and receiving yards in his three-year
collegiate career. Having received poor advice and perhaps led by his own
pride, Bobo skipped his senior season at WSU to enter the NFL draft. After a
poor showing at the NFL Combine, he was bypassed in the draft. He eventually signed a rookie free agent contract with the Raiders.

REGULATING TIME

If a college football player wants to capture the interest of NFL scouts, he can't
do it warming the bench. Players jockey for playing time, and coaches inflict
punishment for everything from cutting corners in a workout or practice to
being late, mouthing off, or any of a variety of other character infractions by
reducing players' time on the field. And when the goal is to rack up statistics
to impress NFL scouts, the worst place in the world is to be on the bench.

    Wes Brown, a four-star recruit, redshirt sophomore running back at
the University of Maryland, described his frustration with the system this
way: "When I got here I was told that Coach Edsel was about good grades
and graduation. But I didn't see him practicing what he was preaching. Which

got under my skin. And like, with me, if I don't trust what you're saying out your mouth, I'm not gonna give two shits or listen to you."

I asked Brown, "So, it was like that when you first got here, but is it still like that, or were you being a little bit immature? Or was it a little bit of both?"

He agreed that maybe he had been acting a bit immaturely. He said, "Yeah, it was a little bit of both. [But] the coaches still wasn't letting us go see our professors and stuff within the times that we had to go see them because of our practice schedule. Coaches tell you to communicate whatever you need. And I'm like, 'Okay.' I tell them I'll be late for practice because I need to see my professor on this day. And even when they know about it, I still get a 6:00 AM?" I paused to clarify whether the 6:00 AM workout was meant as a punishment. "Yeah, punishment," Brown confirmed.

I asked, "So, let me back up. Are you saying the coaches would tell you, 'Go see your professors,' but then they would punish you for doing that? They would tell you to do whatever you need to do for your education and then once you follow through with it, they say that you're not committed to this team, you're missing practice, so now I'm gonna make you go to a 6:00 AM punishment training session?"

Brown reconfirmed, "Exactly. That's why I'm like, 'You know what? I'm not going to this 6:00 AM.'" I was still stuck on the idea of what Brown was telling me. I kept pressing. "Let me make sure I am clear." I said, "You're saying 'I had to go see my professor to go take care of my education,' which is what the coach told you to do?"

"Exactly," Brown said. "Then after that, he's like 'Well, you're not gonna do what you want to do, because this is my team and when the rules are set, the rules are set.' And I'm like, 'Well, you're preaching something that you don't even follow. You're preaching it, but you're not actually doing it.'"

"You said this to the coach?" I asked. Brown nodded. "Which coach?"

"Edsel, the head coach. Then he was like, 'BULLSHIT WES, DON'T BULLSHIT ME!' No one's bullshitting you, I'm telling you straight up how I feel. You guys say 'communicate everything.' Okay, when I was hurt, I had to get surgery my freshman year, they set up the buses for me to get everywhere on campus I needed to be on time, no matter what. The buses got me to study hall late almost every day, and I had a 6:00 AM [punishment workout] for that! . . . I have to take that bus, and it's making me late, and I'm getting 6:00 AMs for that? No, that ain't about to happen! Then Edsel called me the next morning and said, 'Where are you?' I said, 'In bed. I got class today, and I'll be at practice on time.' When I get to the meeting, Edsel pulled me out and yelled at me, so I said, 'Okay. I'll be there tomorrow.' After that, I went there and knocked out two 6:00 AM workouts in a row, then Edsel started being happy. And he came to me and said, 'Now, how hard was that?' I said, 'Yeah, actually it was.'"

During football season, at practice, or while attending organized team events, athletes are dissuaded from doing *anything* else—even if it involves an academic requirement. Tierre, an NFL prospect attending the TEST Combine training academy, recalls asking a coach if he could miss practice to take a make-up test. The answer was an emphatic no. In response to these kinds of student-athlete complaints, the University of Maryland and many other Division I football programs have developed a team leadership council where players can air their grievances. An athlete like Wes Brown is supposedly free to voice his concerns to other players on the council without fear of retribution. But one must wonder, when it comes to renewing a grant-in-aid athletic scholarship or doling out playing time, might coaches react negatively to a complaint?

Former University of North Carolina at Chapel Hill reading specialist Mary Willingham claims Tar Heel football players' schedules are so tightly packed on a typical day that they are often too tired to study. She told me, "[Players] just get a schedule, and are expected to just follow it. Sort of like the military. They really don't have a choice. I think the guys have to check in for breakfast as early as 7:00 AM and then head for 8:00 AM class. They may have a couple of classes in a row before heading over to the center for tutoring. They'd come in for academic support right around noon. They would have a Subway sandwich with them, or they would ask if they could go grab something [for lunch] because they were always starving. [Tutors] were really taking up their [players'] lunchtime, so while other students get a break for lunch, these guys never get a break. When they come in we try to get in a quick hour or 90 minutes to work on a paper or math or something. . . . They had to be somewhere by 2:00 PM [dressed for practice] by that point. So there's all this other stuff going on. [By the end of the day], they were exhausted," she explained. "They've been at practice. They've been yelled at and stepped on, smashed [laughs]. They have ice packs on. . . . It's 7:00 PM and the guys would be like, 'We just got out of practice and we had to be here.

We didn't even get to shower.' That NCAA 20-hour rule is a joke, and it's not much better off-season either."

The situation Willingham describes is all too common for Division I football players, who literally relinquish control over their schedules for as long as they remain on their college football teams. Quotes cited in the *Detroit Free Press* by unidentified University of Michigan athletes align with Willingham's claim. These players alleged that under former head coach Rich Rodriguez, the Wolverine football program regularly exceeded daily and weekly limits, and that quality-control coaches watched supposedly voluntary offseason scrimmages that only training staff should have attended.[14]

Increasingly, surveillance is an integral component of the NCAA Division I football totalizing apparatus. As Goffman noted, within a total institution, a small number of supervisory personnel have a central responsibility to see to it that members comply, and any infraction is likely to stand out against the visible, constantly examined compliance of others.[15] Because even a few misguided 18- to 23-year-olds can place an entire football program at risk of NCAA probation if they refuse to attend classes or maintain the required GPAs, schools employ a small army of compliance officers, academic advisors, and education specialists, class checkers, and other athletic personnel to protect the football program's brand and financial interests from the danger of noncompliant players.

Roland, a defensive back participating at the TEST NFL Combine training program, spoke at length about class checkers at Virginia Tech, patrolling campus to make sure that athletes reported to class.[16] I recalled having seen, when I was a guest lecturer at UNC, a strange man peering through the classroom window; later, I discovered that he was a class checker employed by the athletic department. Athletes at other schools have reported that their athletic departments position "bouncer" type compliance officers near locations frequented by college kids. These officers are tasked with keeping college players out of bars, nightclubs, and fraternity parties. Where class checkers confirm class attendance, the bouncers segregate the players from social situations that may distract a player from his greater purpose.

As happens within total institutions, the subject's social experiences are restricted. Athletes are separated from the general student body at many points throughout the school year. Players are encouraged to focus exclusively on football, which means they are redirected when their attention drifts to other concerns such as part-time jobs, internships, and schoolwork. Major college football players are not explicitly prevented from involvement with extracurricular activities, but activities outside of football are often viewed as distractions by coaches, fans, and sometimes by players themselves.

Cast to the sidelines are the parents, families, love interests, hobbies, friends, potential employers, and any other interest that may distract the athletes from the all-consuming job of playing football. The addition of external pressure affects all players. However, for players with fewer resources, or those who may be uncomfortable talking with people outside of their social class, the loss of connections to their families and friends can be devastating and destabilizing.

Willingham, the Tar Heel education specialist, says, "Athletes really have limited choices in anything they do. . . . Athletes are checked upon all day, and then they get in trouble if they don't do what they are supposed to do." She continues, "[Players] have these little passbooks that have to be filled with these little stickers. . . . When that started, it was like kindergarten or first grade or something. . . . [The passbook] has your grades, it has your progress reports, everything. It's like you are a little kid. Once in a while, [athletes] would come to me and ask if I wanted to see the passbook, and I didn't want to touch it. I'm not signing them in or out. I didn't want anything to do with it. It's a program mandated by football and the academic advisors. It's totally ridiculous."

FISCAL ENFORCEMENT

The term "athletic scholarship" means that in exchange for their participation in the athletic program at an NCAA institution, an athlete will receive a free or highly discounted education. There is no guarantee, however, that the athlete will be able to stay at the issuing university for the entire four to five years of college. Because of the NCAA's One-Year Scholarship Rule,[17] a student has a role on the team from year to year, at the coach's discretion. At the end of each season, a coach can refuse to renew a player's athletic financial aid for any reason whatsoever.[18]

Athletes are keenly aware that they must do everything they possibly can to stay in the coach's favor. Journeymen, in particular, have very little margin for error. If a coach believes a player is taking shortcuts, underperforming, or no longer fits into the team's future plans (read: that another, better player for that position has been identified), financial aid can be withdrawn and issued to another recruit. Athletes and coaches alike recognize that the *threat* of losing a scholarship combined with the overabundance of high school players who didn't make it to college and college players in lower divisions who dream of playing major college football are strong incentives for current players to conform to team and NCAA rules.

A loophole in the One-Year Scholarship Rule incentivizes coaches to ask some players to "grey-shirt,"[19] a questionable practice in which athletes who commit to a college football program will attend school for a semester without a scholarship because that team has over-signed its 85 NCAA student-athlete scholarship allotment. These grey-shirted athletes may take out student loans or may simply sit out the semester. The coach, for his part, is not required to honor any promise to a grey-shirted player; when the time comes, a recruit might simply not receive a scholarship. In that case, though there is no consequence for the coach or football program, the player may lose an entire year of NCAA eligibility just waiting for his chance to play.

Of the damaging things that can happen to an athlete—being asked to grey-shirt, losing his financial support, suffering through academic scandals, and violations of institutional control—almost all are out of the player's control and almost all can lead to his early exit from the tournament.

With nearly every aspect of their lives under observation by the football programs, I wondered how the financial constraints placed on the players by the NCAA affected their lives. The NCAA does not allow student-athletes to receive financial compensation for participating in anything that might allow a player to benefit from his elevated status (such as being paid to sign autographs), or to receive money or anything of value (such as access to a car, a ride downtown, a plane ticket, or a free dinner) that can be deemed as benefiting from his athletic status. Every transaction must be cleared through the school's compliance department. For players from wealthy families, these restrictions pose a minor inconvenience. For a player from a less advantaged background, such restrictions greatly reduce mobility and give the athlete the feeling that he has no choice. For instance, when Roland played for Virginia Tech, he lived off-campus in a shared apartment with three teammates. The athletes would pool their monthly stipend checks to pay rent and to buy ramen noodles and other inexpensive grocery items. Any remaining funds would be sent back home to help ease the financial constraints of their families. With his miniscule stipend, Roland took on the role of "breadwinner." "You do what you gotta do," he said. In Roland's case, he knew that if he didn't send money home his young brother, sister, and daughter would do without basic necessities each month.

The NCAA publicly touts the benefits of playing college sports, but often missing from the public discourse is the recognition that since college football serves as their gateway to the NFL, first-generation college athletes and individuals from lower economic backgrounds are vulnerable to exploitation by an institution that generates large sums of revenues from their participation.

TACIT RULES

It is not my intention to declare that college football players never have choices. To the contrary, football players often assess their situation and develop strategies to excel within the boundaries of the institutional rules.

Although football programs adopt different tactics to coaching athletes, there is at least one universal directive: players are expected to follow team rules without question. Some of these rules are written in the playbook that each athlete receives. The uninitiated quickly learn that there are also unwritten rules. The first is the tacit understanding that the words "voluntary" and "optional" actually mean "mandatory." At Division I colleges such as the University of North Carolina at Chapel Hill, athletes are invited to remain on campus in the summer to participate in voluntary workouts under the watchful eyes of the strength training coach. As a result of having to be on campus, the football players must also attend classes. Willingham shares her insights, "The way I understand it, it [the program] was mandated that football players had to be here for second summer session. Athletes can't exercise a right to wait and report to campus in August at the start of summer practice. . . . I guess that some players would have chosen to not be here at all. One of the people I knew quite well in the summer didn't really want to take classes, he just wanted to play football and he made that very clear. [He] was very, very smart from the standpoint of questioning why the guys don't question the authority. I'm just using him as an example of somebody who absolutely did not want to be here during that time. . . . It just made me think that 'You guys have to be here, it's just part of the deal.' "

Willingham likened football players having to attend the summer session to civilian recruits attending boot camp after going through their initial processing: both groups attend classes, take a battery of health examinations, and participate in strenuous training programs. Thus, like boot camp, the summer session in college football is a vital part of an indoctrination process that reinforces the necessity of following the rules without question.

Willingham's stories about Tar Heel players and the football team summer session program and my recollection of a teammate's conflict with the head coach represent different dimensions of college football as a totalizing institution. Some athletes are acutely aware of the constraints placed on them; others spend little time questioning the sacrifices required to remain in the sport tournament. Then there are athletes like my college teammate who refused to submit to the demands imposed on him by coaches and administrators.

RULES VERSUS RULES

What happens when the coach's directives conflict with the NCAA rules? For instance, the NCAA rules stipulate that during football season, athletes cannot engage in football-related activity in excess of 20 hours per week (8 hours per week in the off-season; hence, what's called the 20/8 Hour Rule).[20] Critics of the NCAA contend that playing major college sports is akin to working a full-time job. In an NCAA survey of 21,000 players, major college football players reported spending an average of 44.8 hours per week practicing, playing, and training.[21] One of the players I interviewed at the TEST NFL Combine training program, Tierre, a former Big 12 conference athlete, said that in the spring of his freshman year a new coaching staff took over at his school and "[they would] put pressure on us to spend 50–60 hours a week doing football related stuff, if they could get away with it."

The existence of the NCAA 20/8 Hour Rule raises questions about the sincerity of such policies. If the NCAA sets the number of hours per week that athletes can work on their craft, why do athletes report that the average time they spend in season actually working in football-related activities is more than double the allotted time? And what about the off-season? As Tierre claims, the off-season hours required by his coaches at the University of Nebraska were at least six times the allowable amount. Because the rules are stated, but not followed or generally enforced until there is an obvious problem, they become a paper tiger—things that appear to be threatening but are essentially ineffectual.

Much like the 20/8 rule, many of the NCAA's rules regarding eligibility requirements (grade minimums and graduation rates) can be skirted, given the proper resources. So, in fact, the NCAA rules are more like obstacles than tools of dominance. But by requiring that the student-athlete performs well on the field and in the classroom, behaves well, and stays financially secure enough to survive without needing an income source, the NCAA demonstrates gross insensitivity to the needs of those athletes in socially and economically vulnerable populations.

DEVELOPMENTAL DELAYS

Indoctrination, power, and control are deeply embedded in the ethos of Division I college football. An unknown risk to players is that participation in this insular world alters, and at times suspends, the usual transition from college to adulthood, in which students are supposedly trained and empowered to make important choices about their futures. By exerting authority over nearly every aspect of football players' lives, coaches and athletic administrators can limit athletes' opportunities to make those choices and develop the skills necessary for subsequent decisions later in life.

While it may benefit the athletic program to employ academic and support staff who proactively address issues as they arise, the practice can rob athletes of valuable opportunities to develop problem-solving and life management skills.[22] Consider a spring semester day at the University of Maryland, when I ran into running back Wes Brown. As we walked to class together, I reminded Brown that he needed to schedule a time to visit during office hours. Brown asked where my office was, and, after giving him the building and room number, I deftly mentioned that it had been listed on the course syllabus. Brown told me that the academic support staff required football players to turn in their course syllabi. I asked why. "We have to check with our academic advisor each week to see what assignments are due. They just tell me what papers or tests I have coming up, then make sure I turn them in." I was dismayed, asking, "You mean to tell me they don't trust you to manage your own schedule?" Brown's reply was simple, yet poignant, "I never thought of it that way."

A few weeks later, I saw KG, a sophomore fullback for the University of Maryland Terrapins, sitting in the African American Studies Department office waiting to speak with the director of Undergraduate Studies. KG had dropped my Race and Critical Analysis class three weeks into the semester, so I asked if he was there to switch majors. "I don't know," he said.

"What do you mean, you 'don't know?'" I pressed.

"I'm not sure." KG looked down at a piece of paper in his hand. "My academic advisor just told me to come here and speak with Mrs. Skeat."

"You're a grown man. It's your education, right?" I asked, trying to make eye contact. "Then how can you let someone else tell you to attend a meeting if you don't question what it's about? If you let others make academic decisions for you, who does that benefit? Will it hurt the academic advisor if he steers you toward something that you are not interested in? Of course not. As a young Black man, you've got to take charge of your own academic future."[23]

Each brush with a student-athlete had revealed withheld opportunities to mature and gain valuable experience. Forcing athletes to submit their course syllabi to academic advisors and scheduling meetings without offering details about their purpose runs in direct opposition to what sociologist Annette Lareau has called concerted cultivation (middle-class parents' practices of scheduling their kids' lives with activities that help prepare the children for white-collar jobs and adult interactions). That scheduling is purposeful and each interaction is laden with agency-building import. Major college football programs' scheduling and control are not aimed at teaching athletes to engage in critical thinking activities or asking questions that challenge the system. Instead, the more an athlete is discouraged from thinking critically and challenging the status quo, the more likely they are to become dependent on the institution.

Coaches think it is too risky to give football players much freedom and responsibility. As a result, athletic department staff members often handle nearly all the players' responsibilities. When teams travel, paid assistants pack the athletes' bags to prevent the possibility that they will forget an important piece of gear, snacks for the road, or anything else that might, in its absence, impair the athletes' ability to play the game. All the football player needs to do is get on the bus. And if the team travels by air, a team assistant is likely to hold onto the whole team's tickets until the whole crew checks in at the gate. Teams are told this practice allows athletes to focus on the matter at hand: winning football games. But is it also true that the equipment manager wants to minimize the chance for error—that an athlete might misplace his ticket, for instance. Thus, this custom communicates condescending messages: "You can't focus on too many tasks at once." "You're not smart/responsible enough to do this for yourself." "You can't handle this job." The encoded meaning demeans and infantilizes athletes.

And consider that college athletes don't earn money through their efforts on the field, but they also don't have the time to work the part-time jobs that help other students build independence. Academic support staff will assist athletes with registering for classes, ordering course books, selecting meal plans, and making myriad other decisions that most young adults are expected to address on their own. Scholarship football players have their room and board paid for and staffers to help them register for class, then understand and process coursework, and navigate their busy schedules of practice, play, and learning. This abundance of support may help major college programs ensure that athletes are "free" to focus on playing football, but it is almost certainly stunting athletes' personal development. The Division I athletic program may be the ultimate "helicopter parent."[24]

It would be irresponsible of me to blame major college football for the failure of athletes to develop substantive transferable skills beyond sports. However, it is reasonable to suggest that coaches and athletic departments create an environment that routes their players toward the course of institutional dependency rather than self-sufficiency (even if it is all too quick to dismiss a player who gets "out of line" as a man who made his own choices).

A MEANS TO AN END

Does the general *habitus* of a young man such as Phillip Bobo, who grew up homeless on the streets of a poor neighborhood, differ from that of a young man who rides to TEST Sports Club in his mother's BMW, hustling to get to his high school football academy sessions after an SAT prep course? Are individuals who grow up with a certain kind of general *habitus* more accepting of an institution's demands than others might be? Are these individuals more vulnerable to manipulation? Is a young athlete with limited social capital or financial resources who has banked his future on an athletic career more likely to willfully conform to, and behave in accordance with, football's officially approved norms—no questions asked?

Athletes may not like being forced to attend summer school or to maintain a 2.0 GPA to remain academically eligible to play, but, in general, some view college football as a means to an end. The majority of athletes I interviewed rarely considered questioning the system. It was easier to follow the rules and dream about playing on the next level. If the NFL is the goal, and conformity is rewarded, why buck the system? Rather than make a fuss or risk being dismissed from the team, Bobo chose to "suck it up," remaining silent as he was injected with an unknown substance and sent back into the game.

I asked former Purdue coach Shoop to name the biggest challenges facing coaches in the winner-take-all environment of major college football. Coach Shoop pointed to the NCAA's 20/8 rule: "Why are we responsible for our players' behavior when our hands are tied? We don't get to spend much time with athletes off the field, yet when they get in trouble, fingers quickly start pointing at us." Coach Shoop believed that more face-time with players would allow coaches to build stronger bonds with athletes, and that a stronger coach/player bond would result in fewer behavior problems. Of course, it's notable that Coach Shoop thinks players who are not under direct supervision will get in trouble. This assessment sheds light on the reach of college football as a totalizing institution. Even if Coach Shoop is correct, the strategy of increasing hours during which athletes would be under direct supervision would further alienate athletes from the rest of campus life by restricting their already limited autonomy.

To justify its stringent rules, particularly given the economic and political climate that encompasses college football today, NCAA president Mark Emmert frequently recites that participation in college sports leads to better grades, higher graduation rates, higher self-esteem, and more fulfilling preparation for life.[25] While this may be true for some scholarship athletes, it's not factual for a significant number of those who participate in revenue-generating sports, such as football at Division I schools.

The reality is that major college NCAA football serves as the de facto feeder system for the NFL, developing the essential physical skills and football habitus athletes will need if they make it to the league. Several of the athletes I interviewed for this book told me that they had no interest in going to college. For them, college football was an unpaid apprenticeship, something

they had to endure in order to play in the NFL. They didn't believe that the
kind of college education they would get while playing football would help
them at this phase in life. If they could start working in the NFL right away,
making money and playing the game without the possible injuries they might
incur playing college ball, many would. "College could wait," they said. But
despite how many athletes expressed displeasure with the collegiate athletic
system, they weren't about to challenge the coaching staff's authority. Instead,
college football players report to campus on time and do whatever is necessary
to remain on the team, to remain in the tournament.

In 2012, Mary Willingham, the academic specialist quoted earlier in this
chapter, went public about shady practices surrounding the education of student-athletes at the University of North Carolina at Chapel Hill: classes that
never met, lectures that never happened, independent study courses in which
the assigned professor never met with students, students who couldn't read
above an elementary school level, papers that only purported to be original
work. Internal reviews found evidence of forged signatures and about 500
grades that had been changed without authorization. Willingham was labeled
a whistle-blower, fired from her supervisory role, and publicly condemned by
university officials, but she shared her displeasure with the treatment of athletes
in her program in several news reports.[26] In one article, Willingham declared,
"I was part of something that I came to be ashamed of. We weren't serving
the kids. We weren't educating them properly. We were pushing them toward
graduation, and that's not the same thing as giving them an education."[27]

If it is true that Willingham is just one of many eligibility enablers at
institutions of higher learning across the country, what does that say about
the validity of the NCAA's argument for not permitting the athletes to earn
money for their work on the field? That is, can we accept the argument that
the reward for *student*-athletes' efforts is a free education? And if an athlete
is over-matched academically, unable to study due to athletic demands, and
forced into fields of study that hold no interest to him but are well-staffed
with people who will help the student acquire passing grades, then what is
that education worth?

The evidence is so clearly stacked against the NCAA's central argument that
many have argued it is time for the college football programs to stop serving
as the developmental league for the NFL. Journalists Taylor Branch[28] and Joe
Nocera[29] have contributed a great deal to the conversation about whether

the NCAA is necessary to the functioning of college football. Branch asserts that the NCAA insinuated itself into the governance of amateur athletics and points to the inherent imbalance of rewards: college football programs generate millions of dollars while there are no guarantees that the athletes' compensation—an education—will hold any real value. In various publications, but most frequently in the *New York Times*, Nocera regularly slams the NCAA for its "double standard," seeking to ensure that college athletes in revenue-generating sports remain unsullied by financial matters—unpaid for their training and play and unable to profit from their elevated status as athletes—while accruing money to the universities and to the organization.

The NCAA and the NFL have worked in concert for years. Sometimes, the ideal outcome is measured by games won, but more often, it is measured in profit. Their cooperation occurs at many levels, too: larger Division I football programs develop the kinds of athletes the NFL values. NCAA rules stipulate that athletes are allowed to remain eligible for up to five seasons while receiving athletically related financial aid,[30] and the NFL requires athletes to be at least three years removed from high school before they can apply for special eligibility or become otherwise eligible for the NFL draft.[31] Even games are scheduled by courtesy to the organizations: in the early days of television, college football was played on Saturday and the professional football games were scheduled for Sunday so as not to split the football audience. In this dance of symbiosis, these two institutions are careful not to step on each other's toes.

The NFL is also privileged in that it is able to draft from a talent pool of college athletes created from a mix of private and public funding and alumni donations.[32] As such, the NFL is able to shed the costs associated with developing talent: trainers, health and other employment benefit costs, facility fees, and salaries for additional coaching staff and players. This scenario works for the colleges, too. They make a significant amount of money in the current arrangement. In addition, coaches play on players' dreams of "going pro" to leverage victories, which brings in more cash, encourages bigger television contracts, keeps the alumni happy, and helps fund ever-higher coaching salaries.

The willingness to endure a protracted apprenticeship and make personal sacrifices for the chance to play in the NFL marks college football players as attractive candidates for a totalizing institution. Like servicemen who attend jump school in order to become paratroopers, football players who attend NCAA Division I football programs forfeit control over their college experience in order to gain the training and skills sought by the NFL. As we have seen, though, some athletes are caught in a state of suspended adolescence,[33] a result of preemptive measures designed by program administrators to improve efficiencies, and are left to suffer and struggle to adjust to life after football.

When an athlete is able to dodge the obstacles surrounding eligibility, conform to the rules of the institution, and play better, harder, and longer than anyone else in his position—then, and only then—may he be *considered* for a job in the NFL. But only 1.6% of college players will make it to the NFL. Ultimately, with the help of Nocera and Branch, an emerging body of research makes one clear point: only three parties largely benefit from the student-athlete arrangement in college football—the college, the NCAA, and the NFL.

6

MASKING THE PAIN IN MASCULINITY

JUST THREE DAYS before I reported to summer camp with the San Francisco 49ers, I attended Sunday service at my nondenominational evangelical church. There were nearly a thousand members in attendance, and tens of thousands of other people across New Jersey watched on cable television. The pastor called me—along with Kenny Breelong, a rookie free agent wide receiver with the New York Jets, and Bill Clark, an undrafted rookie defensive tackle with the Miami Dolphins—to come up on stage so that the congregation could lay hands on us. I felt like everyone was staring as the pastor charged us with being strong role models for Christ. He declared that God had chosen us out of thousands of athletes, and a chorus of "Hallelujah" rose up. He shouted that we had been chosen to evangelize the players of the NFL. "Amen!" By the time he said I was going to take God's message to the good people of the NFL, folks in the congregation were jumping around, praising God for the victory. There I was, a 27-year-old former USFL and CFL athlete preparing to give it my all for one last shot at the NFL. Going to California wasn't a victory ride to me; it was the fourth quarter with time running out. All I could think was, "What the heck am I gonna do if I get cut and let all these people down?" The only thing I could do was put on a brave face and pray the 49ers coaches would see things my way. Odds are always stacked against a rookie free agent trying to break onto an NFL roster.

At camp, all of my energy was focused on learning the playbook and prepping for every repetition I could get on the field. I was acutely aware that journeymen like me were just one play away from a plane ticket home. The coaches needed to see me doing something special each time they reviewed the practice films. Making matters worse (for me, at least), four other free agents and one draft choice were battling for the one or two open positions in the secondary. The 49ers had won a string of Super Bowls, and it would be a battle for me to remain on the roster once veteran defensive back Carlton Williamson recovered from his knee injury.

And when I got cut. The sting wasn't as painful as I imagined. What really hit me was when the general manager thanked me for my services and asked "Where do you want to go?" with that plane ticket; I had no answer. My body went numb. My football career was suddenly done. Over the years, I had been cut four times and bounced back to make another roster, but this was different. This felt final. It was possible that another team would claim me off the waiver wire and offer a contract. But in my heart I knew it was time to move on.

As I sat in the general manager's office, memories of my home church came flooding back. I was horrified. There was no way I could go back and face everyone after that big scene my pastor had made. Those wonderful people were holding me in their hearts and prayers, lifting me up to the Lord, and I had let them down. What would I say when one of them said, "I saw you on TV and you were playing well. How come you're not on the team anymore?"

I was five years removed from college, so moving back to Virginia didn't feel like an option. I couldn't face my congregation or my family, so New Jersey was out. I wanted to hide, but instead I had one night to absorb the general manager's brisk, firm handshake and to let his secretary know where to book that plane ticket.

It's one thing to lose a job. Your ego is bruised and you worry about how you'll pay the bills. But in football, so much emphasis is placed on being the toughest, strongest, fastest, and best *man* out there. To lose a football job is to lose part of that masculine identity. You are still *a* man, but you lost in the sport tournament. You are not *the man*.

I decided to rent a car and visit my younger brother, Charles, detained at a youth correctional facility. Charles did his best to console me, saying he was proud his brother had played in the NFL. He reminded me that a lot of people never even make it that far. No doubt his words were sincere, but the disappointment cut so deep, his words could not soothe the pain. Unsettled, I went to Los Angeles to visit my uncle. After about a week, it dawned on me that I could escape my past in New Jersey by remaining on the west coast. I could create a new identity, never again trying to explain what had happened to my NFL career.

PROFESSIONAL FOOTBALL IS overwhelmingly masculine—among social science scholars like R. W. Connell, it's a bastion of hegemonic masculinity, or "the culturally idealized form of masculine character, which emphasizes the connecting of masculinity to toughness and competitiveness."[1] Physical force and control, occupational achievement, and aggressive heterosexuality are all key components of hegemonic masculinity in American culture.[2] By combining Connell's approach with a traditional understanding of hegemonic theory, sociologist Michael Messner offers a nuanced examination of sport as a social institution.[3] Based on his personal experiences playing and coaching youth baseball and his interviews with retired athletes, Messner concludes that the interests of powerful stakeholders, almost always male, largely shape the structure and values of sports. Scholars who investigate the rewards accrued to athletes in male-dominated sports when they portray themselves as hyper-masculine and hyper-heterosexual routinely cite Messner's work, which establishes football as a hyper-masculine space.[4]

Less familiar in academic circles and in the general public is the way masculinity functions as a mechanism of control in professional football. In the locker room, on the practice field, in team meeting rooms, and in dorm rooms, athletes continuously monitor one another for clues that teammates are part of their "Band of Brothers."[5] In other words, football is an institutional enclave that rewards male athletes for displays of dominance and power. The pressure is so deeply embedded in the *football habitus* that athletes rarely consider the physical risks they take in order to play this "man's game." Pain is proof positive of masculinity—so long as you ignore that pain, push through it, inflict pain in return.

Football offers numerous opportunities for athletes to formulate opinions about and reinforce masculinity stereotypes. From the start, kids are taught that football is a man's game, that it requires toughness and a never-say-die attitude. Players are compared to gladiators and warriors. But besides being able to withstand physical pain and display mental toughness, a football player must know how to conduct himself in the presence of other men. He must not cry or fear his enemy. He must bounce right back up after "getting his bell rung." In short, a football player must always be a man. Maybe a high school coach will console a player when he's down, help him, assuage his doubts, give him a pat on the back. In college? In the pros? No such luck. Football is a man's sport, and men aren't supposed to need help.

H. G. "Buzz" Bissinger's best-selling book, *Friday Night Lights*, chronicled the totalizing culture of high school football in west Texas.[6] His book revealed both positive and negatives aspects of the intense relationship between a community and the young men on the field. He outlined the contours of intense social pressure by following a handful of players; he showed the difficult contradictions produced by the unrealistic dreams of athletes and their fans. Where Bissinger's work presented relationships at the team and community levels, the narrative offered by Phillip Bobo, the former Washington State University and NFL wide receiver, explores how the complexities of race, class, and masculinity can entangle troubled African American athletes specifically. When the culture of masculinity engenders self-censorship, when athletes fear dismissal or reprisal, they are left to shoulder their pain and vulnerability alone.

Bobo speaks about seeking his father's approval through performance on the football field: "The thing is, I told my dad years ago that I wanted to be an actor and he was like, 'All these out of work Black actors. . . . What makes you think you gonna make it?'" In a broader sense, Bobo's acquiescence, his quick dismissal of his dreams in acting or music, was an attempt to cement a relationship with his father, who had only recently returned in his life. In earlier childhood, the father's financial abandonment left Bobo, his mom, and his brother homeless on the streets of South Pasadena. They were food insecure for many of his early years. Bobo depended on the love of his family and his faith in God to help survive these difficult times. Then, in high school, he recalls, "My mom eventually talked my dad into letting me come out to live with him at the start of my sophomore year. Now, keep in mind, I had no desire to be in football. My desires were to be in music and film. I wanted to be in entertainment. The first thing my dad did when I got there was strip me of all that. He made me cut my shag, and my Jheri Curl, all of that. He just stripped me of my identity."

Though he'd landed on his father's doorstep, Bobo quickly learned he was not actually welcome. "My father used to put me down a lot. Called me the milkman's son; said I was too dark to be his kid. I think he hated my likeness, I'm a ghetto Nigger coming to that shit?" Bobo claims his father viewed Black folks from Pasadena as uncultured and stuck in poverty, which may explain why the elder Bobo turned his back on his two eldest sons and his ex-wife. "Pops used to hate anything ghetto, but the irony is that he used to live ghetto even though he denounced it. He hated so-called Niggas, and he saw me as one, 'cause I'm not polished. I came from straight rot-gut-poor-shit." At age 36, Bobo now can reflect on and even assess this tumultuous situation, but back then it was a different, and very painful, story.

Like some other African American males who play sports at predominantly White institutions (PWIs), Bobo learned to mask the hurt and pain of racial and class stigma through familiar tropes of masculinity.[7] His father, Wyatt Bobo, counted several Los Angeles Rams among his acquaintances and business associates: "My pops was pretty good friends with Ron Brown[8] and Eric Dickerson[9] and he was trying to get them to do business with him." No doubt, an adolescent athlete will be captivated by football when a future NFL hall of famer shows interest in his ability. "When my father made me play football those guys became my heroes, which was cool 'cause I was like, I got Ron Brown at my house, I got Eric Dickerson at my house and I wanted to be like them guys. So I started migrating towards football, but I still kept my roots in music."

Despite his best efforts, Bobo never made headway with his father. Bobo established a pattern of self-sabotaging behavior that plagued him throughout his football career. "So the turning point came during my high school junior year," Bobo recalled. "Cheerleaders used to love my older brother, and it was my first experience with White girls. I got to know a cheerleader from my high school that became my girlfriend. And my Pops was always mister flossy. He would make sure he looked good when he was doing his shit. He was never one of those guys who carried guns and all that stuff. He was more like a white-collared criminal-type dude. So my girlfriend at the time used to come see me. So one night he would not let me drive her home, for whatever reason." Bobo took a long pause. "So he took her home, and I never saw her again for months. She just dropped out of school. They ended up going to Vegas together and getting married. She had two kids together by my father."

The code of hyper-masculinity in football taught Bobo how to channel his pain into success on the gridiron. The "tough it out dictum" provided him with the perfect antidote to endure the embarrassment of his father stealing and then marrying his high school girlfriend. "I got through by building a wall around myself. It was a defense mechanism, but it was a complete internalization. I was just living through it. Strictly numb to the whole thing." By the age of 16, Bobo had already experienced a lifetime's worth of pain and disappointment. Living as the brother to his ex-girlfriend's two children served as a constant reminder that Bobo's father had chosen not to stick around and support his mother years earlier. "I don't know how it transpired, but it came back to me that Wyatt was trying to do deals with my ex-girlfriend's parents but her dad wouldn't fuck with him 'cause he sniffed him out," said Bobo. "But her mom loved my dad 'cause he was the most charming, sweetest guy ever, who could talk you out of anything. Evidently he convinced her mom to allow her [daughter] to be with him. So she actually endorsed the marriage. At the time my ex-girlfriend was a senior in high school and Wyatt talks her mom into allowing her daughter to marry him. Who the fuck does that to their child?"

Just as an untreated disease can cause massive internal damage, Bobo's unresolved emotional pain complicated his life for decades. It took years for him to acknowledge that he had hidden behind football and entertainment to suppress feelings of rejection and betrayal. "I felt abandoned by everyone, but I didn't realize it until much later. I was just living in the moment." In addition to shutting himself off from the world, Bobo learned to use his star athlete status to guard against further emotional vulnerability in college.

Besides drawing further into his protective shell, Bobo developed a deep distrust of White people. When asked to explain the roots of his troubles, Bobo responded, "In high school, the girls, the way people was jockin' me and my brother for the way we was rollin', everything seemed manufactured when I was dealing with White people, because the closer you get to people the more questions they start asking—especially White people. They are the nosiest people on earth."

Rationally, Bobo knew his father was to blame, yet he insisted that his father hadn't given him any reason to expect much. Bobo thought the hurt was his fault because he'd trusted the wrong man. He shifted his trust to sport, to his faith. "At that time I was doing a lot of praying. Throughout my life-time I always felt alone, but I always felt that God had my best interest at hand. I always stayed true to what my mom taught me and that was to stay prayerful." These incidents created an emotional vacuum.

Even football players from solid family backgrounds can struggle with the emotional and mental adjustments when they attempt the move from high school to college or from college to the pros. Because the pressure to win in football is enormous, athletes are destined to face trying situations. Challenges may arise in the form of injury, poor performance, or from simply associating with the wrong people. If they lack coping skills, athletes may not be able to handle these routine troubles, especially when they are facing the end of their careers.

College, the NCAA, and the NFL do try to head off these problems by offering athletes a wide range of psychological services. But what happens when athletes choose not to accept or trust professional help? What if counseling is perceived as a sign of weakness or athletes worry that the stigma of mental health problems will hurt their chances of remaining in the game? Some athletes may even feel that accepting help from mental health practitioners is a betrayal of their faith in God. How athletes deal with these issues will have ramifications for the rest of their lives.

In the summer between his college, redshirt sophomore, and junior year, a single event led Bobo to develop a deep, if perhaps unwarranted, resentment toward his college football program at Washington State University. Driving down a long stretch of desert highway outside of Las Vegas, his closest friend from high school, Duncan Boyd, fell asleep at the wheel. Bobo recalls the car flipping several times before landing on the passenger side. "I see it like it was yesterday. We skidding and tumbling in the dirt and we crash. The whole time we're tumbling, I'm just sitting there with my eyes wide open, and neither one of us has our seatbelts on." Boyd had been poised to move from junior college to Division I football, and now he died in Bobo's arms. "I had to make the phone call to his dad, and it fucked me up. We was all like family, every time they'd see me they was like, 'Bobo what's up?' I had to tell them that, and all my friends."

In a matter of minutes, Bobo's life took a dark turn. When the WSU season started several weeks later, Bobo put on a brave face. "My mom called Coach Price and told him what happened. Coach called and gave his condolences or whatever, and I went back to school. Once I got there, it was like it never happened." The years of constant disappointment and resentment had taken such an emotional toll on Bobo that he slipped into survival mode, shielding himself from the outside world. "I basically shut the whole world off since my sophomore year in high school," he told me. "Then it got even worse after Duncan died; then it was like it don't even make no sense. Life don't even make no sense. What the fuck, what is this? You know what I'm saying? I'm watching my best friend die, and I have to explain, I have to take the responsibility to handle all this shit, but I'm not mature. I'm still tore up inside. I still got shit I haven't even dealt with. It was just suppressed. Everything was suppressed. Nobody was close to me, not my boys, nobody. I shut out everybody after Duncan died."

The masculinity and violence of football teaches athletes that mental and physical toughness are paramount, both on the field and off. Phillip Bobo risked an emotional breakdown. He knew he needed help, but he didn't feel he could ask for it without risking his masculinity, his legitimacy on the team. Chances are, if he had received help after Boyd's death, he may have saved his football career. As it was, Bobo left college early to enter the NFL draft. He was passed over, and he ended up signing with the Los Angeles Rams as an undrafted rookie free agent.

BY THE TIME an athlete earns a college football scholarship, he has already had to deal with a fair amount of physical adversity. The ability to play through pain is one way an athlete remains in the sports tournament. The old adage, "You can't make the club in the tub," rings true in locker rooms across the country. If an athlete is constantly in the training room getting treatment for every bump and bruise rather than practicing, he or she will eventually lose the respect of teammates and coaches. The challenge confronting an athlete is to know when to play through the pain, and when to be smart and seek treatment. Not being able to recognize when to speak up and ask for help exposes an athlete to unnecessary health risks that could ultimately jeopardize his or her career. To counteract the risk of athletes trying to ignore pain, coaches rely on trained medical professionals to properly evaluate injuries and determine the appropriate course of action.

The same masculine code that says football players must get up and shake it off or tough it out and play through the pain applies to psychological trauma as well. The risk of long-term suffering is heightened when athletes conceal their emotional pain from the outside world. Phillip Bobo learned how to hide his true emotions at an early age, building walls. Nonetheless, Bobo finds it remarkable that no one in high school or at WSU could see that he was really struggling. They couldn't see over his walls.

"To me, I was like *damn*. Motherfuckers couldn't see the signs back then?" he asked. "Couldn't somebody, you know, come and rescue this little kid way back then? None of all them grown-ups could see what I was going through back then, or y'all just didn't give a fuck? All the people are just gonna assume 'cause you have that athletic ability then you all right. But see, I was so good at having the façade 'cause that's what I learned from my mom and dad. My dad would always tell me 'No matter how broke you are, make sure nobody knows,' You know what I'm saying? With all the things I went through and had pent up inside of me—all the secrets that was holding me and was tearing me apart—there was no way in the world I could tell anyone that my father was in prison or that he fucked my girlfriend. I mean, all those things because they held me in such high regard out there at WSU, because on the surface I handle myself really well. But with handling yourself like that comes a certain responsibility that I just wasn't mature enough to handle."

During Bobo's redshirt junior season, an event of his own doing caused him to harbor even greater resentment toward the Washington State University community. Every so often college athletes will make headlines for stealing, smoking marijuana, or violating an undisclosed team rule. The coaching staff sometimes handle minor infractions internally, and the athlete ends up being admonished for exercising poor judgment. More egregious offenses can lead to an athlete losing his scholarship, a coach getting fired, or even NCAA sanctions imposed on the entire team. In the wake of such scandals, the administration, alumni, and the college football community are left wondering why athletes with such bright futures act so recklessly. Bobo suggests that his self-destructive behavior was a result of immaturity: "You need the preparation to become a man," he said. "You can do it like I did—learn through life's lessons how to become a man—or you can get proper tutelage, 'cause 18 years is plenty of time for you to become a man. You still have some growing up to do, but it's still plenty of time to learn how to get the basics of what a man does. The first thing is take care of your responsibilities, learning to be responsible for what you do, taking care of your actions. I didn't get none of that."

When a high-profile athlete finds himself in hot water, it is common for him to blame others for the indiscretion. The more star treatment an athlete receives, the more reasonable it is that he believes the rules apply to everyone else but to him. Plus the pressure to win can lead coaches and administrators to look the other way when a star athlete lands in trouble. They need the stars on the field.

According to Bobo, the irony of his story is that he swore that he would never do anything stupid enough to ruin his own football career. "When I used to see Lawrence Phillips,[10] I used to say I'd never be like that. Little did I know that I was sabotaging my shit in my own way." Going into his redshirt junior year, Bobo claims that he had worked hard to prepare for a great season. He started the season off with 20 catches over the first three games. At that point in the season Bobo was the leading wide receiver in the PAC 10 Conference. On a Thursday before his team traveled to Fresno State University for a football game, Bobo made what at first appeared to be a minor lapse in judgment.

"I go to Dissmore's, I see these batteries," he chuckles. "I was collecting stuff for the away trip. I went and paid for everything but the batteries. I just stole them, but I had the money to pay for them. Then the dude just came up and said, 'Man I can't let you get away.' Dude just came out and said, 'I know you put the batteries in your pocket.' I was like, 'Come on, man let me get away.' He says 'I saw you stealing more shit a couple of weeks ago, but I let you get away with it 'cause of who you are—but this time I can't.' So we go back and I was like, 'Man you don't have to make a big deal of this shit,' and he says. 'Okay, but I have to file a report for the store.' So he calls the cops, and the cops come do what they got to do, but when you call the cops, it's gonna go over the wire and go to the press. So they come and talk to me or whatever. I'm like, 'Look man, this is real stupid. Can I just pay for the batteries and get out of here?' So they let me pay for the batteries and I left. So I figured it's all done. I mean, my excuse is I forgot to pay for the batteries.'"

In the days that followed, Bobo learned just how rapidly things can escalate when the media get involved. "Right when I got home the phone rings. It was my position coach, and he was like, 'What the hell did you do? Did you steal something?' I was like, Yeah, but I paid for them. It's no big deal.' He was like, 'OK, but don't answer the phone.' And my dumb ass answered the phone, one reporter called after another." Instead of coming clean and telling the truth, Bobo lied. The next day, the coaches called him in and told him to give them the real story and assert himself as a team leader. "They made me stand up in front of the team to explain what happened. I said that I didn't really try to steal the batteries, but they was just there and I put them . . . it just sounded like some stupid shit, but I still lied to them. I made up something, and they knew I was lying because they talked to the store and my story didn't match up." The coaches decided they had to make an example out of Bobo. He was suspended and missed the game against Fresno. "First time I was about to cry over a football game," he remembers.

Making matters worse, he was a high-profile player. His story went national, and Bobo soon discovered his name was flashed across the ESPN cable network. "I was at home Thursday night watching Cal against Kansas State. I had invited a lot of people over. The team had left already to go to Fresno, nobody even knew that I was suspended, I just told them I was hurt. So we sit up there watching the game. We was about 10 deep in my crib, and they cut into the middle of the game. On ESPN: 'This just in from Pullman, Washington. Phillip Bobo has been suspended for shoplifting. Stay tuned.' So I turn around, and everybody is looking at me. And the dude made it seem—like shit, like it was a big deal. Then my phone just started ringing off the hook. My fraternity members that lived back east was calling me, 'What the fuck you done did? You on parole or some shit?' I was just looking at these people, and I said, there you have it. See, 'cause from where I grew up, my dad didn't take responsibility for whatever he did, so I didn't get it. I was used to finagling my way out of it as opposed to handling it." On the heels of the Dissmore's battery incident, Bobo skated through an otherwise unmemorable season.

The NCAA touts the many benefits of participating in college sports, including academic success, healthy living, and elite training opportunities.[11] People love to watch a competitive Big 10 or Pac 12 football game filled with bone-jarring tackles, electrifying punt returns, and gravity defying interceptions. But what happens when a player is suffering emotionally?

By season's end, Bobo had recorded the lowest number of receptions and receiving yards in his collegiate career. After the Stanford game, Bobo acknowledged that playing football started to feel burdensome. "The rest of the year I was just out there catching two or three passes a game, and no touchdowns. I was just going through the motions not really even trying." Mental and emotional health issues are perhaps as prevalent as physical injuries in college and professional football, but few athletes will be granted the time and help they need to address their problems. Once the NCAA's eligibility clock starts, athletes are awarded four seasons to participate in athletics. Likewise, the moment an NFL athlete enters the league, the sand in his career hourglass starts to flow. The stigma associated with mental and emotional health issues, along with the general lack of awareness about them within the football community, can allow athletes to slip into a state of depression without anyone really noticing. In retrospect, Bobo says, "I think

I was depressed. Yeah. As a matter of fact, I think I was depressed the whole time I was there. From the end of high school through college, bro, the whole shit." Perhaps Bobo could have received the necessary treatment if the code of masculinity—both inside and outside of football—didn't maintain "No Pain, No Gain."

In addition to the code of masculinity that drives athletes to take unnecessary risks, the desire to reach the highest ranks of the sports tournament places athletes in danger. I was no exception. During my junior season of college, in a game against Virginia Military Institute (VMI) I pursued a ball carrier as he ran a sweep out of the backfield. When he turned the corner, I rushed to fill the lane from my right cornerback position. Just as I shed the blocker to make the tackle, the wide receiver reached back and clipped my foot. I stumbled headfirst into the ball carrier's powerful thigh as my neck snapped back and everything around me went silent.

The pain from the collision was excruciating. I couldn't get up. At that moment all I could think about was what my high school coach, Tom Higgins Sr. used to say, "No matter how bad the pain is, you better crawl, limp, or roll off that field." He would admonish us to never let the other team have the satisfaction of seeing one of us hurt. But as hard as I tried, I couldn't move. When the team doctor and trainer arrived, they asked if I could move my shoulder. I will never forget my exact words: "Doc, I can't move my arm. It's ripped off my body." It felt like somebody tore off my right deltoid and poured hot-burning coals in it.

The doctor assured me that my shoulder was still intact, then placed his hand just above my elbow and asked me to move my forearm. Only after feeling my fingers move was I convinced that the shoulder had not actually been detached. But I had suffered a traumatic cervical spinal cord and shoulder injury that nearly left me unable to lift my arm.

The doctors at the University of Virginia School of Medicine determined that I had herniated and ruptured a disk between my fifth and sixth cervical vertebrae. The injury included severe nerve damage to the brachial plexus, and torn right deltoid and trapezius muscles. Several spinal bone fragments had broken off and lodged against nerves in my neck. A neurologist delivered grim news: I needed an operation either to fuse vertebrae or to insert a U-bolt and open up a space between the vertebrae in hopes that the disk would heal itself. I opted for the U-bolt; if the procedure was successful, I might, just maybe, play football again.

The evening before the scheduled surgery, a myelogram[12] was performed to exactly locate the injury. The test left me so groggy the next morning that I didn't grasp what the doctor meant when he said the operation was no longer necessary. I recall the doctor explaining that on extremely rare occasions, the body has the ability to heal itself. More clearly, though, I remember that he told my parents my recovery was an unexplained phenomenon, a "medical miracle." Throughout the ordeal, my grandmother Ruth Turner had encouraged me to pray and put everything in God's hands. Her words strengthened and reaffirmed my Christian faith in a way that lasts to this day. Nine months after nearly losing the ability to move my neck or lift my right arm, I was cleared to reenter the sports tournament. Because my neck and shoulder were still weak from playing post-injury, I decided to take some time off after the end of my senior season and attend another semester of school. This decision was both wise and naïve: I knew that more education would help me in the long run, and I actually thought that my football career would be over once teams dug into my medical history.

My own story and many of those I gathered for this book highlight the subtle ways that masculinity is enmeshed in the culture of football in ways that enable major college football programs and the NFL to fulfill their mission of winning games, generating revenue, and affirming the cultural importance of the sports-industrial complex. By using the internal motivation of young athletes hoping for an NFL career, high school and NCAA Division I football programs can develop athletes into finely tuned instruments capable of amazing physical feats, while also transforming them into useful or conforming adults who behave in accordance with the totalizing institution's officially approved norms. The athletes conform to expectations because they know that the football coaching fraternity is a close-knit community in which news travels fast. When a college athlete becomes a legitimate NFL prospect, coaches will tap into their networks to gauge his character and athletic ability. A player's draft status may take a serious hit if his character is called into question or if he is injured. By slipping from high draft status to the middle or lower rounds, an athlete could easily lose millions of dollars in signing bonus money. If a player is deemed a character risk he will slip right off the draft board. Given the pressure on the NFL to clean up its image, one can reasonably ask why any collegiate athlete would admit to injury, mental health problems, or personal indiscretions. Yet each year, college football players find themselves having to explain how they became involved with the law.

For tens of thousands of athletes, the final game of their college football career represents the end of the road. Few athletes will ever wear a football uniform after college. Most will join the ranks of dedicated sports fans and cherish their football glory days. Among the few who are invited to audition for the biggest stage on the American sports scene, even more will be culled before the season begins. Essentially, after college ball, the deck gets reshuffled. The stars and journeymen must once again prove themselves in the sports tournament.

MAKING IT TO THE BIG SHOW

My goal is that I want 10 years [in the NFL], and to walk when
I'm 40.

—Kyle Wilson
2010 New York Jets first-round draft choice

EACH JANUARY AND February, former college athletes attend NFL Combine
training camps across the country. These athletes endure a battery of speed,
strength, and agility tests designed to measure their physical prowess and
their mental and emotional fortitude. Countless hours are spent lifting
weights, catching passes, running suicide drills and sprints, soaking in the
whirlpool, receiving physical therapy treatments, and sleeping in budget
motel rooms, all in preparation for a life-changing opportunity—a contract
to play in the NFL.

Despite public perceptions of selfish athletes throwing lavish sex parties,
exercising poor judgment, and having run-ins with the law, the star and journeymen athletes presented in this chapter hardly displayed such behavior.[1]
Kyle Wilson, a first-round draft selection, and Juleonny Carter, a rookie free
agent, were talented athletes who fought as hard to stay in the league as they
did to earn their initial roster spots.

A STAR IS SIGNED

Perhaps the most interesting aspect of Kyle Wilson's journey to the NFL
is that it nearly didn't happen. At 5'10" and 190 pounds, some doubted that
Wilson was big enough to play in the NFL, but low expectations hadn't
stopped him before. For instance, despite helping Piscataway High School

win three straight state championships, being named first-team All-State as a wide receiver, earning all-area, all-county, all-conference, and all-division honors, Wilson was only considered a two-star college recruit by rivals.com and Yahoo Sports.[2]

Kyle's oldest Wilson brother, Gerry Jr., received numerous scholarship offers but elected to play football and run track at Princeton University. His middle brother, Vincent Wilson, was a standout running back and defensive back who earned a scholarship to the University of Iowa and transferred to the University of Delaware. With the benefit of a strong athletic and academic bloodline as well as an exceptional high school resumé, it was a surprise that college recruiters' phone calls and campus invites never arrived in mass for the youngest Wilson.

Piscataway High School football head coach Dan Higgins was stunned: "For some reason . . . Kyle went under the radar.[3] But he was always one of the most mature and grounded kids on the team."[4] One option to remain in the sports tournament would have been to field offers from lower-tier college programs, where Kyle might have stood out even more. But Kyle and his family understood that playing for a smaller Division I football program might hurt his draft stock. With the assistance of his brothers Gerry Jr. and Vincent, and support of parents Gerry Sr. and Carrie, the family devised a plan to elevate Kyle's recruiting profile. It was Gerry Jr.'s job to make sure that nothing was left to chance.

Gerry Jr. went to work on a grassroots marketing plan: "The first thing I did was create a spreadsheet of the top 50 college programs, then made a comparison of Kyle's high school statistics and the defensive backs on their rosters. Then I created a highlight tape and sent it to each school along with the statistical breakdown. The goal was to garner as much attention as possible." According to Marcel Yates, Boise State University's secondary coach, Kyle had all the attributes he was looking for in a defensive back. Immediately after viewing the highlight film Gerry Jr. had put together, Yates and another assistant traveled the 2,458 miles from Idaho to Piscataway, New Jersey, to offer Kyle a scholarship.[5]

AFTER REDSHIRTING AS a freshman at Boise State, Kyle delivered an impressive performance against the University of Oklahoma in an upset victory at the 2007 Fiesta Bowl. The *Sporting News* awarded him an honorable mention as a Freshman All-American, and, in early November of his senior season, it recognized him as one of 12 semifinalists for the 2009 Jim Thorpe Award.[6] Kyle's collegiate stats and game film suggested success on the next level, but again the Wilson family was unwilling to leave his draft status to chance. According to Gerry Jr., an average of five cornerbacks per year are selected in the first round of the NFL draft. "I needed to try and get my brother in the top five. I pulled a page out of American Express's marketing playbook by inserting my brother into the same conversation as the other top corners. We put together a viral marketing campaign that included stats from all the other guy's fan pages alongside my brother's stats. We wanted to control the material and control the messaging."

In addition to identifying draft trends, Gerry Jr. described his role on Team Wilson as branding: "We used Facebook and Twitter to promote Kyle, since he already had a great body of work." Boise State's undefeated record and victory over Texas Christian University in the 2009 Fiesta Bowl were thrust forward as the main focal point of every conversation about Kyle leading up the 2010 NFL draft.

Perhaps the most indispensable tool in team Wilson's arsenal was a shrink-wrapped, 33-foot recreational vehicle emblazoned in the Boise State Broncos' colors—blue and orange—and plastered with Kyle's image. In Kyle's senior year, his family traveled more than 27,000 miles in the RV, attending every Boise State game and using the vehicle as a centerpiece attraction at tailgate parties. After the 2009 Fiesta Bowl, Kyle was invited to participate in the Senior Bowl. Gerry Jr. made sure the RV was prominently displayed throughout the week. "We wanted NFL scouts to think, 'This guy was at the Senior Bowl, and he has his own RV, video game, and game highlights posted online for people to see.' I got on ESPN to do an interview with Todd McShay at the Senior Bowl. He had a number of questions about the RV."[7]

When Kyle pulled his hamstring prior to the NFL Combine, his participation was limited to the bench press test and attending team interviews with general managers and coaches. Scouts were disappointed that he wasn't able to run, but they were impressed with his bench press performance. Kyle's 25 repetitions of 225 pounds was considered amazing for a man his size.[8] Gerry Jr. recalled, "Kyle had done so much to already prove his worth that he didn't even need to produce at the Combine." Kyle's inability to run at the Combine set the stage for a key workout a few weeks later at Boise State's Pro Day.

FIGURE 7.1: ROBERT "PACKY" TURNER AND KYLE WILSON AT FEDEX FIELD.

Gerry Jr. continued, "All we had to do is post his Pro Day video online. It was one comprehensive, consistent message. Talk to the recruiters, his coach, his family, and you get the same message. Put on your GM hat and ask yourself, 'Where am I going to get the most bang for my buck?' It all adds up to Kyle Wilson. Some people go to family reunions, but we go to football games. We all pulled together to help him live his dream" (Figure 7.1).

Leading up to the NFL draft, Kyle only needed to focus on putting on a top performance for the scouts. Gerry Jr. and the rest of the family each played their part to perfection, and the Jets made Kyle the 29th selection of the 2010 NFL draft. In the culmination of a long journey that began with Pop Warner football, Kyle Wilson became just the second Boise State football player to be picked in the first round.[9]

ANSWERING THE CALL

The transition from college to the NFL is vastly different for star and journeymen athletes. Kyle Wilson is one of the rare athletes to successfully make the leap from being lightly recruited in high school to the first round of the NFL draft. Most young athletes grow up with dreams of hearing their names called by Commissioner Goodell on day one of the draft, but for tens of thousands of football players that dream never materializes. In fact, only 32 athletes are selected in the first round each year. On April 22, Kyle huddled around the television set in his parents home, surrounded by extended family and friends, as the NFL commissioner announced, "With the 29th pick in the 2010 NFL draft, the NJ Jets select Kyle Wilson, defensive back, Boise State University."[10]

After I interviewed both his father and his older brother, Kyle agreed to speak with me about what it meant to live the dream of a star athlete playing in front of a hometown crowd. Kyle recounted the rapid sequence of events leading up to the draft: "During the Combine, you meet with different teams for like 15 minutes each. I had like 16 team interviews prior to the draft. Some teams fly you out to their team facility, then coaches test you by teaching you something and ask[ing] you to give it back to them. I had already remembered some of the stuff I was taught earlier. After the Combine, I visited 10 teams in like two weeks—so you ain't really in good shape. I had to work out on the road and do a little stuff in the hotel."

I asked Kyle about dealing with the demands of school during his final semester at Boise State while simultaneously auditioning for the NFL: "That last semester, I only had six or eight credits left, so I was already done with school. Guys got to figure out what types of obligations they got. Some guys drop school all together, and other guys make it a priority. In between the Combine and Pro Day stuff, you just got to go back and figure it out. Basically, it's just the start of working at being in the NFL as a job." Obtaining his degree and fulfilling a commitment to the Boise State football family were clearly priorities to Kyle; he could have skipped his senior year and headed for the NFL early as a mid-round pick. He looked into it: "I had a pretty good year my junior year, so I submitted my film to the NFL [to] see what they would tell me to do. The request has got to go through your college head coach. It was a complex process that gave me a different perspective of what other people thought. You got to figure out what works. I knew I wanted to shore up things about my game. I had goals that I had set and things I wanted to work on. [I knew] what type of numbers I wanted to put up. Every game, I went out with the mindset that on every play, I could have made the play if I had done something [better]." He decided to remain in school and keep working.

At the culmination of the four-day NFL draft, each team hosts a minicamp so draft selections and rookie free agents can become acquainted with the coaching staff and playbook. Kyle told me how fast it went: "You get drafted, and you get a call that night. They pick you up the next morning. Then you get introduced to the media and all the team staff. I only had a straight weekend to pack up my stuff at Boise State. I took it to the post office on Saturday, then on Sunday I got to the campus and said my goodbyes; then got on a plane that evening. Didn't have no time for nothing else. They whisk you out to rookie minicamp. When you get there, you supposed to have a full team at practice, but they only have like 40 guys, and you ain't in the best shape. You got five practices in three days. All this stuff happens pretty quickly. At that time, you have your playbook and start studying to get ready for the next minicamp and summer camp."

This early phase of the transition from college to the NFL is sink or swim. Suddenly, NFL athletes are expected to manage their own time and set priorities in the off-season. No longer coddled by high school and college programs, NFL prospects are expected to attend the Combine, Pro Day, draft, and rookie minicamps on their own, find a place to live in a new city while continuing to train, and learn the playbook for the upcoming season.

Because it is almost impossible for major college football players to work while attending school, most athletes enter the draft strapped for cash. Sometimes parents or a benefactor provides support, and, for prospective high draft picks, sports agents are willing to arrange for loans or lines of credit leveraged against future earnings.[11] But that money comes at a cost. There are plenty of horror stories of athletes declaring financial hardship within years of exiting the league.[12] Unlike athletes from disadvantaged backgrounds, Kyle's family had the resources and expertise to shield him from unscrupulous agents seeking to exploit vulnerability. Gerry Jr. told me about a typical situation: "One day we were in Sacramento and this agent pulls up in his little Porsche Boxer with the top dropped—suited and booted—and I was sitting there in a T-shirt. I have full tattoos on both arms, and this guy has no idea who I was. You know, the guy really didn't do a thorough job with his homework. He just knew I was Kyle's brother. He shows up and is just trying to evaluate potential athletes and gauge the prospects. We sit down, and he gives me his NFL background, then later in the conversation he asks, 'You know what type of line of credit would your brother be looking for?' I looked at him a little bit confused, and then I said, 'Line of credit? You mean how much money does he need to borrow for something that he doesn't need, based on future earnings that he is not guaranteed?' The guy kind of looked confused, then I had to set him straight and say, 'Look, I have a mechanical engineering degree from Princeton. And I have an MBA from MIT. I'm well aware of debt, line of credit, and all of the above.'" Where journeymen might get a small investment from an agent to pay for Combine training and a small living stipend until they get a contract, star athletes are bombarded by unscrupulous agents and financial con men. Many young men who were raised in low-income homes and have no real experience handling money find these temptations too difficult to resist. Kyle was particularly fortunate.

In addition to needing money for daily expenses, the transition from college to the NFL is filled with practical issues: finding a place to live, buying a car, relocating to a new city, establishing bank accounts and paying bills. These practical issues are even more challenging for the 21-year-old accustomed to having others handle his affairs. Ahmad, a former second-round draft choice for the Cleveland Browns, learned that when he was 11 years old, his mother had put the electric bill in his name. When she didn't pay it, Ahmad was saddled with a bad credit rating that dogged him for years. As an NFL athlete, Ahmad was denied a loan when he went to buy his first home—his credit was terrible.

The transition also means going from the athlete's final collegiate game to his first day in the NFL. Kyle did not sign his rookie NFL contract until July 31—one hundred days after the New York Jets drafted him. During that period, he was expected to attend a nine-week voluntary off-season workout program[13] (see Table 7.1), a three-day post-draft rookie minicamp,[14] a league sponsored rookie symposium,[15] and mandatory team minicamps.[16] From a logistical and financial standpoint, those first 100 days can be astoundingly difficult for an NFL rookie to manage. For Kyle, the stress was fairly low, since he was staying in New Jersey, and rather than borrowing money to pay for temporary housing or to hire a concierge service to help with the logistical challenges of moving, Kyle's family provided the support he needed. At the conclusion of the Jets' organized team practice activities (OTAs), Kyle flew to Orlando, Florida, to continue his preparation for his rookie season. "After minicamp you gotta keep working out to prepare for summer camp. I asked

TABLE 7.1: NINE-WEEK VOLUNTARY OFF-SEASON WORKOUT PROGRAM, OTAS.

Phase 1	The first two weeks of the program consists of activities limited to strength and conditioning and physical rehabilitation only.
Phase 2	The next three weeks of the program consist of on-field workouts that may include individual player instructions and drills as well as team practice conducted on a "separate basis." No live contact or team offense vs. team defense drills is permitted.
Phase 3	In the next four weeks of the program, teams may conduct a total of 10 days of organized team practice activity (OTAs). No live contact is permitted, but 7-on-9, 9-on-9, and 11-on-11 drills are permitted.

some of the vets what I had to do and where to go between camps. I decided to get trained by Tom Shaw at Disney's Wide World of Sports."[17]

As a first-round draft choice, Kyle was dubbed a local hero, and with that title came the expectation that he would be readily available for media interactions and community events. Shortly after the draft Kyle received a phone call from Jets defensive leader Kris Jenkins, making sure he was focused and prepared for what was to come.[18] Two days later, Kyle was standing on the pitcher's mound of Citi Field with his name sewn on the back of a New York Mets jersey, throwing out the ceremonial first pitch before a game against the Atlanta Braves.[19]

Once his rookie season started, the glamour and hype wore off quickly. Virulent Jets fans wanted to see Kyle become one of the top defensive playmakers in the league. Raising expectations, head coach Rex Ryan had a reputation as a defensive guru with an eye for top athletes. The year prior to Kyle's arrival, the Jets had been defeated in the AFC championship game by the eventual Super Bowl Champion Indianapolis Colts. Heading into the 2010 season—Kyle's first—Jets fans and media outlets viewed the team as a legitimate Super Bowl contender.[20] I asked him about living up to such lofty expectations: "Learning how to play in certain situations, that's what's different from how it was in college. You see so much stuff around the league; stuff gets called so inconsistently. You see a penalty that gets called on one play, but that same type of play can go without a call the next time."

"Everybody knows the risk that comes with playing in the NFL," he continued. "Every single day I feel like my job is at risk. I got to do extra stuff every day, 'cause I know I'm gonna get hurt. That's a fact. If you don't take care of your body, then it's a higher risk of getting hurt."

After dropping to the bottom of the depth charts and drawing media criticism in his rookie year, teammates and coaches began referring to Kyle as a "student of the game." In his second year on the team, defensive back coach Dennis Thurman observed of Kyle, "He writes everything down and draws formations, too. Most [guys] don't do it that way." At the time, All-Pro cornerback Darrelle Revis was quoted as saying, "[Kyle] is playing unbelievable for us, and it's only going to get better. He wants it. He wants to be great, and he's on the way to doing it."[21] Although he played in every game of his first season, the organization seemed to question whether Kyle could step into a starting role in year two. He had been known for letting bad plays stick with him. Rather than take a wait-and-see attitude, Kyle took part in a six-week, off-season training regimen with Revis in Arizona. The two cornerbacks pushed one another on the track and in the weight room; they broke down tapes of wide receivers and perfected the art of deciphering body language. Starting his second season, the hard work seemed to pay off. Kyle only had one penalty (of five yards) and he did not allow a long completion or touchdown pass in the first eight games. Kyle told me, "You got to learn from every single thing. It's like taking a test every single day, but you already know what the test is going to be on. 'How do I learn from what I just did?' If you are fortunate enough, you can build on what you did and you can just keep getting better and better. It's a daily grind of what you put on film. Once you take care of things on the field, then things just keep opening up for you. It gets better every single year."

Kyle has been recognized for his many contributions to the community. He made more than 20 visits to New Jersey schools representing the NFL-sponsored "Play 60" program;[22] he drummed up support for the Alliance for Lupus Research; he raised money for the Piscataway High School football program; and he was named the New York Jets Walter Payton Man of the Year.[23] Kyle told me proudly, "I got the ability to effect change and to impact children. . . . Kids are going to look up to you. It's not always about giving money, but sometimes it's about giving of your time, giving kind words, and giving motivation."

As Kyle approached his contract year with the Jets, the New York media buzzed about his future on the team. Critics claimed he had taken a step backward at the inside nickel cornerback slot position, even though Pro Football Focus ranked him tied for first in the league at the position.[24] Head coach Rex Ryan remained steadfast in his public support of Kyle. He told the media he felt Kyle was playing with more confidence than in the past and was expected to have a terrific season.[25] By the start of the next season, however, neither player nor coach was still with the Jets. Ryan was fired after compiling a 46–50 record with the Jets (.479%), and Kyle agreed to a one-year contract to play for the New Orleans Saints.[26] Prior to his final season in New York, I asked Kyle why he loved playing football. The question was meant to gain a sense of what the game represented to a 26-year-old athlete who had already experienced numerous highs and lows in the NFL. "Playing football, that's the only thing for me," he said. "I like to have fun, and it's the only way I know how to express myself. It's sort of like fighting. You are out there using your hands; it's like boxing, you are out there competing. It's fun. Winning is everything. In the NFL you got to win, but if you don't win, then change is gonna come. If you're losing, something has got to change. That's the one constant in the NFL."

While it is true that my career in the American sports tournament was longer than most, my experience as a journeyman athlete was substantially different from Kyle's ascent to the top. Over the course of a year, Kyle's parents, brothers, and other family members had alluded to the various challenges he regularly faced. From the moment he signed a multimillion dollar contract to play in the media capital of the world, Kyle was thrust into the epicenter of the sports-industrial complex. I asked Kyle about the pressure of entering the NFL as a star athlete. He said, "What are the problems, where is the stress? Personally, you got a job to do, and everybody wants something. Everybody needs something. Everybody wants something from you. It comes on a daily basis. At the end of the day, you only got so much to give, and who is going to give back to you? The perception in the league is that I need to be responsible for everyone in my family. 'You are the breadwinner.' It's like winning the lottery. Stuff comes up, 'Who is gonna pay for that? Am I reaching my financial goals? Am I doing what I'm supposed to do?' Money gives you more options, I know that. When you don't have money, then your options are slimmer. It ain't no secret. It's on Sports Center. Everybody knows how much money you make.[27] If I have kids, I don't want them to play football. It's like Biggie [rapper Notorious B.I.G.] says, 'More money, more problems.' My goal is that I want 10 years [in the NFL], and to walk when I'm 40."

If a young athlete's ultimate goal is to sign a first-round, multimillion dollar NFL contract, perhaps Kyle's experience with the Jets can remind us that even star athletes "living the dream" are under intense pressure. If you're on top, you want to stay on top. Even with support from family and close friends, Kyle is the only one who can strap on his helmet and try to live up to the lofty expectations of the NFL. Rex Ryan could not preserve Kyle's position within the organization; nor could a Walter Payton team award or two Marty Lyon awards.[28] The cold, hard reality of the NFL is that winning is all that matters. A football player's true value is measured in wins and losses.

What may matter most for the athlete is what Gerry Jr. uncovered during Kyle's transition from college to the pros. He frames the issue this way, "What is the main difference between a journeyman and a star? A star athlete is awarded a multimillion dollar contract and most often remains in the league long enough to qualify for full retirement, healthcare, and pension benefits. A journeyman athlete on the other hand, [he] rarely plays beyond the league average: 3.3 seasons."

THE JOURNEYMAN'S JOURNEY

Juleonny Carter's transition from college to the NFL was anything but conventional. His college head coach refused to invite NFL scouts to give Juleonny a workout. He even warned Juleonny against pursuing a tryout for fear of embarrassing the program or hurting the chances of several underclassmen who seemed to have more legitimate chances of making it to the NFL. Juleonny's big break came when a former college teammate who played for the Green Bay Packers told the team's head talent scout that he "had blazing speed." When Juleonny learned of the scout's scheduled visit to a nearby university campus, he talked his way onto the field for a workout. The scout clocked Juleonny's 40-yard sprint at 4.3 seconds. He was instructed to run it again. After Juleonny crossed the finish line with another impressive time, the scout told him to stay in shape and wait by the phone.

As an undersized (6'2", 210-pound) linebacker who had played in the NCAA Football Champion Subdivision ((FCS) formerly Division I AA), Juleonny would have to seize every opportunity that came his way. And after watching nearly 240 players get selected in the 1998 NFL draft, Juleonny knew he was fortunate to be among about 150 free agents to receive a free-agent rookie minicamp invitation.[29]

Like other undrafted free agents, Juleonny was offered a league-minimum rookie contract of $200,000. Since the $7,000 signing bonus he received was barely enough to live on between graduation and the start of summer training in July, Juleonny moved back into his mother's home. In accordance with the NFL labor agreement at that time, clubs were permitted to hold a rookie minicamp on one of the first two weekends after the draft in April. Because clubs can invite athletes to use their facilities only during organized team activities, athletes generally need to pay for private trainers or gym memberships during the remainder of the off-season. Higher draft picks can use their signing bonuses to hire trainers and work out at state-of-the-art facilities, but rookie free agents like Juleonny must rely on whatever free or cheap resources are available. "I decided to work with the female track coach at my college," Juleonny told me. "I would spend rainy days out on the track, running by myself or sometimes with the women's track team. I'd go work out every day, 'cause I knew I had to train. I didn't have an agent saying, 'I'm going to pay for you to go to Cris Carter's Fast Program in Boca.' I was like, these are all the resources I have, so I got to make the best of it."

If he wanted to secure a spot on an NFL roster, Juleonny had to fight to stay one step ahead of the competition. At the rookie minicamp, the major difference between Juleonny and the team's top draft picks was that no one on the coaching staff knew much about him: "I was just a name and a number. There was really nothing to know [about me]. Actually, my recruiting scout, the guy who found me, was the only one who knew anything about me. When I started to do good in preseason games, he was always there to congratulate me."

For Juleonny, the challenge of the mental aspects of the pro game was intensified by the team's recent successful run: "The year before I got there, they were winners. The team was all veterans, so the playbook was all a review for everyone else. For me, it's the first time I'm trying to decipher what the codes mean—Sun, Sky, Rainbow, I mean, he's going from Nickel to Dime, to Penny to third down, to goal line, and I'm like, this is like a war strategy—like a pre-conceived war strategy. But what war are we fighting? I was like, 'What the hell is going on?'"

Such disorientation is common for all first-year players, but undrafted free agents basically have to fend for themselves when it comes to grasping the nuances of an NFL playbook. Juleonny says, "Like the first-round draft choice from my year . . . he was a hell of an athlete. But he didn't get pressured like us. Guys in my group, we didn't get a lot of attention." Because teams invest millions in high draft selections, every organizational resource is made available to get them on the playing field quickly. An athlete's draft position, contract, and signing bonus directly correlate to his chance of gaining a roster spot. The combination of the three often determines the length of his career.

The NFL Collective Bargaining Agreement restricts a free labor market. With over $143 million of annual salary cap allotment at stake per team, football is now a year-round occupation for NFL athletes.[30] The competition for roster spots has stiffened to the point that athletes can ill afford to lose their physical edge or mental focus. By the time an athlete makes it to the NFL, he has committed so much of himself to the game that to stay in it, almost no sacrifice is too great. The pressure to hold onto a roster spot never eases, even after an athlete presses his way into the league.

An unintended consequence of the NFL salary cap is that teammates are pitted against one another, trying to secure the largest contract possible. Juleonny described the conflict: "You got to be careful who you trust. I've seen guys try to sabotage their teammates in the middle of a game just to try and get that person cut. One guy might have a bigger contract than the next guy. If you can get the guy cut that's making more money than you and the team gives you his salary, then so be it. In the NFL, it's about surviving."

Despite the long odds faced by journeymen, the salary cap can sometimes work in their favor. It did for Juleonny. When a team has too many high-priced veterans on the roster, management must look for ways to shave salaries. In fact, every year a handful of late-round draft picks and free agents make it onto club rosters *because* they provide cheap labor.[31] Juleonny is sure that's what happened to him: "I scraped in because a linebacker was gonna demand a multimillion-dollar-a-year salary, and it wasn't in the budget. They said 'Okay, you [Juleonny] can play special teams, and you'll play defense eventually,' and that's how I made it." This economic reality also means that journeymen cannot miss a single practice or risk a coach questioning their commitment. An injury, a minor infraction, a broken alarm clock, or a mental lapse during a game can signal the end of a journeyman's career. To illustrate this point, Juleonny recounted: "A friend of mine got food poisoning because they cooked him a bad omelet at [preseason training] camp. He told me the food they had was like lobster and steak, it was all catered eggs; the food we had [at training camp] was like at McDonald's. Bacon, eggs, in the big tins and stuff. He was in Jacksonville, and he got food poisoning. He got cut, and the train kept going. He could have made it, too. . . . Those of us that aren't drafted get one shot in camp. Maybe he shouldn't have ate that lobster, or maybe he shouldn't have ate that steak or them eggs. Maybe something didn't smell right. It's your own fault you got food poisoning."

During both spring minicamps of his rookie season, Juleonny developed a method he referred to as "the cheat," allowing him to master the team playbook quickly. "I would get back to my hotel room after practicing all day then do schoolwork, because I still needed to graduate from college, and then study my playbook until I fell asleep. My cheat was to dream about the plays I just studied. That way, they were still fresh in my mind for practice the next day." Although a large signing bonus can protect star athletes and high draft picks from getting cut, Juleonny and other journeymen look for whatever advantages they can find—like "the cheat"—when fighting to earn a spot on the team roster.

After surviving nine weeks of optional training activities (OTAs) and a grueling four-week preseason training camp, Juleonny's NFL dream was finally realized. Yet, in the daily grind of the season, he barely had time to celebrate. From the first week of September until a play-off loss five months later, football consumed nearly every aspect of his life. A typical workday began at 5:15 AM with an individual weight training and stretching session. That was followed by three film sessions, a special teams practice, a defensive team practice, and a personal weight training and conditioning session (required to help maintain his playing weight). The day ended some 15 hours after it began. Learning a new defensive scheme each week during the season was more mentally and emotionally exhausting than memorizing the playbook in the preseason training camps. Over the first half of his rookie season, Juleonny estimates that he averaged about four hours of sleep per night. Whenever the veterans went out after practice for dinner or drinks to blow off steam, Juleonny headed home to study his weekly special team assignments and the defensive game plan. His evenings usually consisted of reviewing hours of game film before switching to footage of that day's practice.

When his team began facing divisional rivals for the second time, after the season's mid-point, Juleonny's routine was altered slightly. The defensive game plan was adjusted less often, and Juleonny spent most of his time reviewing his notes from games he had played earlier in the season. He could spend a little extra time bonding with his teammates after practice. He could gain a few more hours of sleep each night. "By this point in the season, my body required more time to recover, so I was glad to sleep six hours at night instead of the four hours I was getting when the season started."

Practice Schedule during the Season

5:00 AM Wake up

5:15–6:00 AM Individual weight training session

6:00–6:15 AM Eat breakfast

6:30–8:00 AM Special teams meeting (nonspecial team guys eat breakfast)

8:05–8:30 AM Team meeting and announcements

8:30–10:00 AM Positional meeting, review films; install strategy for upcoming game

10:30–12:00 PM Watch more game film then hit the field for a walk through session

12:00–1:00 PM Eat lunch

1:30–2:30 PM Special teams practice

2:45–4:30 PM Regular practice

4:45–5:30 or 6:00 PM Watch the practice film

6:30–7:30 PM Organized team weightlifting session

7:30–8:30 PM Treatment for any injuries before leaving for the night

Nine months after reporting to his post-draft rookie minicamp, Juleonny's first season finally came to a close. Article 21 of the NFL Collective Bargaining Agreement (CBA) stipulates that each team's official voluntary off-season program can begin by mid-May. Before he knew it, the off-season was over and it was time for Juleonny to participate in optional training activities (OTA) and earn his spot on the team all over again.

Like all young players, Juleonny understood that "optional" really means "mandatory." This was particularly true of the OTAs he picked up between his first and second years in the NFL. "You could skip them if you want to, but your butt would be gone come time for the season. Everything for me was a rough situation. Nothing in my pro career came easy. I couldn't take nothing for granted. The OTAs are very intense. This is another area that you had to prove yourself." In the NFL "Panopticon,"[32] league control becomes self-control and optional becomes mandatory.

Even established veterans know what OTA really represents. After skipping a voluntary minicamp and receiving a stern rebuke from teammate Peyton Manning and head coach Jim Mora, former NFL star running back Edgerrin James quipped, "Hell, I only went to college for two and a half years, but I think I know the meaning of the word *voluntary*."[33]

In addition to a lengthy season, 16-hour workdays, and countless hours working with private trainers, NFL athletes also live in a public fishbowl.[34] Teams are constantly in search of the greatest talent at the lowest possible cost.[35] Given the financial reality of the salary cap, NFL athletes can rarely afford to spend more than six weeks away from their annual training regimen. In the meantime, to protect their investment above and beyond the physical rigors of playing football, the league employs security professionals to conduct extensive background checks and monitor athletes for offensive behavior. Coaches and talent evaluators pore over every second of game and practice film to evaluate each athlete's performance. The pressure to play at a high level acts as a strong incentive for athletes to prove their undivided loyalty. Collectively, these constraints reinforce the Panopticon effect, isolating stars and journeymen from society at large while subjecting them to surveillance, rigorous training, and constant competition.

While the transition from college to the NFL may be more straightforward for the star than for the journeyman, neither path is void of tremendous personal sacrifice. Kyle Wilson might have been rewarded with a multimillion dollar contract as a first-round draft choice, but his performance with the Jets failed to quiet persistent criticism and the ongoing complaints from media, fans, and coaches that he was a disappointing draft pick.[36] Juleonny Carter scraped and clawed his way onto three opening day rosters, but eventually another rookie willing to play for the league's minimum salary replaced him on the team. Neither the star nor the journeyman athlete can afford to relax. If a player loosens his grip on his job, he could be the next one to experience an early involuntary exit from the game.

8

EYE IN THE SKY: DISCIPLINE, CONTROL, AND THE BLACK BODY

WHAT DOES IT mean to play football in the NFL? I presented this question to a group of current and retired NFL athletes. Ahmad (who spoke under the condition of anonymity), a former Cleveland Browns linebacker with three and a half years of service, challenged the public perception of a professional athlete's life as one of ease, luxury, and excess. He said, "The NFL is an illusion. It's a form of modern day slavery. Go to the NFL Combine. You'll never ask that question again. [As a player], you're not in control of your own life."

As a second-round draft choice and former star recruit for Clemson University, Ahmad received over $2 million in bonus money during his career. But the large cash advance did little to prevent him from developing a critical opinion of the league. "If it's all about the money, then you aren't a slave. But when you talk about life, then you begin to see that every aspect of your life is controlled [by the NFL]."

Ahmad believes conflicts between labor and management are rooted in racism: "I feel the reason NFL players have so little control of their careers is because the league is 80% Black and the NFL Players Association is weak.[1] Black people still suffer from a slave mentality in certain ways. You ever read *The Making of a Slave* by Willie Lynch?[2] That's exactly how NFL owners treat Black athletes."[3]

The NFL is the largest employer of African American athletes in professional sports. While Black men represent only 6% of the total US population, nearly 70% of the athletic talent in the NFL is Black.[4] Scholars have argued that this overrepresentation has led to Black youth developing a single-minded pursuit of fame and upward mobility through sports.[5] Compounding the issue of race, league management and club owners are overwhelmingly White.[6] Given the significance of these issues, it is essential to understand how well-paid Black men experience race in the NFL. How do African Americans interpret and respond to being publicly praised for their athletic accomplishments while simultaneously being marginalized and micromanaged by the league? The NFL claims to hold every employee to the same standards, but the racial composition of the players and their interactions with the commissioner's office tend to influence some African American athletes' views on race throughout the league. Additionally, the racial dynamics between labor and management play an important role in determining how the Black athlete transitions to life after the NFL.

By almost any standard, it is difficult for many Americans to conceive of Black male professional athletes as a marginalized group. A simple Google search uncovers dozens of articles and websites that call professional athletes spoiled brats.[7] A *Washingtonian* magazine published in 2010 offers a glimpse into extravagance afforded to some NFL athletes. Among the Redskins highlighted is former quarterback Donovan McNabb, who purchased a 10,000-square-foot house in Great Falls, Virginia, for $2.2 million dollars. By comparison defensive back DeAngelo Hall lives modestly; after signing a six-year, $55 million dollar contract in 2009, Hall paid about a million dollars for a red brick home with five bedrooms, seven bathrooms, a four-car garage, and more than three acres of land in Leesburg, Virginia.[8]

Sociologist Harry Edwards[9] contends that race is but one of many factors that contribute to the marginalization of Black professional athletes. In his account of the Black athletes' role in the civil rights movement, Edwards recalls how US sprinters Tommie Smith and John Carlos used the 1968 Olympics to spotlight racial inequality in sports and in American society.[10] Decades after the image of Carlos's and Smith's raised arms and black-gloved fists left an indelible impression on society, some scholars assert that little in the world of sports has changed. Sociologist Douglas Hartmann[11] extends Edwards's work by concluding that although athletes of color are now handsomely compensated at the elite level, they continue to serve as athletic commodities, either helping teams win or being forgotten about altogether. Though Earl Smith[12] rejects Edwards's and Hartmann's conclusion by arguing that sport has changed considerably in the past 50 years, Cozzillio and Hayman[13] remind us that biases and barriers of discrimination have infused the politics of exclusion into the world of sports. Regardless of the position one favors in this debate, it is important to recognize that a lack of economic opportunity outside of sports plays a significant role in some young men's pursuit of NFL riches.

Chronic unemployment, broken schools, disproportionately high incarceration rates, predatory lending practices, and other social factors have left many Black and Brown young men discouraged about their futures in America.[14] Recent ethnographic studies by Scott Brooks,[15] Reuben May,[16] Loïc Wacquant,[17] and others demonstrate that some young Black males view sports as a means to achieve the American dream. In particular, Wacquant's work examines Bourdieu's concepts of the body as a form of physical capital[18] and sports as a vehicle for upward mobility.[19] A second body of literature relevant for this discussion investigates how Black men understand their social position in relationship to the American dream and workplace discrimination. Sociologist Al Young,[20] who demonstrates how marginalized young African American men interpret their social world, suggests that Black men who regularly leave economically depressed neighborhoods tend to have a wider range of opportunities than those who remain. However, they are also met with more racism, hostility, and institutional obstacles. Sociologist Deidre Royster and others argue that a disproportionately small portion of lower-middle- and working-class Black men will achieve employment and earning parity with their White male counterparts, at a rate no better today than it was thirty years ago.[21] Given that many young Black males view sports as an American institution where meritocracy prevails, much can be gained from an investigation of how Black NFL athletes interpret and respond to their role within the sports-industrial complex.

The complex set of racial dynamics in sport parallels the world of African American corporate executives in the post–civil rights era described by sociologist Elijah Anderson.[22] After conducting six months of intensive ethnographic interviews and observations, Anderson concluded that affirmative action had produced uneven results in the "C-suites." A few Blacks *have* reached upper-level management positions, but most believe it is difficult for them to feel and act as if they are accepted as full participants in the organization.[23] So, too, does the professional African American athlete hold the dual distinction of being identified first and foremost as a member of a historically stigmatized group while simultaneously being cast as a member of the elite social class. Contrary to the notion that professional sports are a gateway to the upper echelons of American society, Ahmad's commentary raises questions about the Black NFL athlete's ability to enjoy the same privileges as his White counterpart.

For example, the reach of the coaching fraternity apropos the NFL vetting process has been discussed in previous chapters. The NFL justifies its extensive interviewing and information gathering as due diligence, part of the process of hiring high-quality and expensive athletes. But at what point is this process too invasive, inappropriate, or discriminatory? According to published reports, former Oklahoma State star wide receiver Dez Bryant said that Miami Dolphins general manager Jeff Ireland, who is White, asked him in a pre-draft interview whether his mother was a prostitute. Bryant, who is Black, said that over time he had been asked similar questions about his family background in team interviews, but he refused to show his emotions. This time was different. After Bryant related his story to reporters, Ireland released a statement through the Dolphins organization suggesting that his job was to find out as much as possible about any player that he may draft. Ireland admitted that he used poor judgment in one of the questions directed at Bryant, but he meant no disrespect—he was just doing his job.[24] A similar incident took place in 2016 when former Ohio State cornerback Eli Apple claimed that at the NFL Combine, Atlanta Falcons coach Marquand Manuel asked whether he is gay.[25]

Scholars further contend that professional sport league officials disproportionately fine and criticize Black athletes for trash talking, taunting, celebrating, and dancing.[26] Sociologist Vincent L. Andrews[27] believes that counter to White male interpretations, for the African American athlete, celebrating is expressing excitement and showing emotions that will be contagious, motivate his teammates, and evoke a positive response from the spectators. Simons argues that the major underlying reason that Black male behavior is often targeted in the NFL is because it poses a threat to White male control of the sport and the right of the predominantly White ownership to define and interpret players' actions.[28] In response to this threat, Caucasian men have made normal African American behavior abnormal and deviant by interpreting the meaning of these behaviors through a White cultural lens.[29] A contemporary example is the public criticism lodged at former Seattle Seahawks defensive back Richard Sherman for trash-talking in a live post-game television interview. Sherman had made the game-deciding play in the Seahawks' victory of the 2014 NFC conference championship game, but his post-game comments saw Sherman being labeled a "thug." When a journalist asked whether being labeled a "thug" bothered him, Sherman, who is Black, responded, "What's the definition of a thug? Really? Can a guy on a football field just talking to people [be a thug?] . . . There was a hockey game where they didn't even play hockey! They just threw the puck aside and started fighting. I saw that and said, 'Ah, man, *I'm* a thug?' What's going on here? So I'm really disappointed at being called a thug."[30] Sherman's comparison between his brash words and the outright fighting considered part of the game in hockey, a predominantly White sport, was apt.

ON APRIL 10, 2007, the New York Giants issued a press release stating that the National Football League announced changes to its long-standing Personal Conduct Policy (PCP) for players, coaches, and other team and league employees. Among other policies, the correspondence indicated that the modifications focused on increased levels of discipline for PCP violations. It included a statement from newly elected NFL commissioner Roger Goodell: "It is important that the NFL be represented consistently by outstanding people as well as great football players, coaches, and staff." Goodell went on, "We hold ourselves to higher standards of responsible conduct because of what it means to be part of the National Football League. We have long had policies and programs designed to encourage responsible behavior, and this policy is a further step in ensuring that everyone who is part of the NFL meets that standard. We will continue to review the policy and modify it as warranted."[31]

In addition to the new PCP, the 2011 players' Collective Bargaining Agreement (CBA) gave the league the right to discipline players for numerous violations. Among the on-field infractions that can result in player fines are flagrant or personal fouls, fighting, verbal abuse, unsportsmanlike conduct, physical contact with an official, throwing a football into the stands, wearing unauthorized logos, and using a cell phone as a prop in a celebration. These fines range from $2,000 for unnecessarily entering into a fight area (that is, stepping into a fight you weren't already a part of) to $100,000 for wearing the wrong logo or amending the correct logo in any fashion.[32]

The NFL Substance-Abuse Policy governs off-field violations such as use of alcohol, drugs, and steroids. Punishment for violations of this policy range from fines and reprimands to suspensions or even lifetime expulsion from the league, depending on whether it is the player's first, second, or third violation. At the conclusion of every NFL investigation, Commissioner Goodell has full authority to impose whatever discipline he believes is warranted.

In what appeared to be a show of solidarity with the NFL, former NFL Players Association executive director Eugene Upshaw[33] added, "The NFL Players Association and the Players Advisory Council have been discussing this issue for several months. We believe that these are steps that the commissioner needs to take, and we support the policy. It is important that players in violation of the policy will have the opportunity and the support to change their conduct and earn their way back."

Commissioner Goodell implemented what attorney David Cornwell and other sports agents label "draconian changes"[34] within his first eight months in office, which begs the question, Why would a labor union that represents multimillion dollar athletes acquiesce to a commissioner's demands and willingly endorse a policy that restricts their employees' freedom? The NFL Players Advisory Council, a six-member committee of veteran players even publicly endorsed Goodell's expanded guidelines for bad behavior.[35] What are the political, social, and cultural conditions that encouraged NFL athletes to accept a policy that, among other things, renders them powerless to file grievances with an impartial third party? The Players Advisory Council's passive stance helped open the door for the NFL to freely discipline and punish athletes without adversely affecting labor relations. In other words, the NFL and the NFL Players Association together convinced the athletes that it is in the best interest of the game for the commissioner to act as the sole arbiter of bad behavior and the ultimate authority on punishment.[36]

Goodell has been credited with increasing the number of fines imposed for on-field infractions and leveling stiffer penalties for off-field violations. After watching dozens of athletes' names appear on police blotters across the country, Goodell essentially took a page from the educational system's playbook and established a "zero-tolerance policy" for bad behavior.[37] As the league's highest-ranking administrator, the White Goodell fills a role familiar to Black men across the country—the czar of discipline or, as Ahmad might call him, the *slave master's overseer*.

After years of personal interactions with professional football players, it is my conclusion that certain Black athletes view the NFL as a racialized institution. Some believe the new conduct policy is yet another attempt by White men to keep Black men "in their place" and protect their investment; others think it's nothing more than a classic labor conflict. The Black athletes I encountered generally employed one of two strategies to deal with the issue of race in the NFL: the Black Nationalism/Afrocentric approach, which appeals to a smaller number of African Americans willing to vocalize their thoughts and ideas, and the Racial Integrationist strategy, which resonates with a larger group of NFL athletes.[38]

Rather than viewing it as a political attitude, some African American athletes are drawn to Black Nationalism for the meaning it offers in their everyday lives. This group believes that Black Nationalism or Afrocentrism is an effective strategy to fight against racist owners, intent on exploiting and marginalizing African Americans. Shortly after beginning field research, I discovered that Black Nationalist/Afrocentric athletes are further apportioned into two smaller ideological subgroups. Certain members of this camp claim that Blacks must unite and fight against the White establishment; others argue that the historic legacy of slavery has left African Americans fractured, incapable of such unity.

The African American NFL athletes who reject the Black Nationalist ideology tend to employ a strategy of Racial Integration. The Integrationist athlete often downplays the effects of race by emphasizing the benefits of hard work and clean living. Individuals in this camp tend to discard the notion that the new NFL PCP has anything to do with race and everything to do with athletes behaving irresponsibly. African American athletes who support racial integration generally believe that playing in the NFL is an honor and individuals have a personal and social responsibility to adhere to the league's guidelines, no matter how restrictive. Racial Integrationists often reason that athletes who display poor judgment draw negative attention to the NFL, which jeopardizes the financial well-being of the entire league. While recording interviews for this study, I noted numerous comments that fit with the Racial Integrationist's interpretation of the racial climate in the NFL. Marcus, a former Phoenix Cardinals kick returner and wide receiver, said, for instance, "I'm sure racism exists in the NFL just like it does everywhere else in society. You can't worry about that though, or else you'll be kicked out of the league in a hurry. Your job is to play football and everything else will take care of itself. I just don't spend too much time thinking about race."

In my interactions with NFL athletes it also became apparent that Racial Integrationists adhered to the neoliberal rhetoric of "personal responsibility" as paramount to fixing problems throughout the African American community. I spoke with dozens of Black athletes who testified that even though they came from poor backgrounds, their circumstances did not prevent them from getting ahead in life. The Black Integrationist athletes in this study felt the African American must "stop making excuses" and "take responsibility for his own actions." When pressed as to how structural inequality affects the poor in America, the Black athletes I spoke with agreed that racism is a difficult obstacle but believed that others in the Black community too often use race as a crutch. Athletes guided by the Racial Integrationist ideology claim that racism has nothing to do with the stereotypical guy in the ghetto, selling drugs to buy Cadillac Escalades. They even thought now-disgraced comic Bill Cosby was right to condemn African Americans for behaving irresponsibly.[39] I explained that Cosby was criticized for promoting conservative views that blame the victim, but one Black athlete reasoned that even as a registered Democrat who voted for Obama, he had to admit that too many Black people would rather complain than work hard to change their personal circumstances.[40] More than four years of fieldwork has led me to conclude that Black athletes who subscribe to the Racial Integrationist ideology believe the best way to avoid racial conflicts in the NFL is to stay out of trouble, collect your paycheck, and head home to take care of your family.

The discovery that Black football players use competing strategies to address the racial dynamics in the NFL led me to consider how race affects athletes during retirement. The data suggests a subgroup of Black athletes view Afrocentrism as a guiding principle in their everyday lives. Afrocentric athletes are skeptical and distrustful of the NFL as a White-owned institution. Black athletes who subscribe to Afrocentrism strongly believe that White owners treat Black football players as commodities to be exploited, then discarded after their bodies are broken and battered. Thus the only way for a Black man to truly survive in the NFL is to sell out to the White man. Afrocentric athletes feel that the White NFL establishment views the enlightened Black man who speaks his mind as a threat that must be contained. Ultimately, they may conclude that racism is the reason their careers will end in disappointment. Many retired Afrocentric athletes believed that their

White counterparts even found greater job opportunities and social resources to draw on after leaving the NFL.

The athlete who adheres to the Racial Integrationist model tends to downplay race as a factor that negatively affects his life after football. The Racial Integrationist is deeply committed to the notion that failure is not an option, and most Black Integrationist athletes believe that the same dedication and perseverance that propelled them into the NFL is exactly what it takes to succeed in every other aspect of life. For them, focusing on structural or systemic racism is counterproductive. The Racial Integrationist would rather concentrate on the things he can control, such as keeping his body healthy and maintaining a positive attitude, than worrying if a NFL general manager or a Fortune 500 corporate manager is racist. Racial discrimination is just one more obstacle to overcome, and the true test of a man's character is how he addresses these challenges. Ultimately, the Racial Integrationist feels he is responsible for whatever happens in life. As NFL alumni, the Racial Integrationists refuse to be considered victims of racial discrimination either during their careers or once they have retired.

HOW RACE WORKS

"Why you think Goodell went after athletes?" asked OD, as we drove on the New Jersey Turnpike headed to Morgantown, West Virginia. OD's oldest son "Red" had just initiated a conversation about his younger brother Oderick's NFL draft status: "It's better to get drafted in the middle to late rounds. That way you get a few years to learn from vets on a good team instead of [being expected] to be the savior for a bad team." Oderick was completing the final month of his collegiate career and preparing for the NFL draft. For several minutes, they bantered about draft picks before OD shouted, "I'll tell you what! With the way Goodell is coming down on brothers, a motherfucker got to play it right these days. This shit ain't like when I was playing. That damn Goodell is a motherfucker, that's for sure."

After a nearly two-minute-long diatribe, OD asked Red a compelling question, "Why you think the first thing Goodell did when he got into office was go after Michael Vick? What is it you do when you want to show that you can't be fucked with? WHAT? You go after the weakest motherfucker around,

THAT'S WHAT. In the NFL, athletes is the weakest ones 'cause they ain't got no say."[41]

One of the first athletes Roger Goodell targeted under the revised PCP was Adam "Pacman" Jones, a first-round draft choice of the Tennessee Titans, who had showered scantily clad dancers with thousands of one dollar bills at a Las Vegas strip club, then gotten into a fight outside the club. A short time later, three people were shot. Jones was suspended for the 2007 season, forfeiting his nearly $1.3 million salary.[42] It is widely agreed that Jones deserved to be punished, though not everyone agrees on the severity of the punishment.

OD's remark had cut to the heart of the structural issues confronting NFL athletes: not only was the NFL Players Association's relatively weak in the disciplinary discussions, but the athletes themselves were relatively weak in the league—always subordinate to management. The financial, political, and legislative success of the NFL has firmly established club owners as powerful members of the social elite class.[43] Billions of dollars in tax incentives and other forms of assistance are granted to them by state and local governments for stadium construction projects.[44] And Goodell was hired to protect the political, social, cultural, and economic interests of the NFL. According to OD, Goodell sent a clear and ultimately patronizing message to the players when he declared that controlling "Athlete Misconduct" was his first order of business. He picked on the weakest group in the game, the players, to make a statement, assign blame, and gain a reputation. If players screwed up under his watch, they owned their behavior and they would suffer public punishment. If there's one thing we've seen, there are always plenty of eager up-and-comers ready to take the spot of any NFL player who doesn't like his contract, his management, his union, his pay, or his surveillance.

CUNY law professor Marc Edelman says of the union that they "have never really succeeded in collective bargaining. Their successes have come in anti-trust actions. . . . [T]hey still have no guaranteed contracts; and they have yet to obtain other basic benefits like a neutral arbitrator for player grievances."[45] OD agrees that NFL players are an exploited, fractured, and fractious group. But he also buys into a fair amount of the neoliberal discourse of personal responsibility. In the four years I spent with him, going to speaking engagements, sporting events, and family outings, I saw how OD's worldview had been based on what he saw during a strict upbringing in the Deep South.

He said his parents "taught us right from wrong." And he reminds his sons that "respect is something you got to earn." And these aren't just aphorisms; OD is wary of the world and believes part of personal responsibility is knowing how to negotiate racism. "Any Black man who trusts another man is a fool. I don't trust nobody completely. . . . That's why I ain't letting that shit happen to my son. When he gets into the league, he ain't gonna go through the same shit I went through with them White boys. They try to get you anyway they can. Man, you have no idea how many people come at you because you play ball. And you know what? That shit don't change—not even when you get out the league."

Besides making athletes marks for unscrupulous businessmen, OD believes the financial windfall that often accompanies a draft pick can cause African Americans to treat one another poorly. "My own relative stole a check and forged my name—even after I gave him thousands of dollars to handle some problems he was having." Thus, Black athletes need to keep a watchful eye on everyone they come into contact with: family, females, agents, team physicians, front office personnel, financial advisors, and the general public. According to OD, all this mistrust stems from the legacy of slavery (many scholars, when considering issues like persistent residential segregation, agree).[46] Of course, the common retort is that African Americans are quick to blame *every* problem on slavery.[47]

Ahmad, who was raised near Jacksonville, Florida, has a more pugnacious outlook on how race functions in the crown jewel of the American sports-industrial complex. Now attempting to revive his career in the Canadian Football League, he has played for the Cleveland Browns and attended training or minicamps with the Detroit Lions and the Indianapolis Colts. To him, the NFL is a racist organization, plain and simple. It exploits Black bodies for profit. Ahmad recognizes, of course, that by playing in the NFL he could earn enough money to "set my family up . . . and give me the freedom I need for the rest of my life." But this financial freedom would exact a heavy toll: "What people don't see is that fact that every day, when I step out on the field, I'm risking my life." On this point, he's right: NFL athletes can suffer long-term damage and illness including traumatic brain injury (concussions, chronic traumatic encephalopathy, memory loss, and suicidal depression) and abnormally high rates of diabetes, high blood pressure, and sleep apnea, which increases the risk of heart attacks, strokes, and daytime drowsiness.[48]

The significant risk of injury associated with playing football coupled with long-term health issues, questionable labor representation, and significant differences in the racial composition of labor and management suggests that Black athletes have plenty of reasons to remain wary of the league. Still, for young men from socially disadvantaged or impoverished backgrounds, the NFL represents an enormous opportunity for upward social mobility. Rather than make waves or be perceived as radical, some athletes just put their heads down and play the game (literally and figuratively). Danita, Ahmad's wife of three years, says, "I just think that when you're making enough money, you just keep quiet and deal with it." Ahmad echoes, "Black athletes reconcile their behavior because they are going to the bank every Monday or Tuesday. They just taking care of their families."[49]

Giving it a radical spin, however, Ahmad states that as long as Black NFL athletes focus on making money, they will have second-class status. The NFL "don't want no Blacks with intelligence. They don't want no one who has any kind of self-awareness." He told me, "The NFL prefers guys that don't think that there is life beyond football. There is a double standard for the Black and White [athletes] on this issue. You could have a White athlete teaching other White athletes about life after football, but they don't want Black athletes to feel that they can do anything other than play football. And that's what the NFL wants: to keep you dumb, deaf, and blind." As you might expect by now, Ahmad feels compelled to speak up whenever he feels disrespected by management. His wife suggests that this outspokenness forced him out of the NFL early and has hindered his ability to land another NFL job: "The system may not understand a guy like Ahmad, because he's loud and can be offensive, and controversial. . . . Honestly, I think that his anti-institution attitude is the thing that has kept him from returning to the NFL."

Perhaps Ahmad was cut from the Browns to make room for players the club felt offered a better chance at winning. Maybe Ahmad truly was a malcontent bent on disrupting team harmony with Afrocentric rants. Or maybe he was a good player, but an outspoken one, and managers saw him as spending too much time fomenting player resentment and not enough time working hard on the field. Whatever the actual reason for his dismissal, Ahmad's precarity now is as much about a lack of job security as it is about race. Without the security of a guaranteed contract, Ahmad and others who accuse management of marginalizing Black athletes may very well find themselves unemployed without due recourse.

Not every Black athlete shares Ahmad's or OD's view that the NFL is unduly hostile toward African Americans players. P-Rock, a former defensive back and teammate of OD's who spent his entire 10-year career playing with the same club, believes there are decent people and racist people throughout the NFL. After he delivered a guest lecture on leadership to a graduate class at Fairleigh Dickinson University, I asked P-Rock to share his experiences with race in the NFL. He said, "I've always been pretty much the type to stick to myself, so I guess our coach was wondering why I didn't act like the other guys on the team. One day in training camp during my second year he told the offensive coordinator to go after me. They ran 12–15 plays at me without a break. Play after play, he just kept coming at me. I was dead tired, but I wasn't gonna let him know it. I just kept battlin' until practice was over."

When P-Rock played, from the mid-1980s through the mid-'90s, it was commonplace for teams to allot 35–40 plays to defense during a training camp practice session. This means that P-Rock had to chase offensive players around the field for 20 to 30 minutes without a break. A coach may apply this kind of pressure when he is looking for a reason to cut an athlete. One misstep, and the coach can easily claim the player does not have mental toughness or stamina required to play in the NFL. I asked P-Rock why he thought the coach had singled him out. "Doc, you know what the coach said to me one day? He said, 'P-Rock, how come you never have nothing to say when I walk by? You don't think I like Black people do you? I ain't got a problem with Black folks. Growing up we had a Black nanny and a Black housekeeper. I've been around Black people my whole life.'" It was clear that P-Rock held no animosity toward the coach; I asked P-Rock about playing so many years for this coach, and he pointed out that the coach was only one man in the organization. He said of the team's owner, "He always treated me with respect. Mr. Mara told me as long as I wanted to play for him, there was always a spot for me. When he died, Mrs. Mara told me how much her husband loved me. She said I was always one of his favorites. I knew I could always count on him for anything."

P-Rock's views on race and sports were, like many other men, shaped by his experiences growing up. He was raised in rural North Carolina, and he says, "I didn't grow up with a father, and sports weren't really part of my family life. One day a friend invited me to play on a baseball team, which was pretty unheard of 'cause Blacks and Whites pretty much stuck to themselves. We played every sport together as kids, and his father took me in like his own son. Even when I continued to get a lot of attention as an athlete and my friend stop playing, his father was right there for me. We are still close to this day. I had my share of run-ins with jealous White folks growing up too. My next-door neighbor hated the fact that I was a better athlete than his son. He did everything he could to hurt me, claiming I was too old to play, trying to get me kicked off of teams, and other stuff like that. But [the neighbor] was right there, standing in line waiting for an autograph with his grandson when they named a road after me in my hometown. That's how it is in sports. As a Black athlete, some folks want to use you for what they can get, and other folks are good decent human beings." P-Rock recognizes that White people wield great power in sports. He understands why OD and some of his former teammates question their motives, yet he chooses to remember, "These are the guys that I've gone to battle with. I won two Super Bowls with these guys. If it wasn't for them, I couldn't lead the life I live today. When one of these guys come calling, I'll do whatever I can." Assimilation can be a powerful tool to reconcile and compensate for differential treatment along racial lines in the NFL.

EYE IN THE SKY

All athletes, regardless of race, are subject to the long shadow of the NFL's surveillance methods. Once an intrusion—or perhaps always an intrusion—it's not going away.[50] As a result of the new PCP and the 2011 CBA disciplinary rules, athletes are constantly monitored throughout the season.[51] The historic legacy of what is known as the "White gaze," though, may mean that African Americans are particularly sensitive to such efforts to monitor their behavior.[52] Philosophy scholar George Yancy asserts that the Black body vis-à-vis the White gaze is dehumanized and subjected to White discipline both to enact punishment and to confirm its a priori debasement. The Black body can be admired for its physical ability and cultivated to generate entertainment revenue, but it must also be corralled and disciplined.

While recounting his three years in the league, former linebacker Juleonny Carter recalls the constant scrutiny: "It's like they take a piece of your soul, man. 'Cause you're trying to impress, but you're trying not to over-exert. You know, you got to stand out from the pack. You know, they're looking to see who's crossing the line last every time. They're looking to see who's cutting corners, who's cheating on their sets, who's keeping the proper etiquette and techniques in lifting. These are all evaluating tools that the draftees don't have to worry about. But me? They're looking for a reason for putting my ass out."

As Juleonny described his experience, I probed deeper to uncover how he dealt with the pressure of knowing that any misstep could cost him his job. Did the pressure ever let up? I know from experience how an NFL player is both publicly admired and privately sanctioned—an exceptional athlete at one moment, expendable labor the next.

In perhaps the most visible of the NFL's oversight mechanisms, on-field cameras track every move made by stars and journeymen alike. Juleonny is sensitive to the ubiquitous gaze, believing Commissioner Goodell and the foot soldiers employed by each NFL club are always assessing him and every other athlete in the league. "There are cameras everywhere," Juleonny said. "People are watching. You know the general manager is hovering somewhere. People are always watching," he says. I asked if he meant in the practice facility, and he said yes. "Cameras are everywhere, and they control every aspect of that place. 'Cause they looking for the cues that they find important to them that they think will make their team stronger." His words called to mind "the Panopticon." I noted, "It seems like what you're describing is like a prison."

"No, 'cause at anytime I could say, 'Fuck ya'll! I'm going home. I don't want to do this anymore,'" Juleonny said. I went further, "No, I mean like a prison compound. You know, like you see on television, when patrol guards are walking around on the tower with guns and watching everyone."

"Ok, yes. In that aspect, yes," Juleonny conceded. "You don't always see them. They are not always up there. You can't always hear them; you know 'CLANK, CLANK, CLANK,' 'cause it's padded up there. But you know they are there."

"There is always an eye in the sky?" I asked.

"There are always cameras," Juleonny affirmed. "So it's—are you working hard even if no one is up there manning the cameras? 'Cause there's always someone on the sidelines taking notes. 'Cause they're gonna see the film at the end of the day anyway. It's just, do you run a little faster when there's cameras and someone watching you?"

"It's like Big Brother," he continued. "That's what it feels like. Is there a camera in the bathroom or what? You start wondering if the coach is thinking, 'What the hell is he doing in there so long?' Shit, man, it's tough."

Toward the end of his rookie season Juleonny tested positive for an illegal substance. Pursuant to Article XI of the Collective Bargaining Agreement and the NFL Constitution and Bylaws, athletes have the right to appeal any fine or suspension for violating the PCP; however, the commissioner has complete autonomy to name an independent panel to participate in deciding appeals and to serve as hearing officer in any appeal.[53] It's easy to see why an athlete may choose to remain silent. For example, aside from filing a grievance or appealing the decision with the NFL, Juleonny's only recourse was to go to court. In weighing his options, Juleonny felt the coaches would look at him more favorably if he just put the situation behind him and started preparing for the next season. Rather than appeal the decision, he accepted a four-game suspension. In the end, the violation cost Juleonny 25% of his $200,000 salary in fines.[54]

While Juleonny and Ahmad were able to remain in the NFL for the average career length, neither athlete played long enough to be vested for retirement benefits. Whether Ahmad's Afrocentric outlook or Juleonny's post-racial, integrationist approach made any difference, both men were out of the league in an average career length of a little over three years. Neither earned enough money to retire comfortably. Playing in the NFL may be a short-term elevator to upward mobility, but in the long term, it's hardly any guarantee of a young Black man's class mobility.

From the owner's perspective, leveling fines and suspending players for violating the PCP can be construed as prudent business decisions protecting clubs from acts deemed harmful to the integrity and reputation of the NFL. Indeed, under the leadership of Commissioner Goodell, revenues have risen significantly.[55] There's quite an enormous investment to protect. But where Goodell's supporters see smart management, many athletes see his tactics as attempts to control and subjugate the Black body. The historical legacy of race in America combined with the vast imprisonment of Black and Brown men and the lack of employment opportunities available to them have left many feeling marginalized and distrustful of a system dominated by White men. The surveillance methods described by Juleonny, racialized comments directed at P-Rock by his coach, and a work environment that allows a White, middle-aged general manager to apparently genuinely ask a 21-year-old Black male athlete if his mother is a prostitute, has led some athletes to conclude that Black men in the NFL are supposed to entertain the masses on Sunday—damage to their bodies be damned—then shut up and take orders in the workplace every other day of the week. One of the highest paid NFL players ever, Minnesota Vikings running back Adrian "AP" Peterson, has openly called the NFL modern-day slavery.[56] At least one reporter went out of his way to spin AP's comment as an overstatement, but AP made no such assertion. Even a well-established Black star knows that there are always racial power dynamics at work in the NFL.

9

THE OWNER'S PLAYBOOK

That's when I really understood that this is just a business. They're not looking out for anything but their bottom line. There's no family, no loyalty.

It's just a money thing.

—Peter Warrick,
Former NFL first-round draft pick

I ask professional athletes, what does it mean that "This is a business," and that you're expendable?

—Dr. Tim Benson,
Clinical Instructor in Psychiatry,
Harvard Medical School;
Medical Director,
McLean Residence at the Brook

We're 32 fat-cat republicans who vote socialist.

—Art Modell, former owner
Cleveland Browns and Baltimore Ravens

THE NFL HAS crafted a thrilling, complete, and compelling entertainment experience, and *diehard* fans can't get enough. The NFL therefore needs highly skilled, studiously disciplined players to deliver its thrilling entertainment. The sport's inherently high injury rate necessitates an abundant supply of *replacement* players, so the NFL is also in the business of advertising "the dream"—showing off the riches and fame that accrue to its star players—and how quickly misbehavior can get a wayward player kicked out of that dream. The average NFL player salary has ballooned to $1.9 million, one of the highest paid professions in America,[1] and even though only a small percentage of players make big money, media reports fawn over signing bonuses and multimillion dollar deals. For a few star athletes, there will even be seven-figure endorsement deals with multinational corporations like Under Armor, Nike, and Coca-Cola.[2] Since the 1987 Super Bowl, every player voted "Most Valuable Player" of the Super Bowl has grinned straight into the camera and shouted "I'm going to Disney World!" Hall of Famers might even cash in years after the 15 minutes of fame granted the average NFL football player is over.[3]

Another indication that professional athletes represent a unique class of labor is the persistent debate around their status as role models and whether they, like royalty, have an obligation to give back to society. The NFL reinforces the narrative of sports heroes as role models by handing out the annual Walter Payton NFL Man of the Year Award, a community service honor, and through its United Way partnership, a program started in 1973 by Commissioner Pete Rozelle to promote the nonprofit while humanizing a league full of rough and tumble men hidden by helmets.[4]

The NFL plays a major role in promoting athletes as physically talented individuals as well as highly paid and esteemed members of society. Yet, for all the social prestige afforded NFL athletes, they are denied meaningful access to the locus of power: corporate headquarters. In reality, athletes are rarely consulted about any substantive issues beyond their collective bargaining agreement and labor disputes.

To think about the unique employer-employee relationship of an NFL player, we must first look at how the NFL became the most influential political, cultural, and economically dominant professional sports organization in the United States. Then we can consider Dr. Tim Benson's[5] question: "What does it mean to be an athlete in the business of professional sports?"

FAT CATS

For the owners, today's game is less about offensive or defensive game-day strategy and more about the economic playbook that rules the NFL. Unlike the rag-tag early days when coaches like George Halas and Curly Lambeau owned the Chicago Bears and the Green Bay Packers, the current crop of NFL owners is made up of almost exclusively White, very wealthy, and incredibly savvy businessmen—billionaire tycoons such as Paul Allen, Robert Kraft, and Jerry Jones.[6] While all of the NFL franchise teams in the league are profitable, 25 of the 32 clubs are valued in excess of $1 billion. Outsiders can see buying an NFL franchise as a vanity purchase, but it's often a great investment.[7] Jerry Jones bought the Dallas Cowboys for an estimated $154 million in 1989, and the team's value skyrocketed to $1.85 *billion* 23 years later.[8] Jones's success encouraged other self-made billionaires to get into the game. These men are prominent business leaders by any standard, but owning an NFL team offers a level of status and power reserved for a very few elites.

While the bone-jarring tackles and high-flying catches excite fans, the owners might be forgiven for their eager focus on business: Will the consumers continue to pay rising ticket prices? Are there enough merchandising choices for women and children? Will broadcast partners pay more fees to air NFL games? How much more money could we make in a *new* stadium? To their dismay, public relations can be far more suspenseful, as domestic violence incidents, concussions, and player arrests continue to make headlines.[9]

BUILDING AN EMPIRE

These days, the NFL's cadre of executives, lawyers, lobbyists, public relations specialists, monitors, and marketers handle many of the issues that worry team owners. But things weren't always so easy. Financial instability marked the early years of the National Football League. Teams formed and folded on a regular basis. During the first half of the 20th century, the NFL survived attempts from other upstart leagues such as the All-American Football Conference and the American Professional Football Association (1946–1950).[10] NFL owners discovered that when they banded together, they could beat back competing leagues by restricting growth in secondary markets.

The NFL hardly had time to enjoy its dominance in professional football before the US Department of Justice (DOJ) filed an antitrust lawsuit in 1953 seeking an injunction against the enforcement of Article X of the NFL bylaws.[11] The DOJ argued that Article X, which restricts telecasts in the home territories of teams playing a home game (i.e., "The Blackout Rule") was an unreasonable restraint of trade and thus violated Section 1 of the Sherman

Antitrust Act.[12] On appeal, Judge Allan K. Grim ruled against the DOJ, determining that relative equality of playing ability was needed to sustain a fan base; otherwise, weaker teams would be driven out of the marketplace and even strong teams would fail financially.[13] Although Judge Grim's ruling favored the NFL, it effectively made room for another crop of competing football leagues.

Lamar Hunt, the son of Texas oil magnate H. L. Hunt, wanted to own a football team desperately. His many requests were denied by the NFL, so Hunt and his friend K. S. "Bud" Adams forged a rival league of eight teams, the new American Football League. The AFL established a "war chest" of funds with which to attract highly skilled players and the best coaches (many were later inducted into the Football Hall of Fame). The AFL's higher player salaries forced the NFL's hand; with NFL owners unwilling to pay more in labor costs, the AFL lured away half of the NFL's first-round draft choices in its first year, 1960.

The AFL also innovated on the field. They issued jerseys emblazoned with the players' names, showed the official game time on the scoreboard, and created a unique business model in which owners pooled television rights to sell them in a single package and then divided revenues equally across all the AFL teams. The American Broadcast Company (ABC) responded favorably by entering into a multiyear contract to broadcast AFL games nationally over five years for $8.5 million. The nationwide television audience was far more valuable than the NFL had yet recognized; the ABC/AFL alliance conferred priceless legitimacy on the AFL as television saturated American family homes in the 1960s.[14]

NFL owners attempted to outmaneuver the AFL by devising their own revenue sharing plan and entering into an agreement with CBS Broadcasting, Inc. As a precautionary measure, the NFL petitioned a federal district court to determine whether their version of a collective television contract violated the 1953 judgment; a district court judge confirmed that it did.

Not long after Alvin "Pete" Rozelle was named NFL commissioner in January 1960, another challenge arose. The AFL and the NFL announced a verbal agreement that neither party would tamper with player contracts. Within a year, the new AFL filed an antitrust lawsuit alleging monopoly and conspiracy by the NFL involving expansion, television, and player signing.[15] The NFL prevailed, but Rozelle and the league recognized that professional sports leagues needed congressional authority to operate as a monopoly in negotiating collective broadcast agreements. The Sports Broadcasting Act (SBA) was designed to exempt the joint sale of television rights from antitrust laws.[16] Rozelle enlisted the help of Baltimore Colts owner Carroll Rosenbloom and his many Washington, DC, insider friends. According to retired New York Giants general manager Ernie Accorsi, who began his career working for Rozelle in the league office, "Rosenbloom was a big donor in the [presidential] primaries—and a friend of Joe Kennedy."[17] On September 30, 1961, President John F. Kennedy signed the SBA into law, and Rozelle's preemptive moves laid the groundwork for future legislation exempting other professional sports leagues from antitrust measures. After an unusually short vetting period, the NFL secured the precious exemption needed to negotiate collective media contracts,[18] with Congress reasoning that it would bring financial stability to the NFL (now a major national employer) and benefit fans, since more cities would be able to support NFL franchises.[19]

Now the NFL had to address the talent drain: the AFL was aggressively scooping up the best players with lucrative contracts. Higher pay in the AFL forced NFL teams to offer higher pay, and soon it was increasingly expensive for both leagues to attract and retain top talent. As the AFL successfully established teams in key, non-NFL markets, the two leagues entered into secret negotiations. Solid business fundamentals prevailed as owners sought ways to control their costs by eliminating competition for players. In 1966, the leagues announced a merger, with the NFL and AFL officially becoming one in 1970.

Rozelle understood that the merger could be interpreted as another possible violation of antitrust laws *and* that it could raise local politicians' eyebrows if it prevented cities from hosting their own football teams. Again, Rozelle presciently devised a plan. When congressmen questioned the implications of a single league holding complete control over the supply of professional football franchises, Rozelle and other league representatives pledged to add new NFL teams. Team owners went one step further and committed to keeping the current franchises in their existing communities.[20]

In October 1966, Congress passed the second provision of the Sports Broadcasting Act (SBA). Though more narrow in scope than the original, the legislation allowed the NFL and AFL to merge without fear of an antitrust challenge. With some additional political wrangling, Rozelle and the team owners successfully convinced Congress to also pass legislation exempting professional football leagues from federal income tax as 501(c)(6) nonprofit organizations. Together, these changes solidified the NFL's position as a monopoly and gave the league extraordinary power to generate and retain revenue.

Next, Rozelle masterfully created a bidding war for NFL broadcasting rights. Upon entering into the first multimillion NFL broadcasting agreement, the television networks had been keenly aware that they must protect their investment by committing the resources needed to promote the game and build a television audience. In a few short years, broadcast partners were both a powerful marketing partner to and a generous source of income for the NFL. Rozelle leveraged these relationships to increase the NFL's national television contract price by 25% in each of his first few years as commissioner. With the AFL-NFL merger in place, Rozelle had the upper hand in renegotiating the 1966–67 season's broadcast rights. NBC had committed $36 million for the right to broadcast AFL games for five years, while ABC was focused on delivering college football. That left CBS as the lone broadcaster bidding for the NFL contract, yet Rozelle refused to back off his demand for a two-year, $37.6 million deal. In fact, he shrewdly announced that if CBS did not accept his terms, the NFL would lease dedicated telephone lines from AT&T and start its own network. Unwilling to risk losing the coveted male, 18–49 viewer demographic,[21] CBS accepted Rozelle's terms.[22] It was in this period that the annual Super Bowl became a financial juggernaut and *Monday Night Football* was established as one of the highest-rated television series ever, particularly among male viewers. In the year of his retirement in 1989, Rozelle completed the largest broadcast deal in television history: a new four-year contract with three major networks, ABC, CBS, and NBC, and two cable networks, valued at $3.6 billion.[23]

With so many legal and judicial victories tucked under its helmet, why does the NFL spend so much time and money in the courtroom? Since 1986, several plaintiffs have sued the NFL under Section 2 of the Sherman Act. While the courts have permitted plaintiffs to offer evidence and have expressly held that abuse of monopoly power acquired as a result of the legislation is not exempt from the Antitrust Act, most have also deemed inadmissible evidence about the reasons the NFL sought the legislative loopholes in the first place. Further, courts have concluded that NFL lobbying efforts related to the passage of Section 2 of the Sherman Act are immune from anti-trust challenges under the *Noerr* doctrine.[24]

One of these plaintiffs, the United States Football League (USFL) filed a 1986 lawsuit against the NFL for alleged monopolistic intent or the acquisition of monopoly power by unlawful means, a violation of Sections 1 and 2 of the Sherman Act, 15 U.S.C. §§1,2.[25] The USFL sought damages of $1.701 billion.[26] Despite ruling that the NFL's unlawful monopolization of professional football had indeed injured the USFL, the jury found that the NFL had neither monopolized a relevant television submarket nor attempted to do so. Instead, they asserted, the USFL's difficulties were mainly due to mismanagement. The jury further concluded that the NFL's television contracts were not unreasonable restraints on trade, that the NFL did not control access to the three major television networks, and that the NFL did not interfere with the USFL's ability to obtain television contracts. In determining that the USFL was primarily responsible for its own failure, the jury granted the NFL nearly unfettered control over the professional football market.

Other court cases have regarded league owners' concerns with preventing internal and external threats to merchandising. Created in 1963, NFL Properties Inc.[27] was generating $100 million annually by 1979, but a rare league misstep led to a confrontation with athletes over merchandising rights. The situation came to a head in January 1983 as the Washington Redskins took on the Miami Dolphins in Super Bowl XVII. Prior to the game, the Redskins' offensive linemen, affectionately known as "The Hogs," created Hogs Incorporated. The linemen capitalized on their momentary celebrity by selling hundreds of thousands of dollars worth of Hogs merchandise. The NFL believed that this unsanctioned merchandise infringed upon their brand and sought a last-minute restraining order to prevent street vendors from selling the unlicensed goods in Los Angeles county (where the Super Bowl would be played), in Washington, DC, and in Miami.[28] In rendering his verdict against the NFL, Judge Charles R. Richey wrote that a restraining order "would appear to invite catastrophe" through "a nightmare of jurisdictional flaws, deprivations of due process, and windfall litigation that could endure for years to come."[29]

The verdict shed light on a glaring hole in the NFL's business strategy. Following Super Bowl XVII, the NFL methodically went about ridding

the market of knock-off merchandise. The league employed security officers to search for contraband among street merchants outside stadiums and
partnered with law enforcement to minimize the pilfering of official NFL
merchandise. Today, the NFL registers at least 20 trademarks, protected by
court order, before each year's Super Bowl. Such successful efforts to build
the NFL merchandise brand and aggressively pursue and shut down illegal
vendors have paid huge dividends.

At the 2010 league owner's meeting, Commissioner Roger Goodell
presented a vision of the league reaching $25 billion in annual revenue by
2027.[30] He told the group that the league would need to add $1 billion in new
revenue each year (building from the 2010 season's $9 billion). Whether or
not the figures are out of reach, they underscore the degree to which Goodell
and team owners seek to expand their business. New York Jets owner Woody
Johnson believes the league has a chance of hitting Goodell's goal: "If we
expand our capital, expand our stadiums, keep renovating and keep all our
capital equipment up to the highest standards, invest in technology, [invest]
in business, it could be done—or more."[31]

The first step may have been the 2010 announcement of a five-year, $1.1
billion agreement with Nike for the exclusive rights to manufacture and distribute NFL merchandise. Insiders say Nike's team projected $750 million in
sales in the first year alone.[32]

CARTEL POWER

The ascension of the NFL has propelled team owners and league executives
into an elite class of individuals who figure prominently in the US sport-
industrial complex. Very few were born into wealth; most rose up through
business, sponsored by elites in the organization they now control. Goodell,
who began his NFL career as an intern in 1982, was given a compensation
package worth $44.2 million dollars in 2012, making him one of the highest
paid executives in the country.[33] According to the NFL Compensation
Committee, Goodell's pay "reflects our pay-for-performance philosophy, and
is appropriate given the fact that the NFL, under his consistently strong leadership, continues to grow and is by far the most successful sports league."[34]
Their cultural clout is also revealed in the cash grants, loans, guarantees, bail-
outs, and special tax breaks granted to them by the government. Federal,

state, and local officials acquiesce to NFL demands with what critics call corporate welfare.[35]

Scholars, including David Meggysey, former St. Louis Cardinal and former director of the NFL Players Association, assert that despite its immunity to the Sherman Antitrust Act, the NFL acts as a cartel, exercising monopoly power in the professional football marketplace and monopsony purchasing power in the labor market and the professional football merchandise market.[36] It certainly seems to fit the definition: a cartel is an association of business (or political) interests that aims to maintain prices at a high level, keep wages low, and restrict competition to the benefit of its members. The cartel's primary goal is explicit government legitimization; a workable "second-best" is benign neglect from the antitrust agencies.[37] The NFL can boast both. And, since Goodell became commissioner in 2006, the NFL has spent over $5.5 million—triple its budget from 2002 and far beyond any other professional sports organization—on lobbying efforts. According to one Washington insider, "The NFL is not just a bunch of guys running around in uniforms and helmets. It's a huge business that's increasingly intersecting with the game of politics."[38]

In addition to fending off external threats from potential competitors, cartels must contend with internal threats to stability and viability. For example, just look at the league's response when team owner Al Davis wanted to move his Oakland Raiders to a new stadium in Los Angeles in 1982.[39] The NFL filed a federal antitrust lawsuit.

A cartel's survival also depends on detecting deviation and gaining buy-in to the rules and punishments governing member organizations (witness the public sanctions leveled against the Dallas Cowboys and Washington Redskins when they violated salary cap rules in 2011) and individual members (consider the Personal Conduct Policy and its many iterations).[40] And the league has always enjoyed the upper hand in labor negotiations, especially since the USFL folded in 1985.[41] Since it is able to approach labor as a necessary but—because of league owner competition—cheap resource, the NFL has effectively lowered the price any league would need to pay for a football player. As Meggysey figures it, the NFL has worked to "rationalize operations" by eliminating competition among franchise owners for players' services and to protect its own markets by freezing out competing professional football leagues that might otherwise enter second-tier metropolitan markets.[42] NFL owners now selectively operate in cities where demand is high, relatively inelastic, and insensitive to price. The league is free to negotiate vendor contracts and stadium construction deals without the hassle of traditional market competition.[43]

A proliferation of stadium renovations and new construction projects has also helped NFL owners immeasurably. The majority of the funding for these projects in the past 20 years has come from public sources. Subsidies for the latest wave of stadium developments were initiated by federal government programs that allowed state and local municipalities to issue tax-exempt bonds, thereby lowering interest on debt and reducing costs for cities and team owners. To gain support for public financing, stadium proponents tout job creation, revenue generation, increased tourism, and the "multiplier effect," an increase in local income that causes still more spending and job creation. It's essentially trickle-down economics, except that sport economists report that state and local politicians commit more public resources to subsidize sports facilities than they get back in tax breaks issued by the federal government.[44] These scholars claim that by 1996 state and local governments typically spent $10 million annually on subsidies. In response to the enormous sum of public subsidies collected by wealthy team owners, researchers are sure that sports stadiums are poor community investments.[45]

While economists, politicians, community groups, and civic leaders debate the merits of stadium subsidies, though, no one questions how attractive the arrangement is for the NFL. In fact, the monopolistic structure of the league allows owners to supply fewer franchises than can meet the demand—the number of cities that want to host NFL teams. Prior to the 1966 amendment to the Sports Broadcasting Act, Congress recognized that a potential bidding war for franchises could break out if the NFL secured the all-important antitrust exemption. The league conceded that adding four new teams was in the best interest of the game. But even with the league expansion to 32 teams, the mere threat of relocation is enough to hold many cities hostage when teams demand more favorable stadium deals. The real "trump card" in this subsidy poker match is the NFL's extensive revenue sharing plan. It creates a huge incentive for teams to seek home stadiums that feature expansive revenue opportunities such as luxury suites, club boxes, elaborate concessions, catering, signage, advertising, theme activities, upscale bars and restaurants, and apartments with a view of the field.[46] Economic predictors suggest a new facility can add an additional $30 million annually to an owner's coffers.[47]

The bidding frenzy that swept through St. Louis and Cleveland in the 1980s is indicative of the lengths that cities will go to attract an NFL franchise. After initially refusing to commit public funds for stadium financing, both cities agreed to pay substantially more to attract new teams than what they had offered old ones to stay put. In 1987, the Cardinals flew the coop for Phoenix, Arizona, after St. Louis refused to pay $120 million toward a new football stadium, but losing the team caused such uproar that within three years, voters agreed to spend $280 million for a new facility—even though the city had not yet secured an NFL team to play in it.[48] And when Cleveland Browns owner Art Modell decided to move his team to Baltimore, it was because he was offered a 30-year, rent-free lease in a brand new stadium *plus* a $50 million cash relocation bonus. Baltimore's leaders also agreed to grant the team a 10% management fee for concerts and other non-football events hosted at the stadium. Shortly after losing their beloved Browns, Cleveland opted to tear down its old Municipal Stadium and build a state-of-the-art facility for $290 million. After securing a new expansion franchise, the city offered a generous 30-year lease, which includes revenues from all stadium rentals. The new tenant agreed to pay for all maintenance and operations but receives an exemption from paying property taxes. Modell, asked about his thoughts on Cleveland's sudden willingness to accommodate a new team, said succinctly, "If they gave me half of what they're doing now, I'd still be in Cleveland."[49] Given the competitive advantages secured with their antitrust exemptions, NFL teams have exploited their position as the dominant player in the US sport-industrial complex. To date, teams such as the Dallas Cowboys, New York Giants, and the New York Jets have systematically carved out billion-dollar stadium deals that far exceed the agreements hashed out by the Cardinals and the Browns in this heady period.

JUST BUSINESS

"I understand it was just business, but it kinda hurt at the time. I know it wasn't nothin' personal, and I probably would have done the same thing if

I owned the team. I mean, guys get hurt; it's a business. You got to find a replacement if a guy ain't gonna be ready. That's just how business is." Like many of his contemporaries in the professional football fraternity, Marcus's Darwinist interpretation of business is harsh but probably correct: for NFL players, it's "survival of the fittest."

At times, athletes' frustration with the business of football and their powerlessness within it is palpable. Some have even expressed betrayal as they told me about getting cut from the NFL. Marcus, whom I met at Calgary's preseason CFL training camp, was still hoping to get back into the NFL, where he'd spent three seasons as kick return specialist and receiver for the Arizona Cardinals. He described the knee injury that sidelined him, talked about having surgery and getting back into shape, and claimed that he'd been ready for action when the team spent a high draft pick on a "fresh pair of legs."

The long odds of earning an NFL roster spot had not deterred Marcus, who played college ball at a Division II school in Nebraska, from pursuing his dream. Like many journeymen, Marcus knew he had the talent; he just needed a chance. In his first NFL camp, Marcus watched veterans get axed for salary cap purposes while others' careers were shortened by injury.[50] Their tragedy gave him his chance, though: when the final roster was announced, Marcus went from relative obscurity to Monday Night Football. Still, Marcus knew already that job security in the NFL was fleeting. Teams are continuously looking to upgrade their rosters. When I played, my teammates would joke about avoiding the "Cut-Man"—football's version of the Grim Reaper. In the pre-dawn hours of training camp, the coaching staff would send an assistant equipment manager or athletic trainer to an athlete's dorm room: time to turn in your playbook and report to the coach's office. An HBO reality series, *Hard Knocks*, even revealed the cruel ritual with the on-camera release of Miami Dolphins tight end Les Brown.[51] For all the struggles and sacrifices athletes like Marcus endure to make it into the NFL, experience teaches them that for players, professional football is a heartless business.

This chapter was introduced with a quote from Peter Warrick, the fourth overall pick in the 2000 NFL draft. Unlike Marcus, Warrick entered the league as a bona fide star. He had earned a consensus first-team Collegiate All-America selection and was named an MVP in the 2000 Sugar Bowl. After a stellar career at Florida State University, Warrick was considered a rare talent who might change the face of the wide receiver position.[52] Warrick went on to post decent numbers in his career with the Cincinnati Bengals but never lived up to the enormous expectation that comes with being one of the all-time great collegiate offensive talents. Released from the Bengals in 2005, Warrick spent a season with the Seattle Seahawks, and then it was over. His entry into the league as a star was far different from journeyman Marcus's, but the two spoke of the inner workings of the league in similar terms. In an interview with Dennis Maley of the *Bradenton Times*, Warrick describes how his tenure with the Bengals unraveled shortly after he suffered a torn meniscus near the end of his third season.[53] Infection caused him to miss nearly the entire 2004 season, and rumors sprang up that Warrick would be released. He told the reporter, though, that head coach Marvin Lewis assured him that he had nothing to worry about. He was blindsided when, the very next day, he was dismissed: "I felt really disrespected by the way that was handled. I gave everything I had to Cincinnati, and just felt like they owed it to me to tell me like a man. Not hearing it everywhere else first, and then just asking not to be humiliated if that was the case. Let me know before I walk in there, you know? Men have pride. That's when I really understood that this is just a business, and they're not looking out for anything but their bottom line. There's no loyalty; it's just a money thing."

Like most of the star athletes I have encountered, Warrick knew his contract could be terminated early but never dreamed it would actually happen. A *New York Times* article reported that his agents, Jim Gould and the former NBA player Norm Nixon, indicated Warrick received more than $10 million in signing and reporting bonuses as a rookie.[54] Contracts with that many zeroes can seduce star athletes into believing they are immune from the fate of journeymen.

The stress of unanticipated retirement is exacerbated by the fact that the average NFL career ends when athletes are in their mid-20s. Ben, a former defensive back drafted by the Miami Dolphins at age 20, typifies this point. Within three seasons of signing a $3.5 million contract, a knee injury opened the door to his dismissal. Despite being highly sought after college stars, Warrick and Ben were no different than Marcus on their last days in the league: getting cut revealed to the young men that professional football only really cares about the bottom line.

The sentiments shared by Marcus, Warrick, and Ben contradict the business principles Commissioner Roger Goodell espouses. According to

Goodell, one of the NFL's most valued assets is its reputation for lawful and ethical behavior.[55] Under Goodell's leadership the NFL instituted an updated compliance plan, which requires every employee to follow good business procedures that comply with the law and reflect the highest standard of ethical behavior.[56] But the message included in the 2012 document is far from the harsh business practices detailed by the athletes. The differences in perspective may, at least in part, spring from football players' conflation of their roles as highly compensated employees with their short-term status of elite NFL athletes. For all their media exposure and public attention, the NFL's players remain in a protracted struggle to gain respect from the league's power brokers. Their interpretation of how business operates is often naïve and skewed. Having completed the indoctrination and socialization processes required of them to make it into the NFL as players, athletes are often reticent to "buck the system," to speak out against management.

And that makes things even more difficult when the inevitable exit comes. As key members of a multibillion dollar sports enterprise, as people elevated to highly coveted occupations, NFL athletes form the sorts of relationships that should carry over into a successful life after they're through playing the game. But more often, their celebrity status dissipates alongside legitimate business opportunities. What does it do to Sunday night heroes, making spectacular plays on the field, when they become socially irrelevant as soon as the ink dries on a business deal made in some posh office?

10

BILLIONAIRES VERSUS MILLIONAIRES:
LABOR RELATIONS

IN APRIL 2010, New Jersey's Piscataway High School became only the fourth high school to have two alumni selected in the first round of the same NFL draft. A year earlier, another of its former football standouts was selected in the first round, too. Clearly, my alma mater's program, under the direction of my former teammate, Coach Danny Higgins, was developing high-caliber players (Figure 10.1). Two of the draftees, Malcolm Jenkins and Anthony Davis, had been recruited by dozens of major college programs before settling on Ohio State and Rutgers, respectively, but the national spotlight took longer to shine on Kyle Wilson, whose unconventional journey to the NFL included a 2,500-mile detour to Boise State before he signed a multimillion dollar contract to play for the New York Jets. I had little doubt that each young man was prepared to play in the NFL, but, as a social scientist, I wondered how they would deal with the business of the NFL—after all, at the end of Chapter 9, we learned that there's a difference between playing the game of football and playing the game as a laborer in a multibillion dollar capitalist juggernaut.

Kyle's father, retired psychotherapist Gerald Wilson, and his oldest brother, Gerry Jr., spoke with me about the family's efforts to help the youngest Wilson prepare for the instant fame and fortune that accompany a first-round draft selection. Gerry Jr. believes the emotional demands of playing in the NFL can be challenging for any athlete, regardless of his family background or support system, "From my vantage point, and I'm speaking from being intimately aware of Kyle's progress, and with my brother Vince's friend Mike Adams (safety, Indianapolis Colts) from Paterson, New Jersey. Mike grew up in a single-parent family, wasn't drafted, and is wildly successful

FIGURE 10.1: PISCATAWAY HIGH SCHOOL PRINCIPAL JASON LESTER, COACH DANNY HIGGINS, GERRY WILSON SR.

both on and off the field. I also have a teammate from Princeton who was drafted that played in the NFL for about seven to eight years, maybe nine, then went back to business school and now works for McKinsey. Plus, I have a mechanical engineering degree from Princeton and a master's degree in business from MIT. I'm using all these as background just to say that I really have not figured out if there is a blueprint for success along those lines."

In his role as advisor and family spokesman, Gerry Jr. met with dozens of owners, general managers, and league executives who had expressed interest in drafting Kyle. He said, "All relationships need to be symbiotic. If it's a business relationship, the symbiotic relationship has to be financial. So when you think about it, there's no free lunch. You know, people are going to do what's in their best interest to run their business or grow their business. I think you may not necessarily realize that until you experience it. You may not experience that because you haven't run a business to date because you're 22 and 23 years old. Plus, you're not thinking of this as a vehicle for the game that you play as the business. But when you come to understand and realize this, then that's when everything starts to fall into place. So that's the issue."

"Again, I think that's another component that some guys don't think about," Gerry Jr. continued; "The NFL is a business, and you are a business as well. They are investing in you. . . . You're paid accordingly like a business. You file taxes in multiple states like a business. And it is an investment like a business, so you should treat it accordingly. A lot of times too, especially from the owner's perspective, this is their play money when they want to show how big their *thing* is—I'll just buy this team. On the flip side, you have athletes that are okay with doing dumb shit like dropping $10K–$20K at strip clubs when the guy who pays them wouldn't even pay that much for a pair of shoes!"

We discussed why some athletes fall into this trap and what could be done to help. "Sometimes guys just don't know better. Then again, some shit just don't change," he replied. "You can't expect somebody—without a severe intervention—that's been smoking weed their whole life who gets a million dollars—to stop smoking when they get into the NFL. That ain't gonna happen. Some guys just won't be able to figure out what the NFL is all about until it's too late." Ultimately, we agreed, for all of their hard work and dedication, most young men were ill-prepared to save and invest money, advocate for better benefits and protections, or plan for life after the league. Beyond hoping for a big signing bonus, the business of playing NFL football seems like something that will take care of itself. And it does—often to the player's detriment.

THE MOST VALUABLE assets NFL athletes possess are their on-field physical talents and mental ability. Since they are ultimately expendable if either falters, athletes understand the sports tournament offers little time to master the particulars of labor negotiation or acquire the business acumen necessary to match wits with white-collar executives and business professionals. NFL athletes are guided by two simple principles: earn as much money as possible—as quickly as possible, because a career-ending injury is always just one play away.

DeMaurice Smith, the current NFL Players Association (NFLPA) executive director, confirmed that athletes are well aware of the risks associated with playing football. According to Smith, the injury rate was 100% (or 4,500 injuries) during the 2012 season. No one comes out unscathed. And in a published interview with journalist Raymond Crockett, Smith claimed that the 2012 season marks the shortest average career length for players in NFL history at 3.1 years.[1] This reality puts pressure on young men to maximize their career earnings in whatever way possible. The short career average ultimately weakens the bargaining power of the NFL Players Association (NFLPA), the union designed to promote and protect the interests of the player, and negatively impacts athletes after they leave the game.

In 1971, Edward Garvey, former NFLPA executive director, declared, "The history of professional team sports in the U.S. is a story of exploitation of gifted athletes by a few wealthy people who call themselves 'owners.' For over a century they have considered the employee-athletes as chattel to be owned, sold, traded, suspended, or fired at their whim." Garvey challenged players, "If all athletes work together, they have a chance to eliminate the draft, the option-reserve-compensation system, and gain real dignity and a fair share of the revenues. If they remain separate, divided, and aloof to the problems faced by fellow athletes, the reserve system of the 1940s will be re-imposed by the conglomerates."[2]

THE NFL-NFLPA COLLECTIVE BARGAINING AGREEMENT (CBA) is the single most important labor document for athletes if measured by its impact during and after their careers. In addition to serving as the legal agreement that sets guidelines for player salaries and other forms of financial compensation, the CBA outlines who receives health, retirement, and disability benefits, and when. Across different iterations of the CBAs over the past five decades, two main structural inequalities have pitted players against each other: the college draft provision and the absence of guaranteed contracts. These contribute a great deal to the striation and fragmentation of the NFL labor pool.

The Entering Player Pool and Rookie Allocation System, better known as the college draft, impacts former NFL athletes well into retirement. Article VI of the CBA stipulates, "No player shall be eligible to be employed by an NFL Club until he has been eligible for selection in a draft."[3] The NFL Management Council has consistently claimed that the economic viability of the league depends upon controlling the movement of players. Club owners believe that unlike other forms of business, profitability in professional sports rests upon the unpredictable outcome of individual games and championship races. Based on this reasoning, without restrictions on player movement, the best players would gravitate toward the largest markets and the most successful teams. Unrestricted movement, the owners claim, would ultimately strengthen certain teams while undermining fan interest and league revenues. According to labor expert Ethan Lock,[4] club owners consistently argue to the courts that the restrictions on player movement are needed to sustain a viable league: the free market would destroy the NFL.

At least one group of athletes believed the NFL draft restricted their earning potential. After the NFLPA dissolved itself in March 2011, 10 players filed a class-action antitrust labor lawsuit against the league. They claimed that, among other things, the draft is equivalent to a horizontal agreement among competitors that divides up a market and allocates exclusive rights to negotiate contracts with new players. Given the high rate of injury and athletes' short career span, players have a strong incentive to secure the highest salary for the most seasons. Eliminating the draft, they asserted, would force clubs to compete against each other to sign the best athletes available on the free market.[5]

The inability to secure guaranteed contracts is another CBA provision with long-term implications for NFL athletes. Section 11 of the NFL Player's Contract states, "During the period any salary cap is legally in effect, NFL clubs have the right to terminate any contract if, in the club's opinion, the player being terminated is anticipated to make less of a contribution to the club's ability to compete on the playing field than another player or players whom the club intends to sign, or another player or players who is already on the club's roster, and for whom the team needs to make room."[6] Though Section 11 prohibits any team from withholding guaranteed consideration, rarely are NFL contracts secured by guaranteed payment.[7] The Salary Cap clause first appeared in the 1993 CBA[8] when the NFLPA acquiesced to owner concerns that free agency would cause salaries to spiral out of control thereby disrupting the competitive balance and threatening the existence of the league.[9]

Since clubs retain the right to release players at any time, there is little incentive to offer guaranteed contracts. Once an athlete is cut, he is no longer entitled to the remaining portion of his salary. If a three-year veteran signs a contract for the league minimum ($630,000) and is released four games into a 16-game season, the CBA stipulates that he is entitled only to compensation for the games he played ($157,500).

In response to the restrictions in Section 11 of the player's contract, high draft picks and noteworthy veteran free agents began leveraging their position in the marketplace to demand multimillion dollar signing and performance bonuses. A signing bonus is, after all, the only currency that provides a measure of financial security when a contract is terminated prematurely. However, because signing bonuses are counted against the salary cap, veterans in search of financial security risk being replaced by lower-salaried players. This practice has become known as salary cap manipulation, allowing teams to restock with rookie free agents or serviceable veterans willing to play for lesser contracts.[10]

In contrast to the NFLPA, the Major League Baseball Players Association (MLBPA) has united its membership on a number of key compensation issues. Decades earlier, the MLBPA successfully won its fight against a salary cap and established a long tradition of guaranteed contracts. Baseball players have secured the most lucrative contracts of all American team sports.[11] Rather than accept Ed Garvey's challenge to develop such a unified approach to bargaining for wage and retirement benefits, NFL athletes have repeatedly elected to pursue individual interests. Why? Do differences in economic philosophy—for instance the individual's pursuit of income maximization versus the collective pursuit—account for the disunity among star and journeyman athletes, or are there deeper systemic issues at work?

A classic ethnographic investigation of a machine shop offers a useful theoretical perspective for considering why NFL athletes support policies that restrict personal freedoms and contribute to their own marginalization. Sociologist Michael Burawoy was compelled to understand why the workers he observed actively participated in the intensification of their own exploitation.[12] Why, he asked, would workers push themselves to advance the interest of the company at their own expense? Surmising that coercion alone could not explain employee behavior, Burawoy offered a two-part explanation. First, management successfully inserted workers into the labor process as individuals rather than as members of a class distinguished by a particular relationship to the means of productions. Second, labor agreed to a system of rewards based on the individual rather than collective effort, shifting the conflict from a hierarchical to a lateral one (worker against worker rather than worker against labor).[13] In the NFL, the salary cap creates an incentive structure that rewards individual players rather than the collective body of labor talent. When an NFL club signs high draft choices or big name free agents to large contracts, they are playing a zero-sum game: the money allocated to those stars is taken out of the pool of money available to the whole player roster.

The NFL has in essence created a stratified system that unequally distributes salaries and health and retirement benefits based on star and journeymen status. Collectively, labor is further divided based on which CBA is in effect when a new cohort of athletes enters the league.

In Ed Garvey's view, the public gripes and court battles of former gridiron stars illustrate how competing interests among cohorts undermine the effectiveness of the NFLPA. These examples also offer clues into how management prospers when athletes are divided. NFL owners have forged an internal relationship driven by a desire to maintain tight control over labor in order to maximize revenues and consolidate power. As long as current and former NFL athletes remain fragmented, they will struggle to find power at the bargaining table.

Scholars Latham and Stewart are credited with conducting one of the few empirical examinations focused on the managerial objectives of the NFL.[14] To broaden the scope of their organizational investigation, I present a nuanced examination of the labor relationship between NFL athletes and their employer. But first, we must look at a few Circuit and Supreme Court rulings—decisions that are less likely to make headlines than an overturned sideline ruling, but which are ultimately far more consequential for players.

Rather than viewing the NFL as 32 autonomous entities, my analysis aligns with Supreme Court Justice William Rehnquist's dissenting opinion from the denial of *certiorari* in the 1982 case *National Football League v. North American Soccer League*. In his brief, Justice Rehnquist argues that sports leagues are single entities, though made up of individual teams: they are the NFL's " 'raw material,' necessary, interdependent elements that could not survive on their own." Rehnquist notes that "NFL teams rarely compete in the marketplace," and that the league's structure is "a matter of necessity."[15] Rehnquist concludes by suggesting, "The NFL is a joint venture, which produces a product that each of its teams could not produce independently; it competes with other sports and other forms of entertainment in the entertainment market."[16] Viewing the NFL as a collective institution in this way makes it possible to highlight the forces and activities that shape the experiences of current and former athletes.[17]

Counterarguments have found favor in the courts on several occasions. In two separate antitrust actions filed against the NFL (*Los Angeles Memorial Coliseum Commission v. NFL*,[18] and *North American Soccer League v. NFL*),[19] courts ruled that teams were separate entities capable of conspiring to violate Section I of the Sherman Antitrust Act.[20] According to legal scholar Myron C. Grauer,[21] both courts erred in rendering these decisions. Finding favor with Rehnquist, Grauer reasons that if teams act as separate entities in instances such as player-restraint cases,[22] they must be considered separate entities in *all* their actions. The key issue before the courts in such cases is competition, and Section I of the Sherman Act holds that the unrestrained interaction of competitive forces will yield the best allocation of economic resources.[23] In spite of this strong language, the definition of competition in sports leagues remains contentious. The American professional sports industry is atypical in that teams within a league want each other to succeed financially. For the NFL, the controversy generally centers on the question of free agency restrictions with regard to labor. Lawyer Richard E. Bartok claims that because any restraint on free agency necessarily inhibits some player movement, the restrictions always will be characterized as anticompetitive.[24] Rather than belaboring the merits of this debate, I contend that either legal interpretation places management at odds with labor over the issue of free market competition. As do most monopolistic business enterprises, the NFL relies upon its political, financial, and cultural influence to maximize profits and limit market competition.

The NFL initially used a system known as the Reserve Rule, which indefinitely bound an athlete to a specific team.[25] Under this system, every player's contract contained a provision stating that the club had the right to renew a player's contract for another year under the same terms. The Reserve Rule also prevented a player from moving to another team of his own volition. In 1947, the NFL granted free agency by replacing the Reserve Rule with the "One-Year Option" rule, which gave teams the same right of renewal, but limited it to a one-time use.

In 1962, R. C. Owens became the first player to take advantage of the rule by switching to another team.[26] Threats of unrestricted free agency then led owners to create the Rozelle Rule. Unilaterally adopted as an amendment to the NFL Constitution and By-Laws in 1963, the Rozelle Rule allowed the commissioner to award compensation from the team signing the free agent to the team losing the player at the commissioner's discretion, unless the two teams reached a prior agreement regarding compensation.[27] The NFL Players Association filed the first legal challenge to the Rozelle Rule in 1976. In *Mackey v. NFL*, the Eighth Circuit Court held that the Rozelle Rule violated Section I of the Sherman Act as an unreasonable restraint on trade.[28] According to Bartok,[29] the court recognized that the owners had a legitimate need to maintain competitive balance in the NFL but concluded that even if restriction enhanced competitive balance, the Rozelle Rule was too restrictive to serve any legitimate purpose. As part of a settlement, the owners and the NFLPA agreed to new free agency restrictions. Although both sides agreed, the 15 players listed as parties in *Mackey v. NFL* objected to the compensation scheme and right of first refusal included in the new CBA.[30] The athletes argued that the proposal failed to address the defects of the Rozelle Rule. Upon court review, the new agreement was approved based on the reasoning that it met the criteria of a valid class action settlement. In his examination of the NFL free agency restrictions, Bartok argues, "In approving the settlement, the court was not required to consider whether every provision of the plan would be reasonable under the Sherman Act or immune by reason of the labor exemption. Therefore, the court's approval is not determinative of whether these restrictions violate the Sherman Act."[31] As a result, the provisions were included in the 1977 and 1982 CBAs (with a change in the compensation system that primarily adjusted for inflation).[32]

On September 21, 1982, the NFLPA went on strike. No games were played for 57 days as the players demanded, among other things, 55% of the league's gross revenues.[33] Ed Garvey recalls that management had "broken" the union in 1974 by taking the position that the league was fighting to protect the reserve system and dominated that year's labor negotiations through "raw power, some illegal actions, and superior resources."[34] But, he writes, management had a much more difficult time dividing the union in 1982: this time, the NFLPA demanded money for *all* players.[35] Instead of relying on the untested theory of free agency and trickle-down economics, the NFLPA convinced athletes that severance pay, insurance pension, and a wage scale were needed for everyone.

A contemporary example of the struggles that continue to plague the union was seen in the retired players' lengthy battle for increased disability benefits. In 2007, former Chicago Bears Coach Mike Ditka and fellow Hall of Fame inductee Gale Sayers testified before the US Senate Committee on Commerce, Science, and Transportation regarding difficulties encountered by retired athletes seeking disability benefits. In response to Ditka's testimony, NFLPA executive director Gene Upshaw was quoted as saying, "The bottom line is I don't work for them [retired players]. They don't hire me and they can't fire me. They can complain about me all day long. They can have their opinion. But the active players have the vote. That's who pays my salary."[36] Lanny Davis, crisis communication specialist for the players' union, also questioned why Ditka would selectively attack Upshaw and the NFLPA while giving the NFL a free pass. The conflict was ultimately resolved after the union endorsed a plan for the NFL to the fund the "88 Plan," a $10 million fund that provides medical benefits for older retired athletes, the permanently disabled, and those diagnosed with dementia, amyotrophic lateral sclerosis, and/or Parkinson's disease.[37]

A second case pitting retired players against the NFLPA was the 2007 merchandising lawsuit. While it is tempting to dismiss the fight over retirement benefits as a misguided attempt by a small group of malcontents to shame the NFLPA into supporting alumni who have fallen on hard times, Hall of Famer Herb Adderley's lawsuit clearly demonstrates the long-standing schism between the NFLPA and NFL former players. Adderley filed suit on behalf of 2,056 players who argued that the union failed to actively pursue sports marketing deals on their behalf. The NFLPA initially appealed a court ruling that favored the retired players, further agitating the former players who already felt alienated by the union. Shortly after taking over as executive director, DeMaurice Smith announced that the NFLPA had dropped its appeal and reached a $26.25 million settlement with the group represented by Adderley. At the time of his election, Smith stated that addressing the rift with retired players was just as important as opening negotiation with the NFL on a new labor agreement.[38]

To gain a deeper appreciation for the contentious relationship some older players have with the NFL and the NFLPA, I spoke with former Buffalo Bills defensive back Jeff Nixon, who manages *The Nixon Report*, a blog that informs former professional football players about important issues. Nixon's concerns echo those expressed by other NFL "legacy athletes." In response to the NFL-NFLPA $240 million agreement to establish a trust for former players, Jeff writes, "It is interesting to note that the NFL Films Settlement has also established a 'Common Good Fund' for retired players in need. But why would they do that if the NFL Players Association can't even find enough former players in need of their [other] trust funds? Why did the NFL put language in the NFL Films Settlement saying that any unspent money from the 'Common Good Fund' would revert back to them?"

"The services are predominantly targeted toward the more recently retired players—many of whom already qualify for numerous other benefits," Nixon continues. "The fact is, the trust just creates more imbalance that favors the recent retirees over the older generation of former players. Unfortunately, the NFL Players Association leadership still doesn't seem to understand why the older generation of former players has lost so much trust in them. They call us the 'Legacy' players of pro football, but sometimes I can't help but feel like it's all just lip service. I don't know about anyone else, but I think the old school players got played again because we put our 'trust' in the NFL Players Association and expected them to do the right thing. They gave the recent retirees a big turkey with all the stuffing and all we got was a wishbone."[39]

Nixon helped me understand the extent to which former and current NFL athletes are competing internally for limited resources. What social scientists call a "cohort effect" arose out of players operating under at least seven different iterations of the CBA.[40] Current and former players must now argue among themselves, since their labor was governed under so many different contracts, and that infighting keeps them from mounting a collective, organized action to demand a single set of concessions from the league.

Consider the 1987 struggle. Labor and management were at loggerheads over the compensation restrictions in the 1982 CBA. Labor came to the bargaining table hoping to provide veteran players with realistic opportunities for free agency by eliminating the compensation restriction. The NFL's Management Council refused to lift its restraints, and the impasse led the NFLPA to declare a strike. Unlike the 1982 strike, the owners had received advance payments to broadcast games, so they fielded teams comprised largely of replacement players. The NFLPA suffered a second blow when 89 players crossed the picket line; they returned to the field because they feared the owners would cut off their annuity benefits. The union's failure to set up a strike fund, dwindling fan support, the network's decision to televise games featuring "scab players," and cracks in union support all convinced the NFLPA to end the 24-day strike.[41] Eventually, the union leadership concluded that collective bargaining was impossible when the "other side" was a monopoly intent on putting a product—any product—on the field and in front of the cameras.[42] Within hours of the strike's end, the NFLPA filed an antitrust lawsuit, *Powell v. NFL*, in federal court, challenging the NFL owners' continued application of the first right of refusal/compensation system and other restrictions on players, even though the previous agreement had expired.[43]

In late January 1988, Judge David Doty sided with the NFLPA in *Powell*. Doty ruled that the 1987 labor impasse had ended any exemption the owners would have for the continuation of their restrictive practices under the antitrust laws.[44] While the *Powell* case was in appeal, the NFL implemented "Plan B" Free Agency, which allowed teams to protect 37 players on the existing roster and allowed the rest to sign with other teams without compensation.[45] During the prescribed period of free agency an unprecedented number of unrestricted athletes changed teams.[46] The NFLPA charged that star athletes and average players faced the same restrictions they had before the new plan, since no player movement was recorded among protected players (only unrestricted athletes changed teams, remember). Court documents from the *Powell* case indicated that none of the top 37 players on each team had the opportunity to establish his worth on the open market. Of the remaining 619 players left unprotected across the league, teams signed 229, with only 149 under contract at the start of the season.[47] After 23 months of legal wrangling, the Eighth Circuit Court of Appeals overturned Doty's ruling and found that the restraints in *Powell* "were exempted from antitrust scrutiny as the exemption survived impasse."

As a result of the *Powell* case, the NFLPA persuaded its members to decertify the union, revoking its (or anyone's) authority to engage in collective bargaining on the players' behalf. When NFLPA informed the Department of Labor of its intent to terminate its status, the purportedly defunct group then paid for a series of court cases filed against the NFL.[48] Rather than wait for the judicial system to untangle the lawsuits, the parties attempted to enter into a new bargaining agreement: the NFL agreed to recognize the nonstatutory exemption for the term of the agreement while stating that no antitrust claim could be filed by the NFLPA until the parties reached impasse or six months had passed, whichever came later. Once both parties settled, the league then agreed it would not assert any antitrust exemption defense based on any claim that the decertification was a sham.[49]

McNeil v. NFL further complicated the battle over free agency in 1990.[50] In the spring, the NFLPA, which players had voted to decertify, financed the lawsuit on behalf of Freeman McNeil and seven other athletes whose contracts had expired. The *McNeil* lawsuit charged that the Plan B rules restricting free agency violated antitrust laws, which in turn provided legal grounds to sue, since the union no longer represented the players.[51] In response, the NFL charged that decertification was nothing more than a ploy to circumvent the *Powell* appellate ruling since the NFL Players Association essentially *functioned* as a union. Realizing the NFLPA's ability to finance further litigation hinged on the players' continued support of the union-backed Group Licensing Authorization (GLA), the league spent over $30 million in direct payments to players for group licensing rights from 1990 to 1992.[52] As a large number of stars began defecting from the GLA for the new NFL Properties deal, the courts handed down several important decisions. First, the NFLPA earned a significant victory in *Powell v. NFL IV*.[53] Second, the 1991 ruling that decertification had nullified the restraints of the CBA meant the NFL was no longer exempt from antitrust laws. Third, a judge for the National Labor Relations Board (NLRB) ruled that the NFL owners had violated labor laws by refusing to allow striking players to return for the third "scab" game during the 1987 strike. Even though the owners elected to appeal the verdict to the full National Labor Relations Board rather than pay $19 million to 1,400 players affected by the lockout, these verdicts set the tone for the completion of the McNeil trial.

On September 2, 1992, a jury determined that the Plan B system was overly restrictive, in violation of antitrust laws. The jury awarded damages of $543,000 to four of the eight plaintiffs; under antitrust law, that amount was tripled to $1,629,000.[54] In fact, while operating without a CBA for five years, the NFLPA strung together a number of antitrust court victories.[55] Two—a $30 million verdict in the 1989 developmental squad case *Brown v. NFL*[56] and the 1992 class action antitrust suit filed on behalf of Philadelphia Eagles defensive end Reggie White[57]—threatened the league's entire salary cap system. Lawyers for the NFLPA finally felt the group had enough clout to force the owners to discuss all the major issues: free agency, the salary cap, and even the abolition of the draft. Lawyers for the league took the position that losses in these cases only meant that Plan B could not continue in its present form; to them, another first right-of-refusal system was still possible. The NFLPA countered by seeking financial compensation for all players damaged under the Plan B system. Again, rather than duke it out in court, the owners and players reached a settlement. Negotiations in November 1992 culminated in a new CBA by January 1993.[58] This agreement finally recognized free agency with two significant caveats: a salary cap would take effect in 1994 and a new refusal-compensation designation would be enacted immediately. Teams could take top-rated unrestricted free agents off the market by designating one player on the roster with the franchise tag and offering him a one-year contract with a modest raise.[59] This compromise did not offer the complete free agency sought by the players' association, but one right-of-refusal player per team was far better than 37 under the old Plan B system. For its part, the salary cap appeased owners concerned with preventing top players' salaries from escalating as sharply as they had in baseball and basketball.

After disbanding nearly four years earlier, in 1993 the union finally regained the right to represent the players.[60] The 1974 strike for free agency and the 1982 work stoppage had finally brought about a major breakthrough for the NFLPA: as a result of a 1993 settlement, athletes who participated in the 1987 strike received back pay plus 60% interest in November 1994. Though only a handful of players from the 1987 strike remained in the league five years later, the NFLPA claims that the 1993 agreement resulted in a 40% retroactive increase for all active and nonactive player pensions.[61] The 1993 CBA also retroactively provided pensions for athletes who played before 1959. The *White v. NFL* court case brought $110 million in damages to athletes who played from 1989 onward. And, after decades of court battles, the NFLPA can now boast that the CBA was extended five times without a major revision between 1993 and 2006.[62] In 2006, the NFLPA and the NFL Management Council ratified the CBA to include an annuity plan for current players, salary guarantees for players with five or more years of service, and significantly increased minimum salaries.[63]

When the six-year CBA extension and revenue sharing plan was initially signed in 2006, it was considered a stunning win for the players' union,[64] thanks to a last-minute compromise on the part of 30 of 32 team owners, who agreed to dedicate a higher proportion of total revenues to player costs. In May 2008, however, the owners unanimously voted to terminate the 2006 CBA at the conclusion of the 2011 season. The league and the players were, again, spoiling for a fight. Roger Goodell justified the owners' position by saying, "The agreement isn't working, and we're looking to get a more fair and equitable deal."[65] The decision to terminate the 2006 CBA centered on a $5.5 billion player compensation clause; approximately 59.5% of the league's $9 billion annual revenue stream. The owners wanted to change that revenue-sharing deal and adopt a system that would distribute a greater percentage of players' salaries toward long-term contracts with veteran players and less to unproven rookies.[66] Gene Upshaw, the NFLPA executive director at the time, told the media, "All this means is that we will have football now until 2010. If we can't reach agreement by 2010, then we go to no man's land. That's what we see as the realistic deadline. I'm not going to sell the players on a cap again. Once we go through the cap, why should we agree to it again?"[67] Both sides remained publicly hopeful that they would resolve their differences before a lockout prevented the players from working,[68] but prior labor conflicts suggest the owners were prepared to dig in.

At the conclusion of the 2010 season, NFL owners made good on their promise to enact a player lockout. Throughout the following spring and summer, both sides remained resolute in their demands for a new agreement. Similar to previous labor disputes, players turned to the federal courts for relief[69] and a nasty public battle played out in the media. Further complicating matters was the untimely death of NFLPA executive director Marvin Upshaw. The players elected Washington, DC-based trial lawyer DeMaurice Smith to head the union and resolve the stalemate so they could return to work. Ultimately, both sides agreed it was in the best interest of the game to reach a settlement, and in August 2011 a new CBA was ratified.

Even after the signing of the 2011 CBA, meant to be a 10-year agreement, questions about the union's ability to establish lasting ties with current, recently retired, and legacy players persist. Critics say the deal significantly increases team revenues while locking young players into unfavorable contracts and pricing veterans out of the league. They also believe the new CBA distributes player benefits unequally,[70] and it did fail to eliminate ceiling and floor salary limits and other significant restrictions on compensation, ultimately suppressing athletes' market value during contract negotiations.[71]

Prior to the 2011 CBA, the salary cap was meant to determine how much money teams could spend on rookies. Under the old agreement, however, general managers and sports agents were allowed to creatively circumvent these boundaries, particularly when it came to high first-round draft selections. To address this loophole, the "Total Rookie Allocation" and the "Year One Rookie Allocation" were added to the CBA. Now, each NFL team is allotted a maximum amount of money to spend on draft picks (the total combined value and length of each rookie contract). Drafted rookie contracts are generally now set at four seasons, with teams possessing the right to extend first-round picks' contracts for a fifth season, while players are prevented from renegotiating their contracts until after their third season. The new rule essentially locks drafted athletes out of the free agent market until after their fourth or fifth season in the league.[72]

Examples of the downward trend in rookie salaries are easy to find. For instance, the agent for University of Oklahoma quarterback Sam Bradford— the number one selection in the 2010 NFL draft—successfully negotiated a record-breaking, six-year $78 million contract (containing $50 million in guaranteed bonuses). A year later, under the new 2011 CBA rules, the Carolina Panthers were able to sign the first overall selection—Auburn quarterback Cam Newton—to a four-year deal worth just $22 million.[73]

A major selling point of the 2011 CBA was that teams would redistribute the money they saved on rookie salaries to veterans with proven market value. Critics and supporters continue to debate the merits of this new rule.[74] As a result of the changing economic landscape, older veterans can no longer expect to cash in on the sorts of short-term, $10–$16 million paydays that were prevalent under the 2006 CBA. Veteran players who sought to prolong their careers pressed the NFLPA to fight for fewer off-season minicamps and less rigorous practices to give their bodies more time to heal, but the new practice and salary rules seem to have had the opposite effect: since the amount teams can spend on salaries is so strictly monitored, teams now place more value on younger players who are thought to be less prone to injury.[75] Younger players come cheaper and they're still healthy.

The salary cap minimum and salary restriction (the salary floor and ceiling) continue to persist as vexing issues for many veterans. The 2011 CBA delineates a seven-tiered system based on years of service. In 2013, the minimum rookie salary was set at $405,000 and escalates until it reaches a ceiling of

$940,000 for veterans of 10 or more seasons. The clause was intended to protect veterans against deflating salaries, but it can also serve as a mechanism to squeeze certain players out of the league. The minimum salary for a veteran entering his seventh year of service is double the rookie minimum ($840,000 compared to $405,000). That means teams can pay two players for the price of one seven-year veteran. Mid-level veteran athletes are leaving the league each year so teams can load up on cheaper young players and a few high-priced veterans. The NFLPA had attempted to offset this loophole by devising an arrangement whereby veteran players can sign "qualifying contracts," which account for about half the amount normally charged against the salary cap. For example, eight-year veterans can sign a one-year qualifying contract for a league minimum $840,000, but the cost against the salary cap is the same as a two-year veteran, or $555,000. While this strategy may seem reasonable for veterans seeking to extend their careers, the $65,000 in maximum bonus money they are allowed to receive offers little protection against the loss of salary if they are injured or released over the course of the season.

Supporters of the 2011 CBA claim the amount of cash spent on players in salaries and benefits rose to 55% of league revenues in 2011. It has also been reported that players were paid more than $160 million per team in cash and benefits in the 2011 season, exceeding the $142.4 million in cap plus benefits during the previous season.[76]

Fans may point out that it matters little if younger athletes are actually displacing older veterans, since the salary cap requires the same amount of money to be distributed to 53 athletes per team anyway. However, my research offers some insight into aging athlete's views on the salary cap issue. Shortly after the city of Houston, Texas, hosted the 2004 Super Bowl, I was invited to attend a fundraising event and retirement party for Santana Dotson, an 11-year veteran who played for three separate NFL teams. Over the weekend, I spoke with Dotson and other veterans about their views on the salary cap. Dotson said he knew it was time to retire after the team offered to re-sign him at a 50% pay cut. It was the first time I encountered an older veteran who freely discussed being low-balled in favor of a rookie salary, but it certainly was not the last. Dotson claims the team turned an injury to his achilles heel into a more figurative Achilles heel in contract negotiations, saying it *had* to draft a defensive lineman in the first round to protect against his injury. With the rookie first-rounder slated to become the new starter, the team told Dotson they could only afford to sign him to a backup player salary. Chester, another 11-year NFL veteran, says he was similarly called on to do the "grunt work" whenever the team needed a big defensive stop, while *his* highly paid rookie "replacement" stood on the sidelines. The rookie was now the investment, and Chester was literally signed to protect it.

NFLPA supporters counter that the retirement benefits available to NFL athletes have expanded significantly under the new CBA. Former players can participate in programs such as the Legacy Benefit and the 88 Benefit, in addition to the Retirement Plan and the Annuity Plan.[77] However, the expanded benefits package contains key restrictions. Retirement benefits are historically tied to the number of years of service athletes accrue in the NFL. Vesting requirements under the Bert Bell/Pete Rozelle NFL Player Retirement Plan stipulate that effective March 31, 2012, a player who does not have three credited seasons[78] shall vest only if he has earned *five* years of service. Since 2012, athletes must play a minimum of five seasons to qualify for retirement benefits. Former players can also participate in the Gene Upshaw NFL Player Health Reimbursement Account, but only if they earned a credited season for 2006 or any later plan year with a salary cap and have a total of three or more credited seasons (with an exception for athletes who last played in 2004 or 2005 and have a total of eight or more credited seasons). The CBA also stipulates that, in the 2011–2020 league years, an annuity allocation will be made for each player who has a total of four or more credited seasons at the end of such annuity years.

You may have noticed the term "vested" in these benefits. These requirements mean the average NFL athlete is excluded from receiving extended health and retirement benefits. According to a recent NFL Management Council analysis of players who entered the league between 1993 and 2002, the average career length for a rookie on his club's opening-day roster is six years. But a report by NFLPA challenges these findings with a counter claim that the average number of accrued seasons is 3.54 seasons for NFL players on the roster as of the first game of 2010 regular season. The simple truth is that the average player does not remain in the NFL long enough to qualify for most retirement benefits. This stratification of the labor market has meant that higher round draft picks (often the "stars") gain greater financial stability through higher annual salaries (with each increase adding to an already higher starting wage than most of their teammates can claim) *and* have better than average chances to secure retirement benefits (since they'll be among the few veterans not replaced with a new class of rookies in their own third, fourth, and fifth years).

Even mid-round selections stand a decent chance of securing contracts that come with signing bonuses or of earning five or more credited seasons. Later round selections and undrafted free agents are paid less from the start and are susceptible to being cut prior to vesting. Though the NFLPA is quick to mention that current athletes receive a much better compensation package than those of previous generations, the union and the NFL Management Council have yet to resolve many of the issues that confront all players who invest years preparing for a NFL career but are denied access to the extended retirement and health benefits.

In his book *40 Million Dollar Slaves*, veteran *New York Times* journalist William Rhoden[79] expands on a theme advanced by former major league baseball star Curt Flood, who famously told sports broadcaster Howard Cosell, "A well paid slave is nonetheless a slave."[80] In recent years, noted athletes such as NBA forward Rasheed Wallace and NFL Hall of Fame defensive lineman Warren Sapp have joined a chorus of professional athletes espousing similar views.[81] Unlike the litany of praises bestowed upon Floyd decades after his legal battles with MLB,[82] Wallace is often labeled a spoiled self-centered brat.[83] In the four decades since Floyd collected his $100,000 annual salary, claims of unfair labor practices and exploitation made by athletes with multi-million dollar contracts have garnered ever less public support.

A *New York Times* "Freakonomics" column asked a handful of sports insiders to comment on the widely held perception that MLB and NFL athletes have different levels of power since baseball has a stronger union, while in football, owners wield greater power, often at the expense of individual players.[84] Sports consultant and author Vince Gennaro, CNBC sportswriter Darren Rovell, and commentator Stan Kasten (president and part owner of baseball's Los Angeles Dodgers) suggested that under the current set of conditions, both athletes and owners are making out reasonably well financially. Sports economist Andrew Zimbalist's response was damning though: "Why would anyone ask this question? The owners organize Major League Baseball and the NFL. The owners in each league elect a commissioner who acts in the best interest of the owners, or, at least endeavors to do so. Each league is a monopoly and exercises significant market power by, *inter alia*, extracting significant public subsidies for the construction of facilities." Zimbalist believes the labor market offers athletes little choice but to bargain with a monopolistic cartel for a share of the profits.

When examining the athletes' position in the labor process, a key question emerges: Once athletes sell their labor power, what do they have left with which to bargain? NFL owners have successfully developed a mode of production that determines and defines their social relations with the athlete. An NFL athlete's social status and relationship with management, coaches, sports agents, and the players' union is largely dictated by his position in the labor process. As Karl Marx put it, once the instruments of labor begin to employ workers, a fact that arises out of social relations, the work process is fixed in the hands of management.[85]

Economists James Richard Hill and Jason E. Taylor argue, for their part, that the most important labor battle for the professional athlete is to eliminate the monopolistic reserve clause and facilitate the higher pay that goes with a competitive environment that values highly skilled workers' services.[86] The advent of free agency has ushered in an era in which professional athletes' salaries and share of franchise rents have increased considerably. Now that the players have largely won the battle for market-based wage determination, Hill and Taylor contend that owners have focused on ways to manipulate that market.[87] The NFL owners' decision to exercise the early opt out clause of the 2006 CBA appears to support this conclusion. Though the salary cap was designed to suppress player wages, the owners were willing to reopen an ugly labor dispute to reclaim a larger portion of the league's $9 billion annual revenues for themselves.

Current NFLPA executive director DeMaurice Smith argues that he and the union exist to fight tooth and nail over benefits that players will need after their football careers are over.[88] While the 2011 CBA has increased benefits significantly for some players, it appears that not all union members are viewed equally. If the benefits package increases the quality of life for *elite* players during retirement, average athletes are systematically excluded from the most coveted resources. Stars and journeymen endure the same extended apprenticeship, from Pee-Wee football through college. Stars and journeymen face the same risks when they take the field. But, due to the structural inequalities of the draft and the absence of guaranteed contracts, journeymen are far more likely than stars to find themselves with minimal resources and limited recourse when they exit the league.

The evidence bears it out: players seem to have divided labor interests along class lines.[89] Although all NFL athletes enter into contractual arrangements to receive wages in exchange for their athletic performance, star players and high draft choices behave like petite bourgeoisie to the journeymen's proletariat. More than 40 years after Ed Garvey's call for solidarity among professional athletes, unvested journeymen continue to struggle for recognition and equal treatment. Going forward, in addition to the push for higher wages and an unrestricted labor market through the elimination of the player draft, elite NFL athletes must decide whether solidarity includes fighting for access to benefits for *all* present, future, and former athletes.

$=$ 11 $=$

FORCED OUT

We got to start looking after each other, 'cause once your career is over, what you got? Who are you then?

Big Al

TIKI BARBER, FORMER New York Giants' All-Pro running back, cruises through New York City in his shiny black Cadillac Escalade, looking as slick as the car while he drops wisdom. Alongside his wife and children, he discusses how he is preparing for the challenges of life after football. In this car commercial and its accompanying website, we see the glamorous and financially secure life of a pro football player.[1] But, as British poet A. E. Housman writes, sports are a young man's game.[2] Football is no exception.

Running backs like Barber tend to have some of the shortest NFL career spans, yet Barber outlasted many of his contemporaries. Born Atiim Kiambu Hakeen-Ah Barber, "Tiki" was drafted by the New York Giants in the second round of the 1997 NFL draft. After 10 seasons, including three All-Pro selections with the team, Barber announced his retirement—one of the few players who can claim to have elected to retire from the game. Writing for ESPN's website, he elaborated: "I've been considering [retirement] for a few years now. It comes to a point where your body just doesn't want to take it anymore. You see other opportunities out there. I'm excited about the rest of my life as well as I am about this football season. So we'll see what happens."[3] At the time of his departure from the NFL, Barber still had two years and $8.3 million in salary remaining on his contract. Still, in another article, Barber said, "Last offseason, I started thinking, 'What do I want my life to be about?'... Football is just a small part of who I am. I have a lot of interests and I've never wanted to be solely defined as a football player. I wasn't that way in high school, I wasn't that way in college, and I won't compromise my ideals to be that way in the National Football League."[4]

In the final years of his career, Barber served as a spokesperson for New York area McDonald's and appeared in national campaigns for Cadillac, PowerBar, and Johnston & Murphy. Almost immediately after his retirement, NBC announced a lucrative three-year, multimillion dollar contract for Barber to appear as a regular on the *Today* show and as a commentator on *Football Night in America*.[5] Barber walked away from a record-setting NFL career with his body still intact, abundant fame and fortune, and a nascent journalism career in the largest media market in the world. This is as close to a Horatio Alger story as a football player usually gets.

But four years away from the game, Barber began struggling. There were reports that his media career was faltering and that his nasty, public divorce had led to financial difficulties.[6] It was soon revealed that, at 36 years old, Barber hoped to revive his NFL career.[7] Many assumed his change of heart was mostly due to the prospect of another six- or seven-figure paycheck, but according to NFL Network and Fox Sports reporter Jay Glazer, Barber said, "After seeing how much fun [my twin brother] Ronde is still having [playing football], it re-ignited my fire, and I'm looking forward to the challenge of seeing if I can get back to the level of where I was."[8] I've never met Tiki Barber, yet his story shows many of the difficulties athletes face during the transition out of football—a game that has defined their existence since middle school.

As we've seen, star athletes and journeymen have different trajectories, but they often face similar challenges. Social irrelevance is as likely to happen to any of the men I interviewed as to Tiki Barber who saw his team go on, in the six seasons after his exit, to win two Super Bowl championships and cultivate a brand new star running back, David Wilson. During the many years of my field research, more than two dozen former players detailed struggles in adjusting to life beyond the NFL spotlight. NFL athletes *are* accustomed to driving exotic cars, popping champagne bottles at the strip clubs, and attending A-list celebrity parties (even those at the lower end of their team's payroll—a clear pathway to financial troubles on its own), but those perks fade quickly when they are no longer NFL athletes. In addition to having their careers truncated by injury or losing their spot on the team roster to younger, less expensive talent or suffering financial hardship brought on by divorce, bad money management, or bum investments, many of the former athletes I interviewed experienced loneliness, bouts of depression, and the loss of identity, value, and/or "master status."[9] A University of Michigan study confirmed my informal tally when it revealed former NFL athletes most frequently reported trouble with sleeping, with financial difficulties, with marital or relationship problems, and with fitness, exercise, and aging.[10] The study concluded that these outcomes strongly correlate with the presence of moderate to severe depression and struggles with chronic pain. And headlines have shown an unnerving number of former player suicides.

Yet personal accounts of NFL athletes confronting the loss of a lifelong dream while simultaneously transitioning to life after football have proven elusive. Former athletes put up barriers with their hubris, expectation of star treatment, and understandable mistrust of the motives of journalists, friends, loved ones, and strangers alike. The fishbowl effect of life in the NFL can help to intensify the emotional stress of an involuntary role exit or forced retirement. As mentioned in Chapter 9, the HBO reality series *Hard Knocks* has provided some excruciating glimpses, as when cable viewers witnessed an athlete's tension mounting as he gets cut and his devastation as he confronts the end of his NFL dreams.[11] My examination of the involuntary role-exit process experienced by NFL athletes offers a unique opportunity to understand the relationship between identity formation and that loss of social status.

Although it is rare for football players to openly talk about the stress of surviving in the NFL, the lack of job security is a source of concern for all but a few high draft selections or noteworthy veterans. I've been in conversations with teammates and overheard athletes in the locker room share these concerns by saying things such as "It's harder to stay in the NFL than it is to get into the NFL," and "Brother, the NFL ain't no joke. Somebody's always out there trying to take your job." Many high-round draft picks and star players receive some form of financial security in the form of signing and performance bonuses. But the NFL Players Association has been unable to secure guaranteed contracts for all their athletes. The collective bargaining agreements, in fact, explicitly state that an athlete can be replaced if another player is expected to make a bigger contribution to the team. Journalist William Rhoden describes this never-ending stream of surplus labor as a conveyor belt; kids as young as 11 or 12 years old climb aboard to begin their journey.[12] Coupled with the lack of guarantees in player contracts, it means that veterans with larger salaries feel expendable (since teams have an incentive to employ younger, less expensive athletes)[13] and that players are encouraged to work *against* each other. Disunity makes it even more difficult for the athletes to coalesce into a negotiating partnership on equal footing with the NFL owners, ironically meaning that the lack of contract guarantees makes it harder for players to secure contract guarantees. The house always wins.

Add the constant threat of career-ending injury (even the fear that treating an injury rather than getting back into the game will make a player seem expendable—recall the player mantra that "you can't make the club in the tub") and most players must confront their physical fragility and career instability each time they enter the field of play.

After playing an average of just 3.3 seasons, most players are released. In addition to frustration, disbelief, and even numbness, many of the athletes I encountered described a sense of loss with being forced out of their most impactful role in life. Unlike basketball, baseball, soccer, or other team sports, when a football career ends, it's generally really over. Tiki Barber's attempt at re-entry aside, the harsh reality of the NFL is that once athletes leave or are pushed out of the door, rarely are they invited back for a curtain call.

As a former football player, I find it easy to empathize with the numerous athletes who shared their stories about the struggles that come with exiting the game. As a sociologist, I want to understand and explain how the social institution of football impacts an athlete's self-identity and how his sense of self affects his social behavior.[14]

Through research with an ethnically diverse group of elite college football players, scholar Ley Killeya-Jones has observed that the athlete role may occupy such a central place in the athlete's self-conception that it dominates the ego identity.[15] Similarly, sport psychologists Taylor and Ogilvie and others suggest that the most fundamental psychological issue that influences adaptation to a career transition is the degree to which athletes define their self-worth in terms of their participation and achievement in the sport.[16] These scholars claim that *unidimensional* athletes are disproportionately invested in their sport participation and often have few fulfilling or meaningful activities outside of their sport.[17] Thus an overly developed athletic identity can leave athletes ill-prepared for post-sport careers.[18] Their strongly football-associated self-identity, reinforced through close personal ties with teammates, can lead to a variety of developmental, psychological, and social issues that may exacerbate difficulties during a forced exit from the league.[19]

Therefore it is reasonable to conclude that during an unwelcomed or forced retirement, the status enjoyed by an NFL athlete will compete with his self-identity for temporal and psychological resources that can result in a role conflict.[20]

Typically, unidimensional athletes experience retirement from sport as a deep loss.[21] The psychological and emotional challenges of playing in the NFL make it counterproductive for athletes to expend energy thinking about retirement while they are working to extend their careers. Despite maintaining a supremely confident persona, the persistent tension of career uncertainty lurks in every locker room of the NFL, threatening to shake an athlete's self-identity at any given moment.[22] Even though they know the game could end at any moment, to consider it, to plan for it is to invite a distraction that could hasten the exit. They're inevitably unprepared for the inevitable.

TYRONE AND JAMAL

Several of the athletes I encountered in the Canadian Football League (CFL) were actively trying to prolong their careers after being involuntarily forced out of the NFL (Figure 11.1). Two in particular embody the concept of the unidimensional athlete: Tyrone and Jamal, 26- and 27-year-old wide receivers who had bounced around the NFL and NFL Europa with limited success.[23] Tyrone's football career typifies the trajectory of a journeyman who teeters on the margins, the chance of earning one of the final NFL roster spots each season always just slightly out of reach. Though he tended to get agitated whenever I broached the subject of retirement, Tyrone opened up one day as we cruised around town in his $80,000 BMW. He had played three seasons in the NFL after being a seventh-round draft pick out of a midwestern university and had probably made between a quarter and three quarters of a million dollars in the league. Now, in the CFL, he was essentially playing on borrowed time. I waited patiently for an opening before asking, "So, what's up when football is done?"

"Hopefully by that time the real estate thing will have kicked in," he said. "And I can let my money work for me."

I pressed: "What about investments? Who handles that for you?"

"My people's got a lawyer," he answered. "I runs things by her before I jump into anything."

FIGURE 11.1: CFL ATHLETES.

"What type of law does she practice?" I asked. "Does she give financial advice or just legal advice? You decide once you know if the deal is legit?"

"I don't really know," Tyrone stared at his side-view mirror, even though there were no cars around. "All I know is that she's been with the family a long time, and I trust her. She's been doin' right by my family, so I trust her."

"That sounds like a good bet. So, you plan to keep on playing for a minute to make cash and invest in real estate?"

"I'm not really thinking about it that deep. Right now I'm playing ball and doing my thing, that's all. So far everything is straight."

Tyrone was a lot like other men I'd talked to who came from humble back-grounds. He credited athletics as his ticket out of a tough southern California neighborhood, confessing that his youth was marked by confrontations with the law, a little drug "dealin' here and there," and a gang initiation. In his view, the gang functioned like a family, and it actually helped further his career: "In my case, we didn't have much money growing up so whenever I needed something, I knew where to turn. Because I was a good athlete, the old heads didn't want me to get caught up. So they protected me from all that mess going on in the streets." That is, gang leaders knew he was talented and protected him on the streets so he could make good on his football dreams.[24] Through hard work and determination, Tyrone earned an athletic scholarship to a perennial major college football powerhouse. For a kid from southern California, that was making it. Tyrone now relishes the spotlight that professional football offers and proudly views his athletic identity as a badge of honor.

He complements his well-heeled but rough-and-tumble reputation with his physical presence. His chiseled facial features, freshly woven braids, and tattoo-covered, muscular physique might mark him out as a model, and rather than wear athletic gear on the streets, he prefers some "flava": sagged denim jeans, Timberland boots or a fresh pair of Jordans, a loose-fitting designer T-shirt, and a matching do-rag topped with an MLB cap atop his cornrow braids. While he remains true to the look of the West Coast hip-hop street culture, Tyrone is a good-natured guy who appreciates fans complimenting his game and loves signing autographs for children. But he looks intimidating, and I was struck over the three months we spent together by how hesitant Canadians were to approach him. Here's a man who's intensely quiet, with his identity on the line every time he takes the field, but to outsiders, he's like a superhero.

Another crucial aspect of a unidimensional football player's self-identity is the need to justify his short-lived NFL career. After hearing that Jamal signed a large CFL free-agent contract the prior off-season, I was curious to learn what caused his NFL career to end prematurely. Rather than acknowledging any shortcomings in his game, Jamal readily recounts a plethora of reasons he's landed in the CFL. Politics and favoritism—two of the most common scapegoats offered by athletes unceremoniously ushered out of the NFL were go-to tales, as when one evening several CFL teammates gathered before a night on the town. Skip and Jamal were playing *Madden Video Football* while Tyrone sprawled across the couch with an attractive young 20-something blonde. In the center of the dining room table in Jamal's well-furnished luxury rental was what seemed like a quarter-pound of marijuana, the main purpose for these post-practice festivities. Jamal took a long, slow drag on a joint and shouted, "Listen partner, you wanna know about the NFL? The NFL ain't 'bout shiiiiiit! You know why? 'Cause them MOTHER FUCKERS don't want nobody to do shit except their own boys! I can go down there right now and rip shit up, but they still gonna hold you back." Jamal continued, "When I was out there in NFL Europe, they couldn't help but bring me to camp 'cause I was the baddest thing out there! When I got to Dallas, them 'FUCKIN' CATS' couldn't do shit wit me, both me and Tyrone fucked them up. Our game was tight! But if you ain't one of their boys, it don't matter. They got too much invested in them." All of which is to say, Jamal was sure that he and Tyrone were top-tier football talent—no one could touch them!— but the NFL would ignore them in favor of players the league had developed through its system.

"See man, this is how it works." Jamal, seen as an elder statesman among the receivers, was on a roll. "If a team spends a high draft pick on someone in your position, that bitch is making the team! It don't matter what you do, 'cause the money is in him. So I said, 'Fuck it! I'll just go on back up to Canada and make my money.' See, up here, I'm the man! I'm the highest paid receiver in the CFL. People in the NFL and the CFL know I'm bad as shit, and that's all that counts. Cats like Tyrone and me; we get our respect from the true ballers. We go at it hard on the field, get all the love we need, and make that money. You don't need no damn NFL to show your shit—and that's how we do!"

Though Jamal is only a year older than Tyrone, his five years of CFL experience and Grey Cup MVP ring make him, in this room, "the man." (The Grey Cup is the name of both the championship game of the Canadian Football League and the trophy awarded to the victorious team playing Canadian football.) After a successful college career, Jamal never quite fulfilled his NFL promise, even after helping his college team win an NCAA Division I national championship made him a hometown hero. Playing in the CFL serves as a nice buffer from people back home who constantly inquire, "Why aren't you still in the NFL?" Jamal's remarks, in fact, represent a well-rehearsed trope of former NFL athletes: since politics alone cannot account for one's absence from the NFL, athletes rely on press clippings and the Canadian Total Sports Network (TSN) to broadcast their CFL exploits to friends and family back home in the states. It's as if they point to the clips and say, "See? I'm so good! Obviously I'm not in the NFL because of politics."

Self-identity is an important but often overlooked concept that affects an individual's experience during the loss of a significant role. As Taylor and Ogilvie point out, the professional athlete's psychological approach to self-identity is a key factor in his ability to adequately transition into the next phase of life.[25] The narratives supplied by Tyrone and Jamal supports Killeya-Jones's assertion that an athletic identity may occupy such a central role that it dominates the ego identity.[26] Tyrone and Jamal expend a great deal of energy crafting and maintaining a celebrated identity designed to reinforce the social status they depend on. They are frustrated and distrustful of a system that failed to deliver for them on the promises of fame, fortune, and public adulation on a grand scale, but they still want those things—they simply have to construct them, building up the identity and doing their best to live it out.

BK

Voluntary role exit is a foreign concept to most NFL athletes—recall that his ability to announce his retirement was one of the most surprising aspects of Tiki Barber's trajectory. For BK, a talented defensive back who played college football in Colorado, the challenge is finding a career beyond football that can offer similar levels of personal gratification and public adulation—and a hefty paycheck (he feels pressure to financially support his family). BK explained that even though his income dropped precipitously after leaving the NFL, his ex-girlfriend "won't give up" her quest for additional financial support for her and their son. He says, "She thinks I'm hiding something, but that NFL money is all gone." Other family and friends expect financial help, too.

During our first encounter at a CFL training camp in Calgary, BK seemed to hide his taut physique under a loose-fitting Nike T-shirt and a pair of baggy athletic pants. His unimposing stature was consistent with his reserved demeanor, both in stark contrast with popular images of a celebrated athlete who set Big 12 conference records for punt returns and interceptions. A few minutes into the conversation, it became clear that BK was once a highly coveted athlete headed for NFL stardom.

BK was such an accomplished talent that he decided to leave college early for the NFL draft: "I really didn't know what to expect. Because I was only 20 when I got drafted, my grandparents had to sign my first contract. I really wasn't prepared for everything that happened though." BK was young, but he had the speed, quickness, and agility to earn a multimillion dollar contract as a second-round draft selection. Having heard about his accomplishments on the collegiate level, I probed to find out why BK was overlooked in the first round of the draft. "The second round was mainly because of my size. If I were three or four inches taller, I definitely would have been a high first-round selection. I would probably still be in the league and made millions more." This statement prompted me to examine an inconsistency I'd spotted in his biography in the official team media guide. Second-round NFL draft choices are routinely given four or five seasons to prove their value.[27] But BK barely lasted three full seasons in the NFL. "I was stupid and kind of took things for granted," he said. "I just figured as long as you could play, then you're safe. The team invests a lot in the first-round guy, so he gets all the chances. With all that money tied up in him, they're gonna do everything possible to make things work. The farther down the line you are, the fewer chances you get. With me, I got paid really good money, but they could afford to let me go 'cause I kept getting hurt on top of screwing up a couple of times."

BK lasted only a few games into his second season before the coaches grew weary of his late night partying and frequent tardiness. The final straw came after he overslept and arrived 45 minutes late for a Monday morning practice. BK recalled, "I just had my best game in the pros and we were out late celebrating at a strip club. I slept through my alarm clock, when I get a call from the team equipment manager. When I arrive, they tell me the general manager wants to see me. I joked and ask him, 'How much is my fine?' and he tells me they're fed up, that's it, I'm done."

After only one and a half seasons, BK's contract was terminated. A wasted draft pick. Like other high-draft selections, BK was immediately claimed off the waiver wire and signed a contract with the New England Patriots for the remainder of the season.[28] With his reputation as a quality punt returner and defensive back still intact, the Patriots would give him a second chance. Injury, however, would prevent a third. In a matter of three seasons, BK was out of the NFL, working as a sales representative for a south Florida marketing company.

The monotony and anonymity took an emotional toll. BK said, "Man, I got bored sitting in that office doing the same thing over and over again every day. I'm used to people knowing my name, being the man. It's a nice feeling when everybody knows who you are." During the two years I spent documenting BK's life, he walked away from a CFL contract and tried to resurrect his career a third time in Arena Football (AFL). Knowing that BK had enjoyed a seat at the NFL table, I was perplexed that he could be content signing a minor league contract with a small midwestern team. His response was simple yet poignant, "I got that itch again. Just couldn't stay away. I'll probably keep playing until that desire's gone." Now that several years have passed, I reflect back on BK's words with appreciation: BK understood that, at 28 years old, he can still play at a high level, but the game will almost always push athletes out before they are ready.

CHESTER

Chester, a physically imposing 35-year-old defensive end, was forced out of the game after a successful, 13-year NFL career. When we met, it was the spring before his final season, and he sensed the end was near. The physical and emotional demands were taking their toll and Chester was contemplating a life without football. Unlike some of his teammates who burned through tons of cash with extravagances like overpriced jewelry or exotic sports cars, Chester had carefully planned for his financial future. According to his close friend Victor, a lengthy NFL career allowed Chester to amass a net worth of over $36 million dollars. That security seemed to free up Chester to think about how, for the first time in over 20 seasons, he was about to embark on a world free of a rigorous annual workout schedule, mashed fingers, twisted ankles, and soaking in tubs of ice water. From Victor's perspective, Chester was infamous for his quirky personality, but his behavior was becoming more erratic as the end of the season grew closer. Victor said, "He must be going through some kind of phase or something; he's usually very good at handling business affairs. Usually when Chester wants to do something, you can count on him doing it. I don't know what's going on with him right now, but it must be something to do with his career."

The good fortune that helped Chester evade serious injury to play well and have a lengthy career did little to appease the uncertainty around his retirement which, while expected, was still what I'd consider a forced exit. On more than one occasion Chester insisted that he could still perform at a high level, but he knew the minimum salary for veterans made him expendable. "I know I can still play, it's just when you start getting up there in age, then you become too expensive. After you've been around for so long they don't want to pay a brother, so I refused to go to camp." I must have looked confused. Chester continued, "Why should I get out there in the hot sun each summer, let them break my body down and get injured for no money? For the last couple of years, I just waited until training camp was over, then start[ed] making calls. Someone always needs a quality veteran defensive end, so they'd invite me in for a workout and I'd get the job." He had never quit hustling, and it was visibly painful that the end was coming.

When I questioned whether he could squeeze out one more season, Chester's patience grew thin, "Damn Robert! You wear me out with all those questions." But he said he had some irons in the fire: "I want to get my entertainment management company off the ground at some point and get a cigar bar rolling soon, but we'll just have to wait and see." I hadn't heard from him for four months when Victor called. For the first time ever, there wasn't a single team willing to offer his friend a contract for the upcoming season. I asked how Chester was doing and why he stopped returning my phone calls; Victor explained that I wasn't alone: "He kinda withdrew from everybody for a while. Chester is an eccentric dude anyway, so it ain't personal. Who knows what that guy thinks sometimes! He was talking about going back to school and possibly finishing his degree, but I'm not sure what he plans to do next." Over the next year, I spoke with Chester sporadically. Our conversations mainly focused on getting his entertainment company off the ground as football played a less central role in his life. While money never appeared to present a problem, Chester was still struggling with finding meaningful ways to occupy his time.

The discontinuity between a player's status as a former NFL athlete and the desire to maintain his identity as an NFL athlete can result in anxiety or anomie.[29] While role transitions due to old age or a loss of health may be difficult to prepare for, those involving status loss, such as the ones that face athletes and fashion models, are often devastating in their own ways.[30]

BIG AL

Big Al exited the NFL in the mid-1980s at the age of 32. After playing for three NFL teams over a span of eight seasons, Big Al was confronted with the reality that the next phase of his life had suddenly begun. In the third year of his retirement, a mutual friend introduced us. Big Al immediately agreed to train me for my impending tryout with the 49ers. The well-built, handsome, African American former tight end greeted me with the same generosity and respect that I have since witnessed him extend to many others over the years. At that point in his life, Big Al was attempting to reconnect with the political community and business leaders he met while playing for the New York Giants early in his career. In addition to establishing his new life outside of football, Big Al was readjusting to living with his wife and children, from whom he'd been separated in the final few seasons of his career so the kids could stay in their schools in New Jersey, while he played in San Francisco.

Apart from Big Al's kindness and warm personality, the thing that stands out about him is his desire to help former NFL athletes "get paid." He takes every opportunity to remind his NFL brethren that maintaining a high pro-file and remaining active in the community is the most important way to cash in on their celebrity status. From his perspective, former players need to leverage the only real bargaining chip they still hold after they're out of the game: their status as NFL alumni. Big Al tries to organize three or four events each month to help former players earn extra cash for celebrity guest appearances. I jumped at the chance when he invited me to join his celeb-rity basketball team for a fundraiser at a public school in Harlem; I was still a young athlete trying to make the leap from the CFL into the NFL, but I was excited to play alongside the esteemed alumni listed on Big Al's roster. When I asked which retired guys usually come out for these events, Big Al explained, "Most of these guys act like teenagers. The young guys won't show up for a gig because they don't need the money, and the older cats would rather complain about what the NFL ain't doing for them. I tell them to come on, 'All you got to do is show up, say a few words, sign a few autographs, and get paid.' And you know what they say? 'Brother Al, why don't you talk to the NFL and get them to kick in some cash so you can pay us some real money?' Hell, they owe us at least that much; after all we did for them." According to Big Al, former athletes suffer when they live in the past like that. They aren't current players and they don't command the same hefty appearance fees, but a couple dozen smaller paydays are a good supplement to their income.

Big Al is also convinced that the NFL's racial dynamics contribute to the animosity and resentment some Black former athletes hold toward the league. In his thirty-year association with the NFL, Big Al has witnessed Black alumni struggle in retirement. His point brought to mind the late Philadelphia Eagles star strong safety Andre Waters, whose career encompassed 156 games during the 1980s and '90s.[31] He had achieved the pinnacle of success in American

sports, but his life after football was full of struggles to establish a new identity and overcome unfulfilled expectations and bouts of depression. Waters
believed that after all of his on the field success, the league would embrace his
knowledge, experience, and desire to teach young athletes. What bothered
him was that he didn't mean anything to the NFL the moment he couldn't
play anymore: "Nobody knows the game like players, but the guys who get
into coaching and scouting right out of college, they're getting experience
while we're out there playing. When we're done, nobody wants to hire us."
After Waters participated in the NFL intern-coaching program, a few small
college programs made offers, but Waters said he often ran into college
coaches who resented him as an ex-NFL big shot.[32] Waters died at age 44 in
November 2006, reportedly from a self-inflicted gunshot wound to the head.

As my friendship with Big Al grew, I began to grasp how serving as an
NFLPA union representative in the early 1980s had shaped his identity. He
risked his own reputation in a player's strike, and he continues to believe that
there is strength in numbers, despite the blows he suffered in his own career.
While we traveled on the I-95 highway from New Jersey to Maryland, Big Al,
then in his mid-50s, offered the following account of the struggle for higher
wages and racial equality during his playing days:

> Man, the first time we went on strike in 1982 we caught some serious
> hell. My career never really recovered because it was up to me to
> decide if our team should support the strike. I had general managers
> and coaches telling me that I would never work again if the strike went
> through. We were fighting for our fair share of the pie and the NFL
> really tried to stick it to us. They don't give a damn about the players.
> Look how they treat us when we're finished playing, especially the
> Black guys. It's pretty much like they use you up and throw you away,
> unless they can use you to make them look good.

We were headed down the freeway on our way to a mid-summer cookout at
linebacker LaVar Arrington's home to celebrate the signing of his $68 million
contract extension with the Washington Redskins.[33] Big Al continued:

> Yeah, the money has changed, but it's still the same old NFL. These
> young cats think things are different because the money is better now,

but look how many athletes is still struggling once they get out. I mean, you put your time in, make your money, and after you finish playing, then what you got? The league don't give a shit about you. These young brothers don't understand that it ain't just about the money. What good is the money when your body's all beat up? The NFL keeps on rollin' without you. This shit ain't changed. All we thinking about is the money, but we don't understand that it's about more than the money. Don't nobody in the NFL give a damn about you once you gone. It's time for us to come together 'cause it's hard out here these days. We got to start looking after each other, 'cause once your career is over, what you got? Who are you then?

In the years since his retirement, Big Al has sought to establish several programs so former NFL athletes can get involved with the community, yet something always seems to derail his plan. Once, shortly after relocating his family to the southwestern United States, a city official from a town in central New Jersey contacted him about establishing an afterschool basketball program for at-risk kids. The councilmember said that the city had secured a small grant to fund a pilot program and needed an experienced director to help get things started. The work was pro bono but came with the promise of a substantial salary if the program was deemed a success after the six-month trial period. Big Al and his wife discussed the opportunity and decided the program was worth his time, so long as the city agreed to pay his living and travel expenses. For a season, things went well. The city council lauded the program as an alternative to the allure of street gangs and selling drugs, but then tried to persuade Big Al to return the next season without a salary. "That's why I don't like dealin' with folks like that," he said. "They're always crying about how bad things are in the minority community, but when it comes time to put money on the table, they start crying that Black athletes are making all this money and should be giving something back to the community, which is all well and good, but we have to eat, too. I got a family to take care of. I can't be messin' with these folks no more." The incident left Big Al dejected and questioning if the whole thing was nothing more than an elaborate game of bait and switch.

For all his ability to avoid pitfalls, Big Al still seems caught up in a protracted battle of how he believes things ought to be in retirement and the reality of how they actually are. In one respect, Big Al believes being an NFL alumnus provides the currency needed to sustain a successful career in community service. Yet his appeals for financial support from the business community and public officials often lead to empty promises. He has yet to earn the educational credentials that would validate his desire to head a community service organization, and while I have had lengthy discussions with him about returning to school and finishing his degree, writing a business plan, applying for 501(c)(3) nonprofit status, and gaining the management experience needed to head a government-sponsored community-based program, Big Al seems content trying to leverage his status as an NFL alumnus to establish life beyond football. So far, his strategy has yielded mixed results. It's been the sort of protracted struggle that so many NFL football players encounter when attempting to reconcile their athletic identity with their new status as a former athlete.

D. MAYES

I had never heard of Derrick Mayes before a business associate passed along his phone number. My colleague suggested the former Super Bowl champion would be great to interview for my research. The first thing that impressed me when Derrick and I met was the business-like manner in which he approached our conversation (Figure 11.2). Unlike nearly every other professional athlete I encountered, Derrick made a point of turning off his cell phone to offer me his full attention.

Derrick explained that in his fourth NFL season, he had been called into the Seattle Seahawks' general manager's office and was questioned about his involvement in an Internet start-up company. The general manager wanted to know if this outside business interest would compromise his ability to concentrate on the field. Derrick said he was told, "The team pays you to play football. The owner does not like hearing that one of his players is running around town talking to venture capitalists." To this former professional athlete, Derrick's account seemed plausible, but in my role as an ethnographer, I wanted verification. Interviewing the team's general manager was out of the question, so I sought confirmation from Paul Berrettini, Derrick's long-time business associate and former roommate at Notre Dame.[34] Paul explained that ever since college Derrick has schemed about ways to build a business empire. Like many investors in

FIGURE 11.2: ROBERT "PACKY" TURNER WITH SUPER BOWL XXXII CHAMPION, WIDE RECEIVER DERRICK MAYES.

the late nineties, Paul said his friend saw the Internet as a great way to get in on a ground-floor opportunity. Paul noted that Derrick also started a media production company while playing in the NFL. After locating news articles and watching video clips produced by his company, I was convinced that Derrick was serious about approaching football as a business entrepreneur. Although athletes like Big Al, Chester, Peter Warrick, and BK struggled with the harsh realities of life once their professional football careers ended, Derrick Mayes seems to represent those men who take a page out of the owner's playbook in planning for the future.

One particular statement Derrick made during our initial meeting offered profound insight. "When I was in college, Coach Holtz used to say that everything we ever needed in life was right in front of us, we just had to go out and get it," he said. "I have seen so many guys just waste their time making excuses when all they have to do is recognize that all the resources they'll ever need have already been given to them."

After breakfast, we walked in a chilly New York City spring rain to continue the conversation in my office. As the discussion transitioned toward exploring business opportunities, I nearly forgot that Derrick was a retired

NFL athlete and not a Wall Street executive. Only after I began to introduce him around the office did his identity as an NFL athlete take center stage. Glen, the exuberant 26-year-old office manager, jumped out of his seat to shake Derrick's hand: "Super Bowl XXXI, I remember you! You had a nice career, not long enough, but pretty good. I always wondered what happened to you." Glen proved to be a wealth of information as he offered an oral history of Derrick's athletic career. "You're one of only a couple of guys to ever be a captain for the Notre Dame football team.[35] You hold the record for most career touchdown catches at Notre Dame. You were drafted in the second round and played in two Super Bowls in five years. Right?" Glen revealed that he was a big fantasy football fan, to which Derrick chuckled, "And I probably lost you a lot of money during my career."

Later that afternoon, I asked Derrick why his pro career only lasted five seasons. In contrast to many of the other athletes I interviewed, Derrick was both mature and insightful. Only four years removed from playing in the NFL, he said, "I never considered myself to be a 'football player.' I'm a guy who played football, but I never allowed myself to be defined by the game. As a matter of fact, I've always known that football was going to be my springboard to bigger and brighter things. I chose to attend the university that I did because of the alumni network."

I must have looked skeptical that he'd devised such a sophisticated plan as a high school student, but Derrick shrugged, "Growing up, my father owned a successful printing business, and mom was well respected as a schoolteacher back in Indianapolis. One of her students was [former NFL star] Mark Clayton. When I used to visit Clayton, he showed me how the game really works. Those were some crazy times, the things I saw coming at him was something else. Even though I was only in high school, I could still see that you better have a plan because that shit he was dealing with wasn't real. He used to tell me to make sure not to get caught up in all the hype when it was my turn."

After Derrick transitioned out of the NFL, he moved to Los Angeles and used his bachelor's degree in communications to establish an entertainment production company. He tapped into his Notre Dame alumni network to develop a college football TV show and start a weekly TV-online football journal. "Honestly, I never intended to be in the NFL forever. I knew that football could open doors to take me where I want to go in life. So I developed a plan early in life and just stuck to it."

Today, Derrick actively seeks to retain and leverage his elite status whenever possible. He thinks of an NFL pedigree as a calling card that opens doors and gives him access to people with money and power. As our relationship began to take hold, I sensed that Derrick was frustrated with athletes who lacked the savvy to leverage their NFL status into a tangible job or other means of making money. "One of my college football buddies that has a much bigger name than me rang a couple of weeks ago and asked who he could call on to sponsor his entertainment business. I mean, shit! You're fuckin' Mr. NFL, godamnit, and you're calling me for help? People should be begging to receive your phone call." When Derrick contacted me about a fundraising campaign for the Walter Camp Football Foundation to provide scholarships for high school athletes, I offered to introduce him to a colleague who manages the high net worth division of a major Wall Street investment firm. When we arrived at my colleague's office I casually mentioned that Derrick earned a Super Bowl ring several years earlier. Derrick took my cue and declared that he and the firm's CEO were alumni of the same university. Soon, the CEO was on speakerphone, exchanging pleasantries with his fellow Notre Dame grad, encouraging Derrick to call him on his personal phone if he needed anything. As we exited the building, Derrick told me: "This is what it's all about. Coming out of high school, I could have gone to damn near any school in the country. I'm talking about *contacts*—shit, a degree from ND plus playing in the NFL? You can't beat that."

Even with a well-conceived retirement plan in place, Derrick experienced a turbulent exit from the NFL. Derrick's voice trailed off a little when he recalled being shuffled around four teams over the course of five seasons. He'd been traded once, then released by another team, but Derrick still attempted to extend his career by signing with a third and fourth team. That effort was thwarted when he failed a physical examination. Eventually, he filed a grievance with the NFL for disability benefits. Even with the support of his family and the guidance of a senior member of the NFL alumni association, Derrick Mayes, the highly touted second-round draft choice with a great education and a network to be envied, was still disappointed when a knee injury forced him out of the NFL.

GQ MAGAZINE COVER shots and ESPY (Excellence in Sports Performance Yearly) awards are evidence of how prominent sports figures can ascend to the upper stratum of American culture.[36] Yet the hidden costs of climbing the social ladder through professional sports often go unnoticed.[37] Multimillion dollar contracts and insider photos from exclusive parties only tell a small portion of the complex story of using sports as a vehicle to traverse social boundaries.

As former Miami Dolphin BK suggests, anytime an NFL athlete walks out his front door people who want something bombard him with requests. Athletes struggle with the financial confusion caused by earning big paychecks (or other people assuming the paychecks are bigger than they are) and how to cope with the uncertainty brought about from encounters with unscrupulous individuals: "When I started playing in the NFL, everything came at me so fast. Football wasn't the problem. I could always play the game. It was all the off-the-field stuff. The money, girls, fans, everybody wants a piece of you."

The narratives presented in this chapter recount various strategies used by athletes confronted with an involuntary exit from the NFL. Tyrone and Jamal represent individuals who experienced the disappointment of rejection and still find it inconceivable that they might not possess the physical attributes required of a star athlete in the NFL. Rather than preparing for an inevitable exit, both athletes sought refuge and reprieve (however temporary) in the CFL. The apparent lack of forethought toward cultivating transferable skills outside of football appears to be partially responsible for their desire to continue playing in NFL Europa and the CFL.

BK and Chester offer glimpses into the lives of athletes who express an overriding desire to hold onto a celebrity role that offers exceptional social and personal gratification rather than concede that time has come to let go and move on. Both athletes testify that the difficulty of adjusting to the mundane rituals of civilian life was compounded by their unwelcomed exit from professional football. Big Al's story is an example of a prolonged struggle to disengage from a role that continues to inform and shape his life, 25 plus years after retirement. And Derrick Mayes's story shows how carefully cultivated social support networks can play a prominent role in framing how an athlete understands and experiences his celebrity identity. Additionally, Derrick's narrative offers clues regarding how an athletic identity can be leveraged to harvest the cultural and social capital that elevates status even in retirement.

Each season, hundreds of young athletes enter the NFL driven by the overarching belief that their athletic ability and self-confidence will bring them the spoils of celebrity identity. They're rarely thinking about life *after* football; they've only just achieved their big break. For the athletes involved in this study, forced or unexpected retirement is a stressor and a threat to their social status and self-identity. Once time runs out on the scoreboard, it can take years for some athletes to heal from the physical and emotional experience of getting forced out.

═══ 12 ═══

PREPARING FOR, SURVIVING, AND THRIVING
BEYOND THE NFL

IN THE 1994 film *The Shawshank Redemption*, Brooks Hatlen is so unsettled by the prospect of being released after 50 years in prison that he threatens to kill another inmate.[1] We learn that prison—a total institution that takes decision making away from its inmates by regulating sleep, mealtimes, workouts, and other aspects of life, and enforcing its logic and rules through authority figures—has left the gentle and studious Brooks terrified of the outside world. Morgan Freeman's character reasons that inside prison, Brooks is an educated man and an important person; outside the walls, Brooks is just a used-up, old ex-con with arthritis in both hands. Of course, I am not suggesting that the NFL functions as a penitentiary (it would certainly be a gilded cage!), but the dialectic relationship between the institution and the athlete indicates that transitioning to life off the field is a similarly overwhelming, isolating, and imposed reentry process.

Years of social conditioning teach the NFL athlete how to relate to the world as a football player, first, last, and always. Football consumes nearly every aspect of his life from his first youth game through retirement. The pathway from high school through college football is particularly constrained for those who will earn a spot on an NFL roster. For 48 to 50 weeks each year, college athletes are housed in an institutional setting wherein coaches and administrators structure every moment. By the time an athlete enters the NFL, he has undergone an intense, prolonged boot camp designed to indoctrinate him into the cultural, social, and physical expectations of professional football. Given all this, it was no surprise that during my field research, I observed former athletes experiencing a sense of loss or emptiness upon realizing—if not accepting—that they no longer have the social prestige or the locker-room camaraderie of current NFL athletes. Worse, the role of "NFL player" is a defined one; society does not have a well-defined role for the former elite athlete. The retired player is on his own, without a playbook.

DR. HARRY EDWARDS, introduced in the preface, grew up in East St. Louis, Illinois. The Supreme Court's *Brown v. Board of Education* (1954) decision meant he was among the first African Americans integrated into his district's predominantly White schools. Edwards has spoken of the inappropriate ways in which Black students were guided to sports at the newly integrated institutions of higher learning. Instead of being held accountable academically, African American athletes were advanced to the next grade, year after year, without being educated. In college, Edwards was again a minority: a student-athlete on a predominantly White university campus. These experiences led Edwards to explore the relationships between race, sports, and society as both a sociologist and an activist.[2] A central focus of his work has been, he says, "the development of effective strategies for neutralizing racism in sport and the implementation of programmatically intelligent approaches to overcoming the tragically disproportionate influence of sport in the Black culture."[3]

In November 1968, Edwards organized the Olympic Project for Human Rights (OPHR) with four aims. First, to stage an international protest of the persistent and systematic violation of Black people's human rights in the United States; second, to expose America's historical exploitation of Black athletes as political propaganda tools on national and international stages; third, to establish a standard of political responsibility among Black athletes vis-à-vis the needs and interests of the Black community, devising effective ways that athletes address those demands; and fourth, to make the Black community aware of the "hidden" dynamics and consequences of their sports involvement.[4]

The fourth aim of the OPHR remains among Edwards's most resonant contributions.[5] Studies show that in comparison to their White counterparts, African American males are deliberately and intensively socialized into sports by family and the larger community, who, however unconsciously, limit their exposure to other hobbies and role models and push sports as a possible career path early in life.[6] Edwards expanded these ideas in a 1988 article for *Ebony* magazine, claiming that Black families have unwittingly become accessories to and major perpetrators of the tragedies of sports involvement for Black athletes by setting up their children for personal and cultural underdevelopment, academic victimization, and athletic exploitation in service to a cultural trope: that Black men are natural athletes (and, by extension, maybe not well inclined to much *else*).[7] This overemphasis on sports as a way out of poverty, as a quick route to social and cultural mobility, can lead to the creation of unidimensional athletes,[8] men with singular identities who are all but set up to fail when faced with an involuntary role exit. Getting cut would be tough for anyone, but after a lifetime pointed at a specific role, the removal of that role can leave former athletes suffering.

According to Edwards, the Black community also suffers when so many of its youth are under-educated and lacking in transferrable skills. Those African American males who stake everything on sports careers are choosing a professional path which, inevitably and immediately leaves out hundreds and thousands of hopefuls along the way. Where is the eagerness to train to become the doctors, the lawyers, the businessmen, the teachers, the nurses, and the bankers that healthy communities need? As early as 1978, Edwards was positive that sports and an overemphasis on sporting achievement for Blacks created an institutional minefield, shrouded by naiveté and ignorance, and "comes to approximate a racist nightmare more so than the dream come true it is proported to be."[9]

The social climate that framed the sports industry at the start of Edwards's career is very different from the hyper-capitalism-based market that drives the sports-industrial complex today. Size, speed, skill, and talent are but a sliver of what is needed to succeed in the sports tournament now. Junior and high school athletes with access to top-notch coaching and training facilities may be rewarded with greater exposure to gatekeepers such as rivals.com and other ranking websites. These resources are often secured through scholarships, social connections, or family support.

Rasheed and the other athletes at OD's Connecticut High School football camp brought to mind Edwards's analysis of African American athletes and studies around class inequality in sports.[10] These athletes taught me that race, social class, and masculinity operate on multiple levels in the world of football. A sport that privileges young African American men offers little benefit to that group when they lack access to the necessary coaching, equipment, or training facilitates to excel; rather than provide the promised ladder of social and class mobility, the advantage in the sport tournament has clearly shifted to athletes with access, privilege, or exposure. Due to the expansion of the sports-industrial complex, it has become prohibitively expensive for Black youth from poor or working class families and underserved communities to compete in sports other than football and basketball, further adding to their marginalization.[11]

Divergent experiences between Black and White youth in education and sports are also influenced by structural inequalities in school and neighborhood resources. Black students make up an ever-increasing proportion of urban public schools, particularly those schools with high levels of low-income families. Often, these youth attend schools with insufficient budgets, inadequate equipment and facilities,[12] limited access to and opportunity to participate in a variety of sport activities,[13] and inadequate and marginalized physical education programs.[14] White students are more likely to attend schools in suburban and rural areas and less likely to attend schools in high-poverty communities.[15] In short, most schools today are culturally, ethnically, economically, and racially segregated, and the education and development they are able to provide to their students are unequal, to say the least.[16]

On the professional level, enormous salaries and signing bonuses made possible by the development of 24–7 sports media, 1993 CBA provisions that link salaries to broadcast licensing fees, and the build-up of seemingly endless ancillary businesses that aid in the production of excellent athletes have all made the pot of money bigger and more all-encompassing. Given that the NFL still retains a lofty perch atop the sports-industrial complex, is it any wonder that certain groups of Americans find the promise of fame and fortune just as seductive today as ever?

Sport may have changed a great deal, but Edwards's warning of the "hidden" dynamics and consequences of an overemphasis on sports as a way out of poverty or to obtain increased social status seems to hold true. These dynamics will, at least as often as not, lead to tragic outcomes for the individuals and communities, and that is still very much worthy of investigation. In this book I have attempted to update and reinvestigate Edwards's observations, tracing the contours of a changed field of play as well as the sorts of raw power, greed, White domination, and economic (dis)advantage that still carry weighty consequences for athletes—perhaps, especially, the former ones.

IT CAN BE DONE . . .

Not every athlete is unprepared to deal with the business side of the NFL. In Chapter 11, we met former Green Bay Packers wide receiver Derrick Mayes, but he represents a handful of athletes I encountered who had developed a plan to capitalize on their NFL status. Like most Division I football players under the age of 40, Derrick did not work in college before signing his first NFL contract; unlike most, his father owned a small business (electronics), and, though Derrick spent far more time in locker rooms than boardrooms, each night at the dinner table he heard his mother and father talk about the challenges of running a small, minority-owned business in the Midwest. Derrick remembered learning that "you never get ahead in life working for a paycheck," and he told me, "My entrepreneurial spirit came from Dad." By the time Derrick set off for college, he had already formulated a plan for his career. You may recall that he chose his college carefully: "One of the main reasons I went to Notre Dame was because of the alumni connections. I knew playing there would give me connections to alumni all around the world. My plan was never to stay in the NFL for 10 years. I wanted to make a name for myself, make some money, then start working the alumni networks after I got out of the game." Derrick not only dreamed of finding himself in an NFL huddle; he dreamed of meeting potential investors.

Another advantage Derrick had was that his household emphasized education over athletics. His mother taught at a high school that produced numerous Division I NCAA football players while she was on the faculty. She saw firsthand how college recruiters could seduce naïve young African American athletes with promises of the NFL. After each season, her former student, Dolphins' wide receiver Mark Clayton, would visit Mrs. Mayes. Learning from his stories of triumphs and troubles, Derrick's mother was determined that her son would not have to rely on football to get a college education. Derrick laughed, "Anytime a recruiter started talking about playing in the NFL, my mom just shut the conversation down. Mom knew what was up from back when Clayton was being recruited. I basically didn't have a choice. She told me I was going to Notre Dame." Derrick also claims that before signing his scholarship, coach Lou Holtz arranged for him to speak with four Notre Dame football alumni about their work experiences after leaving the game. Derek said his family taught him to enjoy sports but also to use it for a bigger purpose: "I never wanted football to define me."

Another student-athlete's story stood out to me: Roland, who told us, in Chapter 4, about being humiliated along with his fellow players when they arrived late for class. He had another professor, the great African American poet and activist Nikki Giovanni, who, he recalled, "asked five students to describe their typical day on campus," then "requested that a football player stand up and describe his normal day." Roland detailed how Giovanni's gesture helped the athletes develop a sense of pride that they turned into motivation to work even harder in her class. Her approach validated him and his experience as an athlete on campus; he felt recognized and invigorated, not demeaned and judged.

Within a few weeks, my encounters with Derrick Mayes and with Roland drove home the need for educators, coaches, and athletic department staff members to encourage football players to ask questions, demand information, and think critically. All college students should be held accountable for their coursework. All college students should be allowed to pursue their preferred course of study rather than whatever an academic advisor suggests will make it easier to maintain academic eligibility. All college students should have a copy of their syllabus rather than surrender it to academic advisors the way Wes Brown did. All students should know why their presence is requested in an academic advising meeting. And while the institution is ultimately responsible for these sorts of individual experiences, I encourage all college athletes, parents, and guardians to begin asking questions, to take charge of their academic affairs. I encourage the athletes to pack their own gear bags, carry their own plane tickets, and seek out internships. As we have seen, the young men who meet an extra demand—adhering to the rules and strictures of a highly demanding sport while also balancing their daily lives, schedules, and education—are better prepared when it comes time to exit the totalizing institution.

Kyle Wilson has benefited a great deal from the support and solid business advice of his family. It is too soon to see if his carefully laid plans will come to fruition. But, as his brother Gerry Wilson Jr. said, it is imperative that NFL athletes recognize that they are in a symbiotic business relationship with the league. They need to see that *they* are the business. They need to invest in and take care of themselves and make smart decisions with regard to how they spend their time and money.

Either the restrictions that the NCAA holds over athletes regarding their financial well-being, their academic eligibility, and their time need to soften or the NFL needs to develop its own developmental league, divorced from the college farm system. Likewise, the NFL Players Association must find a way to eliminate their class-based system and create a fair and equitable means of distributing resources to every athlete who served his lengthy apprenticeship before brandishing the NFL shield. This is neither a tale of personal responsibility nor of a totalizing institution continuing its support and control from youth to old age. Instead, it's a caution that capitalism, in reducing individuals to expendable labor, can be brutal, even for some of the toughest men out there.

AFTER NEARLY SIX months of silence, OD called. He was under a lot of stress. In addition to the usual family issues, OD was once again fighting his former attorney over unpaid legal fees related to his disability benefits case. In the years since his retirement, OD has joined lawsuits against the NFL and NFL Films Inc. (Figure 12.1). for trademark infringement,[17] and he has added his name to a list of more than 4,800 named player-plaintiffs in the 242 concussion-related lawsuits filed against the NFL.[18] His bouts with depression and chronic pain led me to fear that my good friend might suffer from chronic traumatic encephalopathy (CTE).[19] CTE can only be diagnosed through an autopsy (a macabre explanation for why it seems former football players who commit suicide increasingly tend to do so in ways that will not prevent autopsies of their brains), and that is hopefully far in the future. But I worry about OD. As a former athlete and a sociologist, I feel it is my duty

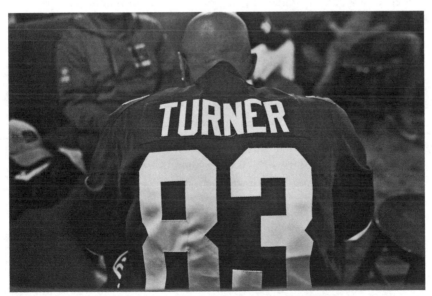

FIGURE 12.1: FORMER NEW YORK GIANT WIDE RECEIVER #83, ODESSA TURNER.

to conduct health disparity research that can identify factors that impact the long-term health and well-being of football players dealing with the lingering stress, chronic pain, and mild traumatic brain injury (mTBI) that come with the heady high of playing at the most elite level. It's the least I can do for the dozens of brave souls who have entrusted me with their life stories.

FINAL THOUGHTS

As I consider my friendship with OD, I find he has given me perspectives on my manhood, my Blackness, and my identity as a football athlete. If I had not played this game and pursued the stories of other professional athletes, I would never have experienced his friendship. Moreover, these years of field research have given me the opportunity to look into the eyes of dozens of professional football players and see that we share an unspoken bond. Nobody can take that away from us. We are honored to know each other, to understand some core experience of training, competing, winning, and brotherhood. We see each other in a way no one else really can. Of *course* we want to share experiences with the next generation (Figure 12.2).

This is my first reaction to the question others often ask me: Would I allow my child to play football? And a second broader question to football professionals as a whole, as framed by my graduate school mentor and personal friend Professor Bill Kornblum, is "How do NFL athletes feel about their children playing football? With all the problems NFL athletes experience during retirement, why would anyone want his child to play football?"[20] It has taken me years to formulate an answer to this question, and I'm still unsure that I can truly explain it, but I'll try: a former professional football player may desire his son to play football simply because he wants him to develop a personal relationship with the game, too.

No words can express what it feels like to line up on defense at the twenty yard line knowing my teammates are counting on me to make a big play. While 65,000 people are going nuts, inside my helmet is the quietest place in the stadium. I remind myself to breathe as the quarterback takes the snap. Is it a run or a pass? He fakes a hand-off, drops back, and looks my way as Vince Goldsmith, our defensive end busts through the line. The quarterback barely gets the pass off. It's a timing route. The receiver and I both dive for the pass. The ball skips off the turf just beyond our grasp. Time runs out as their offense

FIGURE 12.2: ROBERT "PACKY" TURNER AS A VOLUNTEER COACH FOR 4TH & 1 FOOTBALL CAMP.

turns the ball over on downs. Calgary Stampeders victory! I don't remember much else about that game, but that play still gives me chills. Probably because I got to fulfill my lifelong dream of playing with a team of superior athletes and men who believed in me.

As I've argued in this book, the game cannot currently be removed from the system. Edwards's work from the 1960s continues to this day and has become even more of an uphill battle. At this point, the sports-industrial complex may not be dismantled in the way that he would have desired. But the advantage I have (and have hoped to share with readers) is an understanding of this institution. If I had a son (or daughter) who brought home a permission slip, I could sign it, secure in knowing that he would have an opportunity to experience the camaraderie, discipline, and joy of the gridiron. And if he ends up on the receiving end of recognition from high school and college coaches, I can guide him in a way that many parents cannot or do not.

I possess the requisite resources to ensure that high school and college football coaches, the NCAA, university athletic programs, and unscrupulous sports agents or team doctors will not exploit my child for his athletic acumen. I can sleep easy at night knowing my child's fate would not rest in the hands of a football recruiter or coach who might promise the moon, then leave for a better job before the season even starts. Nor would I be concerned that an academic advisor could steer my child to take bogus classes or pursue a meaningless degree. In short, my child's academic future would not depend on football or any other sport for that matter. While injuries are part of the game, the threat of losing an athletic scholarship due to a concussion would not prevent my child from attending or completing college.

Injuries—particularly head injuries—are what lie behind the queries of whether I would let my son play. I take them seriously—seriously enough that my career is dedicated to investigating their relationship to football and its long-term impact on men's mental and physical health. OD is perhaps a perfect case study for those who want to argue that the game is too dangerous, especially for young children. I see things differently. From my perspective, that really isn't the question. Yes, some children and men most certainly are at risk of head trauma playing football.[21] But I prefer to focus on the longer-lasting outcomes of a game that offers tremendous opportunities for some, while simultaneously exploiting others. Football, much like society at large, is fraught with structural inequalities. I desire to focus my scholarship, time, and energy on understanding what can be done for those young athletes most vulnerable to the pitfalls of the totalizing institution of football. I look forward to the day NFL owners, the NFL Players Association, NCAA administrators, university officials, physicians, researchers, and parents join forces for a safer game. From my perspective, the most valuable resource we can give Cody, Rasheed, Juleonny, OD, and future generations of athletes is the support they need for a healthy, successful transition to life after football.

NOTES

PROLOGUE

1. R. O. Crockett, "Business: NFL Players Chief Shares Realities of Pro Football," *Roger Crockett: Business. Leadership. Diversity*, October 22, 2013, retrieved February 24, 2015, from http://rocrockett.com/2013/10/business-nfl-players-chief-shares-realities-of-pro-football/. Conversely, Commissioner Roger Goodell argues that statistics indicate athletes play an average of 6.1 seasons, and those players on a roster on the first day of the season average a total of almost 10 seasons in the league. NFL Communications, "What Is the Average NFL Player's Career Length? Longer Than You Might Think, Commissioner Goodell Says," *NFL Communications*, April 18, 2011, retrieved April 24, 2015, from https://nfllabor.wordpress.com/2011/04/18/what-is-average-nfl-player%E2%80%99s-career-length-longer-than-you-might-think-commissioner-goodell-says/.

PREFACE

1. W. C. Mills, *The Power Elite* (New York: Oxford University Press, 1999).
2. E. Goffman, "On the Characteristics of Total Institutions," in *Symposium on Preventive and Social Psychiatry*, pp. 43–84 (symposium sponsored jointly by the Walter Reed Army Institute of Research, Walter Reed Army Medical Center, and the National Research Council, April 15–17, 1957) (Washington, DC: US Government Printing Office, 1958).
3. J. N. Duru, "The Fritz Pollard Alliance, the Ronney Rule and the Quest to Level the Playing Field in the NFL," in *Race in American Sports Essays*, ed. James L. Conyers, pp. 204–233 (Raleigh, NC: McFarland, 2014). T. Moore, "Struggling with Diversity," *cnn.com*, February 2013, retrieved December 28, 2015, from http://www.cnn.com/2013/02/01/opinion/ozzie-newsome-nfl/.
4. Michael Lewis, *The Blind Side: Evolution of a Game* (New York: W. W. Norton, 2007).
5. T. M. Bourne, M. Smith, and E. Stoff, Producers, and J. L. Hancock, Director, *The Blind Side*, Warner Bros., 2009.
6. Oliver Stone, Director, *Any Given Sunday*, Warner Bros., 1999.
7. Adam "Pacman" Jones, a former first-round draft choice for the Tennessee Titans showered scantily clad dancers with money at a Las Vegas strip club. Just minutes

after "making it rain," Jones was involved in a fight inside the club. He was severely punished for his actions by new NFL commissioner Roger Goodell.

8. M. Foucault, *The Foucault Reader* (New York: Pantheon, 1984), pp. 83; M. Foucault, *The Archeology of Knowledge* (New York: Harper Torchbooks, 1972). (Original work published in French in 1969.); M. Foucault, *Discipline and Punish: The Birth of the Prison* (New York: Pantheon Books, 1977). (Original work published in French in 1975.); M. Foucault, *The History of Sexuality*: Vol. 1, *An Introduction* (New York: Pantheon Books, 1978a). (Original work published in French in 1976.); M. Foucault, *Pouvoir et Corps* [Power and body], in *Quel Corps?*, pp. 27–35 (Paris: Maspero, 1978b); M. Foucault, *The History of Sexuality*: Vol. 2, *The Use of Pleasure* (New York: Random House, 1985). (Original work published in French in 1984.); M. Foucault, *The History of Sexuality*: Vol. 3, *The Care of Self* (New York: Pantheon Books, 1986). (Original work published in French in 1984.); M. Foucault, "Technologies of the Self," in *Technologies of Self: A Seminar with Michel Foucault*, ed. L. H. Marin, H. Gutman, and P. H. Hutton, pp. 16–49 (Amherst: University of Massachusetts Press, 1988). Rail and Harvey point out that while Mauss first published the essay "Bodily Techniques" in 1954, Foucault is credited with placing the body at the forefront of the research agenda in the social science and humanities. G. Rail and J. Harvey, "Body at Work: Michel Foucault and the Sociology of Sport," *Sociology of Sport Journal* 12, no. 2 (June 1995): 164–179.

9. L. J. D. Wacquant, "Pugs at Work: Bodily Capital and Bodily Labor among Professional Boxers," *Body & Society* 1 (March 1995): 65.

10. J. Katz and T. J. Csordas, "Phenomenological Ethnography in Sociology and Anthropology," *Ethnography* 4 (September 2003): 275.

11. M. A. Messner, "White Men Misbehaving: Feminism, Afrocentrism, and the Promise of a Critical Standpoint," *Journal of Sport and Social Issues* 16, no. 2 (September 1992): 136–144. M. S. Kimmel, *The Gender of Desire: Essays on Male Sexuality* (Albany: State University of New York Press, 2012).

12. Kimmel and Messner also contributed significantly to the study of the gendered socialization of male athletes and male workers in male-dominant work settings. As settings go, there are few more male-dominant fields than American football. Further, as populations go, not many other endeavors reward masculinity and machismo more than the American football system does.

13. CBS Pittsburgh, "Dinkins: Players Are Seen as Commodities, Not People," *CBS Pittsburgh*, March 16, 2011, retrieved December 25, 2014, from http://pittsburgh.cbslocal.com/2011/03/16/dinkins-players-are-seen-as-commodities-not-people/.

14. Wacquant, "Pugs at Work."

15. Whenever possible, the quotes utilized throughout this manuscript are reported verbatim. However, several of the narratives contained here were edited for the sake of brevity and privacy. I assigned proper names as pseudonyms to protect the identity of the participants when requested.

16. H. Edwards, "Sport within the Veil: The Triumphs, Tragedies and Challenges of Afro-American Involvement," *Annals of the American Academy of Political and Social Science* 445, no. 1 (September 1979): 116–127, 116.

17. I will return to these themes in later chapters when I explain why the love of the game is about far more than an obsession with competition.

18. In C. Stack, *All Our Kin: Strategies for Survival in a Black Community* (New York: Harper & Row, 1976), Stack debunked the misconception that poor families were unstable and disorganized. In C. Stack, *Call to Home: African-Americans Reclaim the Rural South* (New York: Basic Books, 1996), Stack examines the return of a half million Black Americans to the rural South decades after the great northern migration (1916–1967).

CHAPTER 1

1. Crime rate in East St. Louis, IL: murders, rapes, robberies, assults, burglaries, thefts, auto thefts, arson, law enforcement employees, police officers, crime map. *City-Data .com*, 2015, retrieved January 10, 2015, from http://www.city-data.com/crime/crime-East-St.-Louis-Illinois.html.

2. United States Census Bureau, *QuickFacts: United States*, 2015, retrieved January 10, 2015, from http://quickfacts.census.gov/qfd/states/17/1722255.html.

3. The NFL athletes' struggles are presented in greater detail in Chapter 10.

4. The collective bargaining agreement (CBA) is the single most important document that impacts athletes during and after their careers. In addition to serving as the legal agreement that sets guidelines for player salaries and other forms of financial compensation, the CBA outlines who receives health, retirement, and disability benefits.

5. P. S. Torre, "How (and Why) Athletes Go Broke," *Sports Illustrated*, March 23, 2009, retrieved June 16, 2015, from http://www.si.com/vault/2009/03/23/105789480/how-and-why-athletes-go-broke.

6. K. Carlson, J. Kim, A. Lusardi, and C. F. Camerer, "Bankruptcy Rates among NFL Players with Short-lived Income Spikes" (working paper No. 21085, National Bureau of Economic Research, Cambridge, MA, 2015).

7. W. Nack and L. Munson, "The Wrecking Yard," *Sports Illustrated*, May 7, 2001, 19.

8. F. Litsky, "Giants Welcome a Needed Rest," *New York Times*, October 2, 1990, retrieved January 1, 2015, from http://www.nytimes.com/1990/10/02/sports/giants-welcome-a-needed-rest.html.

9. R. E. Bartok, "NFL Free Agency Restrictions under Antitrust Attack," *Duke Law Journal* 2 (April 1991): 503–559. Owners unilaterally imposed Plan B free agency for the 1989–1990 season, which allowed NFL teams to protect 37 players on a 45-man roster. The remaining unprotected players became completely unrestricted free agents without receiving compensation.

10. A former Heisman Trophy winner and others have made similar claims about the CFL versus the NFL. Google Groups, "CFL Is More Fun Than the NFL," 1995, retrieved January 2, 2015, from https://groups.google.com/forum/#!topic/rec.sport.football .pro/MCyMfphnhqM; A. Russell, "CFL Rules That Are Better Than the NFL's," 2014,

retrieved January 2, 2015, from http://www.thesidelinesports.com/cfl-rules-that-are-better-than-the-nfls/.

11. OD attended Northwestern State University from 1983 to 1986 and was drafted by the Giants as the 112th player selected in the fourth round of the 1987 NFL draft.

12. P. A. Janquart, "Lawyer Can't Take Fees From Retired NFL Players' Pensions, 11th Circuit Says," June 30, 2011, retrieved March 2, 2018, from https://www.courthousenews.com/lawyer-cant-take-fees-from-retirednfl-players-pensions-11th-circuit-says/.

13. Forbes.com reported the 2013 revenues for the NFL would be somewhere just north of $9 billion, but the commissioner intends to reach $25 billion in annual revenue by the year 2027. M. Burke, "How the National Football League Can Reach $25 Billion in Annual Revenues," *Forbes*, August 17, 2013. Maguire argues that the "sport-industrial complex" has structural, institutional, ideological, cultural, and social dimensions that include a number of key groups including state agencies, transnational corporations, nongovernmental agencies, and sport associations. J. Maguire, "Performance Efficiency or Human Development? Reconfiguring Sports Science," paper presented at the Idrett, Samfunn og Frivillig Organisering Conference, Oslo, 2002, pp. 3–4; J. Maguire, "Challenging the Sports-Industrial Complex: Human Sciences, Advocacy and Service," *European Physical Education Review* 10 (October 2004): 299–322.

14. DiMaggio and Powell describe an organized field as one of those organizations that in the aggregate constitute a recognized area of institutional life. According to the authors, the virtue of this unit of analysis is that it directs our attention to the totality of relevant actors. Thus, the field idea comprehends the importance of both connectedness and structural equivalence. P. J. DiMaggio and W. W. Powell, "The Iron Cage Revisited: Institutional Isomorphism and Collective Rationality in Organizational Fields," *American Sociological Review* 48 (April 1983): 147–160.

15. H. Edwards, "Dr. Harry Edwards, Sociology of Sports Origins," *Youtube*, July 20, 2009, retrieved July 2, 2015, from https://www.youtube.com/watch?v=1ipyAYsb5Bg.

CHAPTER 2

1. J. E. Rosenbaum, "Tournament Mobility: Career Patterns in a Corporation," *Administrative Science Quarterly* 24, no. 2 (June 1979): 220–241.

2. J. E. Rosenbaum, "Tournament Mobility."

3. Pop Warner Little Scholars Inc. is a nonprofit organization that provides youth football, cheer, and dance programs for participants in 42 states and several countries around the world. The organization consists of approximately 425,000 young people ranging in age from 5 to 12. Pop Warner is the largest youth football, cheer, and dance program in the world.

4. "Estimated Probability of Competing in Athletics beyond the High School Interscholastic Level," National Collegiate Athletic Association, Indianapolis, IN, 2018, retrieved from http://www.ncaa.org/about/resources/research/probability-competing-beyond-high-school.

5. According to the USDA, active means a lifestyle that includes physical activity equivalent to walking more than three miles per day at three to four miles per hour, in addition to the light physical activity associated with typical day-to-day life.

6. Research suggests that former college football players are more likely than the general population to have problems with obesity later in life. With this risk factor, they appear to be at greater risk of developing obesity-related diseases such as hyperlipidemia, obstructive sleep apnea, and possibly hypertension. J. D. Higgs, "Obesity and Obesity Related Diseases in Former Collegiate Football Players," *Medicine & Science in Sports & Exercise* 40, no. 5 (2008): 533.

7. In February 2008, espn.com reported that a high school athlete called a press conference and falsely announced his decision to accept a football scholarship to the University of California at Berkeley. Cal head coach Jeff Tedford stated that he had never even heard of the young man. Tedford further commented to the Associated Press, "I've talked to other coaches who have had people saying they've committed to their programs who they're not even recruiting, and it just seems like this thing is getting so big and egos are getting so involved . . . people want to have an identity or whatever. To get to that magnitude that I read about is really kind of unfortunate." G. Wojciechowski, "College 'Recruit's,' Lie a Tale Gone Horribly Wrong," *ESPN*, February 9, 2008, retrieved February 25, 2008, from http://sports.espn.go.com/espn/columns/story?columnist=wojciechowski_gene&id=3236039.

8. Tom Brady, starting quarterback for the New England Patriots, has won five Super Bowl championships and was selected as the Super Bowl Most Valuable Player (MVP) on four separate occasions. Cam Newton won the Heisman Trophy in December 2010. He was the first player selected in the 2011 NFL draft by the Carolina Panthers.

9. Mayo Clinic, "Performance-Enhancing Drugs and Teen Athletes," March 11, 2015, retrieved March 2, 2018, from http://www.mayoclinic.org/healthy-lifestyle/tween-and-teen-health/in-depth/performance-enhancing-drugs/art-20046620.

10. B. Cook, "Does Pro PED Use Put Pressure on Young Athletes to Do the Same? Surveys Say Yes," July 30, 2013, retrieved March 2, 2018, from https://www.forbes.com/sites/bobcook/2013/07/30/does-pro-ped-use-put-pressure-on-young-athletes-to-do-the-same-surveys-say-yes/.

11. J. Whyte, "Are Student Athletes Taking Steroids?" Blog, April 20, 2011, retrieved from https://www.huffingtonpost.com/john-whyte-md-mph/student-athletes-steroids_b_850952.html.

12. Mayoclinic.com; Centers for Disease Control (CDC.gov); www.dosomething.org, "11 Facts about Steroids."

13. M. Baker, "Growing Problem: High School Linemen Have Grown Massively over the Last 40 Years, a Trend Health Experts Worry Will Have Serious Consequences," *Tulsa World*, September 27, 2007.

14. C. L. Ogden, C. D. Fryar, M. D. Carroll, and K. M. Flegal, "Mean Body Weight, Height, and Body Mass Index, United States 1960–2002," Advanced Data from Vital and Health Statistics No. 347 (Atlanta, GA: National Center for Health Statistics, Centers for Disease Control and Prevention, 2004). According to the Centers for

Disease Control and Prevention, the average 17-year-old boy increased in weight by 11%, growing from 150 pounds in 1966 to 166 pounds in 2002.

15. Farrell is a recruiting analyst for rivals.com, which claims to be the number one authority on college football and basketball recruiting.

16. Information provided by the rivals.com prospect database, https://n.rivals.com/news/rivals-com-football-team-recruiting-rankings-formula.

17. A detailed report on Oliver's athletic potential can be found at maxpreps.com, Rutgers.scout.com, or rivals.com, https://www.rivals.com/barrier_noentry.asp?sid= 1014&script=%2Fcontent%2Easp&cid=818807.

18. OD is one of the professional athletes hired to teach position skills at the TEST Sports Football Academy. He was charged with the one-on-one wide receiver versus defensive back drills designed to test an individual's skill level.

19. Alfred Lord Tennyson penned "The Charge of the Light Brigade" in 1854 to memorialize the British troops' suicide charge in the Battle of Balaclava (Ukraine) on October 25, 1854, in the Crimean War. An English-language newspaper, *The Examiner*, published the poem on December 9, 1854.

20. The biggest complaint logged by dozens of high school athletes and parents who participated in this research was directed toward their high school coaches. Many athletes expressed frustration with their coach's lack of experience or inability to guide them through the college recruiting process.

21. T. O'Toole, "For College Coaches, It's Substance over Style," *USA Today*, February 6, 2006, retrieved March 15, 2008, from http://www.usatoday.com/sports/preps/football/2006-02-06-recruits_x.htm.

22. O'Toole, "For College Coaches."

23. C. McNally, "Marketing Kiehl Frazier," *Public Broadcast Service: Frontline*, March 2011, retrieved January 24, 2015, from http://www.pbs.org/wgbh/pages/frontline/2011/03/marketing-kiehl-frazier.html.

24. ESPN, "CBS Announces National Signing Day Coverage," January 25, 2012, retrieved from https://forum.huskermax.com/vbbst/index.php?threads/espn-cbs-announce-national-signing-day-coverage-peat-to-announce-on-espnu-3.29112/.

25. In October 2013, the Division I Board of Directors adopted five new recruiting rules including those that prohibited school staff members from attending an all-star game or activities associated with those games and established a dead period when in-person recruiting can take place. M. B. Hosick, "Division I Adopts Football Recruiting Summer Access Rules," *National Collegiate Athletic Association*, October 30, 2013, retrieved January 25, 2015, from http://www.ncaa.com/news/football/article/2013-10-30/division-i-adopts-football-recruiting-summer-access-rules.

26. M. Sherman, "Football's Future Is Heating Up: Prospects Like Jabrill Peppers Are under More Scrutiny Than Ever Before," *ESPN*, June 19, 2013, retrieved January 25, 2015, from http://espn.go.com/college-sports/recruiting/football/story/_/id/9393522/college-football-recruiting-espn-300-prospects-feel-pressure.

27. Since the events surrounding the Jerry Sandusky scandal, Penn State had five football coaches, either full-time or interim between 2011 and 2014: Joe Paterno, Tom Bradley, Bill O'Brien, Larry Johnson, and James Franklin. B. Difilippo, "Penn State

Students Adjust to Series of Coaching Changes," *Centre Daily Times*, January 23, 2014, retrieved January 25, 2015, from http://www.centredaily.com/2014/01/23/3999628/penn-state-students-adjust-to.html.

28. T. Fornelli, "The Friday Five: College Football Coaches on the Hot Seat in 2015," *cbssports.com*, January 23, 2015, retrieved January 24, 2015, from http://www.cbssports.com/collegefootball/eye-on-college-football/24986149/the-friday-five-top-coaches-on-the-hot-seat-in-2015.

29. The APR is a Division I metric developed to track the academic progress of teams during each semester and is based on academic eligibility of the players. K. Bradley, "N. C. State Fires Football Coach Tom O'Brien; Vanderbilt's James Franklin Likely Target," *Sporting News*, November 25, 2012, retrieved from http://www.sportingnews.com/ncaa-football/news/4347642-tom-obrien-fired-nc-state-wolfpack-coach-search-james-franklin-vanderbilt. A similar situation occurred at the University of Nebraska when Bo Pelini became the first coach in the history of a Power 5 program to be fired for on-field performance after winning 67 games versus 27 losses in his first seven seasons. M. Sherman, "Nebraska Fires Coach Bo Pelini," *ESPN*, December 2, 2014, retrieved January 26, 2015, from http://espn.go.com/college-football/story/_/id/11958376/nebraska-cornhuskers-fire-bo-pelini.

30. Head coach Lou Saban has been accused of promising that recruit Landon Collins would one day earn a multimillion dollar NFL contract if he decided to play for the University of Alabama Crimson Tide. C. Schultz, "One Mother of a Recruiting Battle," *The Mag*, January 27, 2012, retrieved March 2, 2018, from http://www.espn.com/college-football/story/_/id/7492921.

31. D. Ivers, "Newark Had Nation's Third Highest Murder Rate in 2013, FBI Says,"*nj.com*, November 17, 2014, retrieved from http://www.nj.com/essex/index.ssf/2014/11/newark_had_nations_third_highest_murder_rate_in_2013_fbi_says.html. With a murder rate of 40 per 100,000 people, Newark is the third deadliest large US city after Detroit and New Orleans. H. Havrilesky, "People Compare the Social Conditions in Newark to What Is Depicted on the HBO Series *The Wire*—But True," *Salon*, September 20, 2009, retrieved from https://www.salon.com/2009/09/20/brick_city/.

32. In 1984, Fryar became the first wide receiver ever to be drafted as the top overall pick by the NFL. That same year, Kenny Jackson was the number four overall pick in the first round, and Jonathan Williams was the seventieth selection in the third round.

33. M. McCarthy, "Fans Tell the Story in NFL's New Campaign and Contest: Free Super Bowl Tickets Will Go to Community Group as Large as 62," *Adweek.com*, August 1, 2014.

34. A. Crupi, "NFL Kicks Off 'Together We Make Football' Campaign: Fan Contest Launches in Tonight's Thursday Night Football Tilt," 2013, retrieved July 1, 2015, from http://www.adweek.com.ezproxy.gc.cuny.edu/news/advertising-branding/nfl-kicks-together-we-make-football-campaign-152541.

CHAPTER 3

1. United States Census Bureau, *State and County Quickfacts* (Monroe City, Louisiana Quicklinks) (Washington, DC: US Department of Commerce, 2010). According to recent survey data, some 96.7% of the 652 students at the high school OD attended 30 years before

identify as African American. Statewide data indicate that a typical school in Monroe has 26.6% African American students; thus OD's high school has a drastically different ethnic distribution compared to other schools in the city and in the state (44.9%). In addition, recent census data indicate the median household income in Monroe City is $29,158 and approximately 90% of the students who attend the same high school that OD did are eligible for free and reduced-price lunch, which reflects the situation OD encountered when growing up there. Needless to say, OD hailed from humble beginnings.

2. DatabaseSports.com, "NFL players born in Louisiana," 2011, retrieved September 14, 2016, from http://www.databasefootball.com/players/player_bystate.htm?state=LA. The town of Monroe has produced its share of NFL talent. Some 45 athletes—including White and Smith—from the Monroe area have played in the NFL, an impressive number for a town of only 49,421 residents.

3. ESPN.com, Press releases: "Looking Back, Back, Back . . . ," *ESPN*, September 6, 1999, retrieved January 15, 2015, from https://espn.go.com/espninc/pressreleases/chronology .html.

4. ESPN Media Zone, "ESPN, INC. FACT Sheet," 2015, retrieved January 15, 2015, from http://espnmediazone.com/us/espn-inc-fact-sheet/.

5. ESPN Media Zone, "ESPN, INC.: 1998 in Review," January 2, 1999, retrieved January 15, 2015, from http://espnmediazone.com/us/press-releases/1999/01/espn-inc-1998-in-review/.

6. C. Patterson, "2017 National Signing Day Announcement Times, Schedule. TV channel, live stream, February 1, 2017, retrieved March 2, 2018, from https://www .cbssports.com/college-football/news/2017-national-signing-day-announcement-times-schedule-tv-channel-live-stream/.

7. The National Football League comprises 32 teams equally divided into two conferences, the National Football Conference (NFC), and the American Football Conference (AFC).

8. James R. Walker references sociologist P. Hoch, *Rip Off the Big Game: The Exploitation of Sports by the Power Elite* (New York: Anchor Doubleday, 1972), to support his argument that fandom is redirected by hyper-commercialized media sports coverage to service the consumer consumption that drives the US economy. J. R. Walker, Foreword, in *Sports Fans, Identity, and Socialization: Exploring the Fandemonium*, ed. A. C. Earnheardt, P. M. Haridakis, and B. S. Hugenberg, pp. i–x (Lanham, MD: Lexington Books, 2012); Hoch, *Rip Off the Big Game*; Earnheardt, Haridakis, and Hugenberg, *Sports Fans, Identity, and Socialization*.

9. J. Vrooman, "The Economic Structure of the NFL," in *The Economics of the National Football League*, pp. 7–31 (New York: Springer, 2012).

10. Use of the term *social timetables* is based on Neugarten's investigation of the meanings of age in the 1950s and early 1960s. A. L. C. Journey, "Studying Lives in Changing Times," *The Developmental Science of Adolescence: History Through Autobiography* (Psychology Press, 2013), 134. B. L. Neugarten, *The Meanings of Age: Selected Papers* (Chicago: University of Chicago Press, 1996).

11. After decertifying the NFLPA and earning a legal victory in the 1992 McNeil case, the players recertified the NFLPA and successfully bargained with the NFL Management Council (NFLMC) for free agency in 1993.

12. P. Yasinskas, "Combine Star Mamula Was Burdened by High Expectations," *ESPN*, February 19, 2008, retrieved January 18, 2015, from http://sports.espn.go.com/nfl/draft08/columns/story?id=3252718.

13. P. Thamel, "Pro Football: Finishing Schools Helping Prospects for N.F.L. Draft," *ESPN*, 2004, retrieved January 18, 2015, from http://sports.espn.go.com/nfl/draft08/columns/story?id=3252718.

14. "Sports Performance Training," *Cris Carter's Fast Program*, 2008, retrieved January 18, 2015, from http://www.myspeedtrainer.com/fp/.

15. D. Picker, "N.F.L. Prospects Head to Boot Camp," *NYTimes*, February 8, 2007, retrieved January 19, 2015, from http://www.nytimes.com/2007/02/08/sports/ncaafootball/08speed.html?pagewanted=all.

16. An example of education and sports values can be found on the Virginia Tech Athletic Department Mission Statement at http://www.athletics.vt.edu/mission.html.

17. B. McGrath, "The Jersey Game: Will High-School Football Become a Big-Money Sport?," *The New Yorker*, January 2, 2012, retrieved January 20, 2015, from http://www.newyorker.com/magazine/2012/01/02/the-jersey-game.

18. WAMU, "The Big Business of Youth Sports," *On Point*, August 31, 2017, retrieved from https://wamu.org/story/17/08/31/the-big-business-of-youth-sports/.

19. P. DiMaggio, "Classification in Art," *American Sociological Review* 52, no. 4 (August 1987): 440–455; B. H. Erickson, "Culture, Class, and Connections," *American Journal of Sociology* 102, no. 1 (July 1996): 217–251.

20. R. A. Peterson and R. M. Kern, "Changing Highbrow Taste: From Snob to Omnivore," *American Sociological Review* 61, no. 5 (October 1996): 900–907.

21. IMG Academy, "IMG Academy Is the World-Leading Provider of Integrated Academic, Athletic and Personal Development Training Programs for Youth, Adult, Collegiate and Professional Athletes," 2015, retrieved January 20, 2015, from http://www.imgacademy.com/.

22. S. Wieberg, M. Hiestand, T. O'Toole, and E. Smith, "Texas' Longhorn Network Raising Some Concerns around Big 12," *USA Today*, July 21, 2011, retrieved January 15, 2015, from http://usatoday30.usatoday.com/sports/college/football/big12/2011-07-20-texas-longhorn-network_n.htm.

23. Bishop Dullaghan Football Camps, "Home: Bishop Dullaghan Football Camps," 2008, retrieved January 20, 2015, from http://www.bishopdullaghan.com/.

24. *Bid* is slang for a prison sentence.

25. K. K. Beamon, "Are Sports Overemphasized in the Socialization Process of African American Males? A Qualitative Analysis of Former Collegiate Athletes' Perception of Sport Socialization," *Journal of Black Studies* 41, no. 2 (November 2010): 281–300.

CHAPTER 4

1. NCAA documents show that institutions under investigation frequently have good policies and procedures but fail to monitor the program sufficiently, http://www.wralsportsfan.com/unc/story/8442723.

2. G. Klein, "NCAA Hands USC Two-year Bowl Game Ban, Major Scholarship Reduction in Football," *Los Angeles Times*, June 9, 2010, retrieved January 7, 2015, from http://articles.latimes.com/2010/jun/09/sports/la-sp-usc-20100610.

3. According to the *Milwaukee Journal Sentinel*, the average per-player operating expense for each of the 12 teams in the Big 10 is $35,673, based on statistics released under the Department of Education's Equity in Athletics law, http://www.crainscleveland.com/article/20111121/BLOGS04/111129980 & http://ht.ly/7AayI.

4. J. New, "A Competitive Disadvantage," *Inside Higher Ed*, November 19, 2014. The NCAA sets minimum admission eligibility standards but allows individual schools to establish special admission practices for athletes who do not meet normal or standard entrance requirements.

5. A. Scher Zagier, "College Admissions Exemptions Benefit Athletes," *The State*, December 31, 2009, retrieved March 6, 2013, from http://www.thestate.com/sports/article14369456.html.

6. S. Wieberg, "Athlete Advisors Fear New NCAA Eligibility Rules Spur Cheating," *USA Today*, July 9, 2009, retrieved March 4, 2013, from http://usatoday30.usatoday.com/sports/college/2009-07-08-athlete-advisers_N.htm.

7. P. Thamel, "Athletes Get New College Pitch: Check Out Our Tutoring Center," *NYTimes*, November 4, 2006, retrieved May 25, 2013, from http://www.nytimes.com/2006/11/04/sports/ncaafootball/04ncaa.html?pagewanted=all&_r=1&.

8. Mary Willingham and Jay Smith co-authored *Cheated* (Lincoln: University of Nebraska Press, 2015).

9. P. Thamel, "Athletes Get New College Pitch"; J. Barker, "Univ. of Maryland Plans $155 Million Athletic Complex That Combines the Old and the New," *Baltimore Sun*, November 17, 2014, retrieved February 14, 2015, from http://www.baltimoresun.com/business/bs-bz-terps-athletic-complex-20141117-story.html.

10. Northwestern State Official Athletic Website, "Graduate 'N' Club Hall of Fame," 2010, retrieved December 28, 2014, from http://www.nsudemons.com/hof.aspx?hof=192&path=&kiosk.

11. QB often serves as an acronym for Quarterbacks.

12. Journal Publishing, "Safety Measures: Hogs' Hewitt Lives Dream of Playing at Division I [Library], October 1, 2007, retrieved March 1, 2018, from https://www.thefreelibrary.com/Safety+measures%3A+Hogs%27+Hewitt+lives+dream+of+playing+at+division+I-a0169960289.

13. K. A. Davidson, "Why Don't Colleges Care about Athletes' Grades?," *Bloomberg View*, August 22, 2014, retrieved February 14, 2015, from http://www.bloombergview.com/articles/2014-08-21/why-don-t-colleges-care-about-athletes-grades.

14. Davis publicly acknowledges making the statement attributed to him but claims his former players did not fully understand the point he was making. A second player, former University of North Carolina defensive tackle Tedreke Powell, made a similar claim on a Greensboro, NC, radio station. *Time* magazine posted Davis's response to the allegation online: "I said that, OK, in the context that I made that statement one time, and it was a poorly phrased context, but I said it half comical and half in the form of 'stop complaining,'" Davis says. "Your days are long. It's a long, hard day.

You've got to practice, you've got to study, you've got to go to class, you've got to take notes, you've got to do extra work. If you wanted to just get an education period, and you didn't want to play in a high profile football program, and you didn't want to chance to go to the NFL, you should have gone to Harvard. It was totally kind of halfway joking and halfway whimsical, comical, and halfway saying 'hey guys, I hear you. I know being a student-athlete in a Division I major college program in any sport is harder than just being a student.' If you just wanted to be a student, you should have gone to Harvard, you know?" S. Gregory, "Is a Bad College Education Illegal for the NCAA? Former North Carolina Football Player Michael Mcadoo Is Suing the School over Sham Classes. Does the Case Have a Shot?," *Time*, November 12, 2014, retrieved February 16, 2015, from http://time.com/3578603/unc-academic-fraud-mcadoo-lawsuit/.

15. According to the NCAA, the APR is a Division I metric developed to track the academic achievement of teams during each semester. Each athlete receiving financial aid earns one retention point for staying in school and one point for being academically eligible. A team's total points are divided by points possible then multiplied by 1,000 to equal the team's Academic Progress Rate. In addition to a team's current-year APR, its rolling four-year APR is also used to determine accountability. NCAA, "Academic Progress Rate Explained," 2015, retrieved March 1, 2018, from http://www.ncaa.org/aboutresources/research/academic-progress-rate-explained.

16. Bryant was drafted in the fourth round of the 1999 NFL draft by the Detroit Lions.

CHAPTER 5

1. In his ethnographic inquiry into the social structuring of bodily capital and bodily labor through boxing, L. Wacquant, *Body & Soul: Notebooks of an Apprentice Boxer* (New York: Oxford University Press, 2004), 315–319 applies Bourdieu's dispositional theory of action to establish the concept of a *pugilistic habitus* as a means of understanding the initiation into a practice of which the body is at once the seat, the instrument, and the target (Wacquant, *Body & Soul*, p. 16). To acquire the practical ability embodied in the skillful behavior of a pugilist, Wacquant spent three years training at a west side area boxing gym: he served as a corner man, fought in a regional Golden Gloves tournament, and lived among poor African Americans in a south Chicago neighborhood.

M. Desmond, *On the Fireline: Living and Dying with Wildland Firefighters* (Chicago: University of Chicago Press, 2007) followed a similar path of investigation to reconstruct the practical logic of firefighting. Desmond focused on the distinction between a general and specific *habitus*; the former is recognized as a system of dispositions and a way of thinking about and acting in the world that is constituted early in life, while the latter is acquired later in life through education, training, and discipline within particular organizations. He suggests that for most crew members, class-inflected masculine dispositions were formed during their upbringing in rural America. Desmond then argues that this general country masculine habitus guides how these firefighters understand the world around them while influencing how they codify sameness and differences and how the forest service crafts and amplifies this quality into a specific firefighting habitus that makes workers deployable.

2. E. Goffman, Asylums: Essays on the Social Situation of Mental Patients and Other Inmates (New York: Anchor Books, 1961); E. Goffman, "On the Characteristics of Total Institutions: Staff-Inmate Relations," in *The Prison: Studies in Institutional Organization and Change*, ed. R. D. Cressey (New York: Holt, Rinehart and Winston, 1961).

3. Goffman, *Asylums*.

4. In his seminal collection of essays, *Asylums*, Erving Goffman suggests that "every institution captures something of the time and interests of its members, or has encompassing tendencies" (p. 4). In considering different institutions of Western society, Goffman noted, "Some are encompassing to a degree discontinuously greater than the ones next in line" (p. 2).

5. "The National Collegiate Athletic Association," in *Division I Manual: October 2014–15*, ed. NCAA Academic Membership Affairs Staff (Indianapolis, IN: NCAA, 2014).

6. In this chapter, I will focus on Division I players because they are the ones most likely to be recruited by the NFL. Making it onto a Division I football program's roster is the first big hurdle in a player's pursuit of a professional football career.

7. Bill Walsh, "How to Indoctrinate New Players into Your Program," August, 2007, retrieved from http://www.gridironstrategies.com/articles01.php?id=17. This article has been shared extensively in coaching circles over the years since it was written. The principal at Gridiron Strategies: X's & O's Newsletter offers Walsh's memorandum to online subscribers of the newsletter.

8. At the time, Coach Tom Osborne received heavy criticism for not kicking Phillips off the team permanently. W. McDuffy, "The Mysterious Case of Nebraska's Lawrence Phillips," *Bleacher Report*, October 2, 2010, retrieved February 20, 2018, from https://bleacherreport.com/articles/480074-mysterious-case-of-lawrence-phillips.

9. C. Gaines, "College Football Reaches Record $3.4 Billion in Revenue," *Business Insider*, December 17, 2014, retrieved October 10, 2015, from http://www.businessinsider.com/college-football-revenue-2014-12.

10. C. Isidore, "College Football's Profit Tops $1 Billion for First Time," *CNN Money*, December 29, 2010, retrieved March 2, 2018, from http://money.cnn.com/2010/12/29/news/companies/college_football_dollars/index.htm.

11. According to *USA Today*, the average annual salary for head coaches at major colleges (not including four schools that moved up to the FBS in 2012) is $1.64 million, an increase of nearly 12% from the 2011 season. E. Brady, S. Berkowtiz, and J. Upton, "College Football Coaches Continue to See Salary Explosion," *USA Today*, November 19, 2012, retrieved March 2, 2018, from https://www.usatoday.com/story/sports/ncaaf/2012/11/19/college-football-coaches-contracts-analysis-pay-increase/1715435/.

12. P. Myerberg, "The Quad Countdown: No. 54 Arkansas," *The New York Times College Sports Blog*, July 6, 2008, retrieved March 10, 2015, from http://thequad.blogs.nytimes.com/2008/07/06/the-quad-countdown-no-54-arkansas/?_r=0.

13. NFL scouts often use an athlete's 40-yard dash time to determine his football speed.

14. A. P. Education Writer, "Not a Game, a Job: NCAA Athletes Work Long Hours," *Sporting News*, September 3, 2009, retrieved March 2, 2018, from http://www.sportingnews .com/ncaa-football/news/114880-not-game-job-ncaa-athletes-work-long-hours.

15. This latter category, which Goffman (*Asylum*, p. 1) refers to as total institutions, is distinguished from the first group in that "their encompassing or total character is symbolized by the barrier to social intercourse with the outside world."

16. Nick Jones, program coordinator for return objectives and class checking at the University of Georgia, claims that every Division I university has some type of class checking, and in some cases graduate assistants, student workers, and counselors are employed to check classes. D. Clark, "Class Checkers Combat Athlete Truancy," *The Red&Black*, November 18, 2011, retrieved February 16, 2015, from http://www .redandblack.com/news/class-checkers-combat-athlete-truancy/article_045e7e6f-9c6b-56da-8103-460d5186bd14.html.

17. A report by the *Chronicle of Higher Education* revealed that one year after the NCAA adopted a policy to allow schools to offer multiyear financial aid to athletes in 2012, only six schools in the six major conferences signed at least 24 multiyear scholarships across all sports. The report claims that programs tend to prefer single-year scholarships with the option to renew annually.

18. A *Los Angeles Times* article reported that Andrew Baumgartner, a walk-on wide receiver, tried out for the UCLA football team and played well enough to earn a scholarship. After catching touchdown passes in victories over the University of Oklahoma and the University of Washington, the next season Baumgartner received a letter from the Bruins football team that his scholarship would not be renewed. According to the *LA Times* article, the UCLA football program did not renew the scholarship for Baumgartner's senior year because that money was needed for top freshman recruits and it could not be wasted on a senior who wasn't as talented. B. Plascheke, "He's No Walk-Off," *Los Angeles Times*, August 13, 2006, retrieved January 7, 2015, from http:// articles.latimes.com/2006/aug/13/sports/sp-plaschke13/2.

19. The NCAA does not officially recognize the practice of grey-shirting. Grey-shirted players either do not attend school in the fall or enroll part-time and pay their own tuition. The school may honor its original commitment and offer the player a scholarship the following semester, but the school is under no obligation to do so. L. Thiry, "College Football Recruiting 101," January 28, 2015, retrieved from http:// www.latimes.com/sports/usc/uscnow/la-sp-usc-football-recruiting-101-20150128-story.html.

20. For a full account of the NCAA Division I 20/8 rules, see the Duquesne University coaches' guide to compliance, http://www.goduquesne.com/m/compliance/duqu-school-bio-compliance-coaches.html or the Purdue University Athletic Compliance website http://www.purdue.edu/athletics/compliance/pages/current_students/ Attachment_A.pdf.

21. B. Wolverton, "Athletes' Hours Renew Debate over College Sports," *Chronicle of Higher Education* 54, no. 20 (January 2008): A1.

22. A similar phenomenon may occur when well-intentioned parents hover over their kids without allowing them to experience the pain associated with maturation.

T. Elmore, "Tollbooth or Roadblock? Why Generation iY Kids Are Getting Stuck in Adolescence," in *Generation iY: Our Last Chance to Save Their Future*, ch. 4, pp. 53–72 (Atlanta, GA: Poet Gardner Publishing, 2010).

23. Sociologist Annette Lareau is credited with creating the term "concerted cultivation," which is a type of childrearing practice of middle-class parents. The main advantage of this form of childrearing is that parents teach children life lessons through organized activities that help prepare them for white-collar jobs and the types of interactions that white-collar workers encounter. Forcing athletes to submit course syllabi to academic advisors and scheduling meetings without offering details about the purpose of the meetings is in direct opposition to the concept of concerted cultivation. A. Lareau, *Unequal Childhoods: Class, Race, and Family Life* (Oakland: University of California Press, 2003).

24. A similar phenomenon may occur when well-intentioned parents hover over their kids without allowing them to experience the pain associated with maturation (Elmore, "Tollbooth or Roadblock?").

25. NCAA Research Staff, "NCAA Research Trend in Graduation Success Rates and Federal Graduation Rates at NCAA Division I Institutions," *National Collegiate Athletic Association*, 2011, retrieved October 4, 2014, from http://www.ncaa.org.

26. P. M. Barrett, "UNC Fake Classes Scandal: Key Administrator Agrees to Tell ALL," March 6, 2014, retrieved February 16, 2015, from http://www.bloomberg .com/bw/articles/2014-03-05/unc-tar-heels-fake-classes-scandal-administrator-will-tell-all#r=most; D. Dodd. "UNC Whistleblower Willingham: Academic Sins Not Isolated," *cbssports.com*, February 11, 2014, retrieved February 16, 2015, from http://www.cbssports.com/collegefootball/writer/dennis-dodd/24439378/ unc-whistleblower-willingham-academic-sins-not-isolated.

27. M. Burns, "Willingham: Never Wanted to Be UNC Whistleblower," *wral.com*, December 3, 2014, retrieved February 16, 2015, from http://www.wral.com/ willingham-never-wanted-to-be-unc-whistleblower/14242192/.

28. Taylor Branch, "The Shame of College Sports," *Atlantic*, October, 2011.

29. Joe Nocera, "Let's Start Paying College Athletes," *New York Times*, January 1, 2012, retrieved from http://www.nytimes.com/2012/01/01/magazine/lets-start-paying-college-athletes.html?pagewanted=all&_r=0.

30. Information obtained from the NCAA rules compliance website, http://www.ncaa .org/wps/wcm/connect/public/NCAA/Eligibility/Remaining+Eligible/.

31. NFL Eligibility Rules, https://www.nflregionalcombines.com/Docs/Eligibility rules.pdf. According to a 2004 lawsuit filed by Maurice Clarett, the NFL Management Committee and the NFLPA negotiated a collective bargaining agreement (CBA), which comprises 292 pages, 61 articles, appendices from A through N, and 357 sections but does not contain "the Rule." The lawsuit claimed that "the Rule" is not the product of a bona fide arms-length negotiation between the NFL and the NFLPA. Federal Judge Shira Scheindlin initially ruled that the NFL could not bar Clarett from participating in the 2004 draft. This decision was overturned by the United States Court of Appeals for the Second Circuit, and then denied by the Supreme Court on appeal. M. Scheinkman, "Running Out of Bounds: Overextending the Labor

Antitrust Exemption in *Clarett v. National Football League,*" *St. John's Law Review* 79, no. 3 (2012): 1–35.

32. Frey and Eitzen argue that major college athletic and professional sports have become institutionalized for the purpose of entertaining society and generating revenues. I expand upon the analysis of these scholars to include some Pee Wee or Little League and high school football teams as young athletes increasingly rely upon these organization as a means of securing athletic scholarships. J. H. Frey and D. S. Eitzen, "Sport and Society," *Annual Review of Sociology* 17, no. 1 (August 1991): 503–522.

33. Similar to what Ortiz described as Spoiled Athlete Syndrome; major college football players can be stuck in a state of Suspended Adolescence when coaches, academic advisors, and athletic department officials become overinvolved in their daily lives. The pampering of athletes can lead to expected star treatment, belief that others will take care of their needs, and that special status should open doors, impress others, excuse offensive behavior, and explain inappropriate activities. S. M. Ortiz, "Using Power: An Exploration of Control Work in the Sport Marriage," *Sociological Perspectives* 49 (Winter 2006): 527–557.

CHAPTER 6

1. R. W. Connell, "An Iron Man: The Body and Some Contradictions of Hegemonic Masculinity," in *Sport, Men, and the Gender Order,* ed. M. Messner and D. Sabo, pp. 83–96 (Champaign, IL: Human Kinetics Books, 1990).

2. H. Brod, "The New Men's Studies: From Feminist Theory to Gender Scholarship," *Hypatia* 2, no. 1 (Winter 1987): 179–196; Connell, "An Iron Man"; S. Jeffords, *The Remasculinization of America: Gender and the Vietnam War,* vol. 10 (Bloomington: Indiana University Press, 1989); M. Kaufman, *Beyond Patriarchy: Essays by Men on Pleasure, Power, and Change* (New York: Oxford University Press, 1987); M. S. Kimmel, ed., *Changing Men: New Directions in Research on Men and Masculinity* (New York: Sage, 1987).

3. M. A. Messner, "White Men Misbehaving: Feminism, Afrocentrism, and the Promise of a Critical Standpoint," *Journal of Sport and Social Issues* 16, no. 2 (September 1992): 136–144, retrieved from CSA Sociological Abstracts database.

4. As of February 2017, M. Messner, *Power at Play: Sports and the Problem of Masculinity* (Boston: Beacon Press, 1992) had been cited 1,853 times, and M. Messner and M. Kimmel, *Men's Lives* (New York: Macmillan, 1989), had been cited 991 times (Source: Google Scholar, https://scholar.google.com/scholar).

5. *Band of Brothers* is a 2001 American war drama miniseries based on historian Stephen E. Ambrose's 1993 nonfiction book of the same name (New York: Simon & Schuster, 2017). The series dramatizes the history of the "Easy" Company throughout their involvement in World War II. Major Dick Winters struggles to keep his men alive, which requires them to work together as a tight unit and sacrifice self-interests in the pursuit of getting the job done, https://en.wikipedia.org/wiki/Band_of_Brothers_ (miniseries).

6. H. G. Bissinger, *Friday Night Lights* (Reading, MA: Addison-Wesley, 1990).

7. Bryson suggested that sport rituals cultivate male dominance by linking maleness to highly valued and visible skills, and by linking maleness with the positively sanctioned use of aggression, force, and violence. According to Jansen and Sabo, football is one of the most highly stylized displays of the contrasts between manly men and vulnerable women in contemporary American culture. L. Bryson, "Challenges to Male Hegemony in Sport," in *Sport, Men, and the Gender Order: Critical Feminist Perspectives*, ed. M. A. Messner and D. Sabo, pp. 173–184 (Champaign, IL: Human Kinetics, 1990); S. C. Jansen and D. Sabo, "The Sport/War Metaphor: Hegemonic Masculinity, the Persian Gulf War, and the New World Order," *Sociology of Sport Journal* 11 (March 1994): 1–17.

8. Ron Brown earned a gold medal at the 1984 Los Angeles Olympics as a member of the 4 x 100 meter relay team. He also placed fourth in the open men's 100-meter dash at the same Olympic games. Brown went on to play in the NFL for the Los Angeles Rams and the Oakland Raiders from 1984 until 1991.

9. Eric Dickerson was inducted into the NFL Hall of Fame in 1999.

10. Lawrence Phillips, a former star running back for the Nebraska Cornhuskers and a former NFL first-round draft choice of the Saint Louis Rams, has had numerous troubles with the law. Phillips made national news in college when he assaulted his ex-girlfriend by grabbing her by the hair and dragging her down a stairwell. J. Murray, "Nebraska Ought to Be Ashamed," *Los Angeles Times*, November 9, 1995, retrieved from http://articles.latimes.com/1995-11-09/sports/sp-973_1_nebraska-player.

11. National Collegiate Athletic Association, "The Value of College Sports," *NCAA*, 2014, retrieved February 28, 2015, from http://www.ncaa.org/student-athletes/value-college-sports.

12. A myelogram uses X-rays and a special dye, called "contrast material," to make pictures of the vertebrae and the fluid-filled spaces (known as subarachnoid spaces) between them. A myelogram may be performed to determine the cause of arm or leg numbness, weakness or pain, or narrowing of the spinal canal; to find a tumor or an infection that is causing problems with the spinal cord or nerve roots; to determine the extent of inflammation of the membrane that covers the brain and spinal cord; and to explore general issues involving the blood vessels that are connected to the spine.

CHAPTER 7

1. A summons filed in Hennepin County, MN, alleged that members of the Minnesota Vikings had engaged in butt groping, sex toy usage, assorted oral favors, and topless lap dancing with women during a 2007 sex boat scandal. C. Lingebach, "Smoot Opens Up about Planning Scandalous Love Boat Party," *CBSDC*, December 28, 2013, retrieved April 24, 2015, from http://washington.cbslocal.com/2013/12/28/smoot-opens-up-about-planning-scandalous-love-boat-party/.

2. D. Jackson, "Piscataway (N.J.) Turning into NFL High," *theganggreen.com*, April 23, 2010, retrieved March 18, 2015, from http://forums.theganggreen.com/threads/piscataway-nj-may-be-turning-into-nfl-high.56147/.

3. K. Armstrong, "Piscataway Coach Dan Higgins Churning Out NFL Talent, One After the Other," *Daily News: Sports*, May 1, 2010, retrieved March 18, 2015, from http://www.nydailynews.com/sports/football/piscataway-coach-dan-higgins-churning-nfl-talent-article- 1.448509.

4. Jackson, "Piscataway (N.J.) Turning into NFL High."

5. G. Bishop, "Kyle Wilson's Can't-Miss Play for Attention," *The New York Times*, April 23, 2010, retrieved March 18, 2015, from http://www.nytimes.com/2010/04/24/sports/football/24jets.html?_r=1.

6. On October 21, 2009, *Sporting News* magazine announced its midseason All-American team, which featured Wilson as a cornerback on the first team unit. Prior to being honored by *Sporting News*, Wilson was named one of the 20 quarterfinalists of the Lott trophy and during the preseason he was named to the watch list for the Bronco Nagurski Award, Chuck Bednarik Award, and the Jim Thorpe Award. Wilson was also named to the 2009 Preseason Playboy All-America Team. Boise State Broncos, "Wilson Named to Sporting News Midseason All-American Team," broncosports.com, 2009, retrieved from http://www.broncosports.com/sports/m-footbl/archive/bosu-m-footbl-2008.html.

7. Todd McShay joined ESPN in 2006 as a football analyst and provides in-depth scouting information on college football players, including the nation's top NFL draft prospects. ESPN Media Zone, "Bio: Todd McShay Commentator, College Football and NFL Draft Analyst, Sideline Reporter," *ESPN Media Zone*, 2015, retrieved March 15, 2015, from http://espnmediazone.com/us/bios/mcshay_todd/.

8. N. Hodjat, "2010 NFL Draft, Cornerback Big Board," *Real GM*, April 19, 2010, retrieved March 3, 2018, from https://football.realgm.com/analysis/1242/2010-NFL-Draft-Cornerback-Big-Board.

9. Boise State Broncos Athletics, "New York Jets Pick Kyle Wilson in the First Round of NFL Draft," 2010, retrieved April 7, 2015, from http://broncosports.cstv.com/sports/m-footbl/spec-rel/042310aaa.html.

10. jetsfan.com, "ESPN Crew Breaks Down Kyle Wilson.mov," *Youtube*, July 25, 2010, retrieved March 20, 2015, from https://www.youtube.com/watch?v=dHGDagL0W3E.

11. According to a report by Fox Sports, firms such as Virginia-based AGR Sports Funding, that specializes in lending to professional athletes, offer loans as high as $250,000 with interest rates as high as 30%. C. Corbellini and J. Schwarz, "Locked-Out Players Line Up for Cash Loans," *foxsports.com*, May 15, 2011, retrieved February 4, 2015, from http://www.foxsports.com/nfl/story/nfl-lockout-leads-to-players-taking-out-cash-loans-with-huge-interest-rates-051511.

12. Five days after New York Lender Pro Player Funding LLC notified Vince Young that he was in default of a nearly $1.9 million loan that was obtained in his name during the 2011 NFL lockout, the quarterback sued both his former agent and financial planner for stealing money. G. Rosenthal, "Vince Young Sues Former Agent for Stealing Money," *NFL: News— Around the NFL*, June 12, 2012, retrieved April 2, 2015, from http://www.nfl.com/news/story/09000d5d829c19ca/article/vince-young-sues-former-agent-for-stealing-money.

13. The NFL collective bargaining agreement stipulates that the voluntary nine-week off-season program is conducted in three phases.

14. Each club is allowed to host a rookie football development period for seven weeks. During this period, no activities may be held on weekends, with the exception of one post–NFL Draft rookie minicamp.

15. The NFL Rookie Symposium for all drafted rookies is a weekend-long event that includes presentations, videos, and workshops based on the principles of NFL history, total wellness, experience, and professionalism. Other topics covered over the weekend include player health and safety, decision making, mental health, substance abuse and domestic violence prevention, nondiscrimination, and maintaining positive relationships. NFL Player Engagement, "Rookie Symposium," 2013, retrieved April 3, 2015, from https://www.nflplayerengagement.com/life/rookie-symposium/.

16. Head coaches hired after the end of the preceding season are entitled to conduct an additional voluntary veteran minicamp. Any voluntary minicamp for veteran players must be conducted prior to the NFL draft, but no earlier than Week 3 of the club's off-season workout program and after at least one week of the two weeks of Phase 1 activities that the clubs may hold pursuant to Article 21 of the collective bargaining agreement. National Football League, "NFL Announces Dates for Offseason Workouts," *NFL: News—Around the NFL*, March 28, 2013, retrieved April 3, 2015, from http://www.nfl.com/news/story/0ap1000000155146/article/nfl-announces-dates-for-offseason-workouts.

17. Coach Tom Shaw offers the Elite Level Training Package for professional athletes, which is available year round. The ESPN Wide World of Sports Complex is a 220-acre athletic complex located at the Walt Disney Resort and includes nine venues that host numerous amateur and professional sporting events throughout the year. T. Shaw, "Top Speed. Top Performance," 2015, retrieved April 4, 2015, from http://www.coachtomshaw.com/.

18. A. McCullough, "Jets First-Round Pick Kyle Wilson Throws Out First Pitch at Citi Field," *nj.com*, April 25, 2010, retrieved April 4, 2015, from http://www.nj.com/jets/index.ssf/2010/04/jets_first-round_pick_kyle_wil.html.

19. S. Brennan, "New York Jets First-Round Pick Kyle Wilson in Dream Situation with Darrelle Revis and Rex Ryan," *Daily News: Sports*, April 25, 2010, retrieved April 4, 2015, from http://www.nydailynews.com/sports/football/jets/new-york-jets-first-round-pick-kyle-wilson-dream-situation-darrelle-revis-rex-ryan-article-1.170321.

20. R. M. Herold, "New York Jets 2010 Schedule: Are They Legit Super Bowl Contenders?," *BleacherReport*, September 14, 2010, retrieved April 4, 2015, from http://bleacherreport.com/articles/461093-new-york-jets-2010-schedule-are-they-legit-super-bowl-contdenders.

21. R. Cimini, "Pats, Take Note: Wilson's No Weak Link," *ESPN*, February 1, 2013, retrieved April 6, 2015, from http://espn.go.com/new-york/nfl/story/_/id/7216909/new-york-jets-kyle-wilson-flourishing-working-darrelle-revis.

22. NFL PLAY 60 is a campaign sponsored by the NFL to encourage kids to be active for 60 minutes per day in order to help reverse the childhood obesity trend. NFL Properties LLC, "NFL rush-play 60," 2015, retrieved April 9, 2015, from http://www.nflrush.com/play60/?icampaign=rush_footer_play60.

23. R. Laughland, "Kyle Wilson Earns Jets' Walton Payton Award," *247sports*, January 9, 2014, retrieved March 3, 2018, from https://247sports.com/nfl/new-york-jets/Article/Kyle-Wilson-earns-Jets-Walton-Payton-Award-105064375; C. Frankel, "Kyle Wilson Is Jets' Walter Payton Nominee: Cornerback's Latest Community Venture at Essex County College," *Jetspodcast*, January 9, 2014, retrieved April 4, 2014, from http://www.newyorkjets.com/news/article-5/Kyle-Wilson-Is-Jets%E2%80%99-Walter-Payton-Nominee/cb56ead6-2a37-4bfa-a143-1b1b1bf05644.

24. B. Costello, "Kyle Wilson Useful in the Slot—for Another Year, at Least," *New York Post*, June 18, 2014, retrieved April 6, 2015, from http://nypost.com/2014/06/18/kyle-wilson-useful-in-the-slot-for-another-year-at-least/.

25. K. A. Martin, "Rex Ryan Has High Expectations for Kyle Wilson," *Newsday*, August 18, 2014, retrieved April 6, 2015, from http://www.newsday.com/sports/football/jets/rex-ryan-has-high-expectations-for-kyle-wilson-1.9091103.

26. N. Underhill, "How Big Was Saints Guard Jahri Evans' Pay Cut? Contract Details Show It's Pretty Hefty, Will Provide Substantial Salary Cap Savings," *The New Orleans Advocate*, April 8, 2015, retrieved April 6, 2015, from http://theadvocate.com/sports/saints/12013594-123/how-big-was-saints-guard.

27. The Associated Press reported on April 1, 2010, that Kyle had signed a five-year contract to play for the New York Jets worth a total of $13 million. The deal was also reported to include about $7 million in guaranteed money over the life of the contract. B. Pareso, "Jets Sign Kyle Wilson to 5-Year $13 Million Contract," *Long Island Press*, August 1, 2010, retrieved April 7, 2015, from http://archive.longislandpress.com/2010/08/01/jets-sign-kyle-wilson-to-5-year-13-million-contract/.

28. T. J. Brennan, "Locker Room View: Team Awards Day," *New York Jets*, December 23, 2014, retrieved April 7, 2015, from http://www.newyorkjets.com/news/article-7/Locker-Room-View-Team-Awards-Day/4ad85bfe-1b9d-4b0a-8a61-85655026479c.

29. Players who are not drafted in the NFL's annual draft of amateur players are also considered to be unrestricted free agents and are free to sign contracts with any team.

30. The NFL team salary cap was set at $143.28 million for the 2015 season. K. Patra, "NFL Salary Cap Will Be $143.28 Million in 2015," *NFL: News—Around the NFL*, March 2, 2015, retrieved April 7, 2015, from http://www.nfl.com/news/story/0ap3000000475775/article/nfl-salary-cap-will-be-14328-million-in-2015.

31. J. Fitzgerald, "Bit-Name Players Fear Salary Cap Casualty Fate," *Sporting News*, December 17, 2014, retrieved April 16, 2015, from http://www.sportingnews.com/nfl/story/2014-12-17/nfl-salary-cap-casualties-2015-larry-fitzgerald-andre-johnson-adrian-peterson-sam-bradford-tamba-hali-free-agency-details.

32. Foucault identified the major effect of the Panopticon, which suggests a control over those observed to the extent that individuals begin to discipline themselves. M. Foucault, *Discipline and Punishment: The Birth of the Prison* (Harmondsworth, Middlesex, UK: Peregrine, 1979); A. Manley, "Surveillance, Disciplinary Power and Athletic Identity: A Sociological Investigation into the Culture of Elite Sports Academies" (PhD diss., Durham University, 2012).

33. M. Silver, "Nothing Optional about 'Voluntary' Workouts," 2008, retrieved November 22, 2015, from http://sports.yahoo.com/nfl/news?slug=ms-thegameface052308.

34. Scholars argue that public knowledge of the personal lives of athletes is greater today than it has ever been as a result of the ubiquitous reach of entertainment media and the unprecedented public access to the lives of sports celebrities. W. J. Brown and M. A. C. de Matviuk, "Sports Celebrities and Public Health: Diego Maradona's Influence on Drug Use Prevention," *Journal of Health Communication* 15, no. 4 (June 2010): 358–373.

35. Teams are constantly in search of the next Russell Wilson or Jimmy Garoppolo, starting quarterbacks for the Seattle Seahawks and the San Francisco 49ers, draft picks that proved to have exceptional value. After leading his team to an 11–5 record in his rookie season, Wilson was slated to be the lowest paid starting NFL quarterback in 2013. One season after naming Wilson the starter, the Seahawks traded quarterback Matt Flynn. The move allowed the Seahawks to eliminate Flynn's three-year $20.5 million dollar contract from the salary cap. M. Maiocco, "Full Details of Alex Smith's Contract," *nbcsports.com*, March 23, 2012, retrieved January 16, 2014, from http://www.csnbayarea.com/blog/matt-maiocco/full-details-alex-smiths-contract.

36. R. Cimini, "Kyle Wilson Is Gone, and the Jets' 2010 Draft Is History," *ESPN*, April 2, 2015, retrieved April 24, 2015, from http://espn.go.com/blog/new-york-jets/post/_/id/50314/kyle-wilson-is-gone-and-the-jets-2010-draft-is-history.

CHAPTER 8

1. D. Zirin, "Big League Blues," *The Nation*, October 28, 2009, retrieved from https://www.thenation.com/article/big-league-blues/, claims the National Football League Players Association (NFLPA) is generally considered the weakest union in professional sports.

2. In 1712, William Lynch, a slave owner in the Caribbean Islands, was allegedly brought to Virginia to share with other slave masters his secret to controlling slaves: set them against one another. Due to several inaccuracies and anachronisms, some historians consider it to be a hoax. https://en.wikipedia.org/wiki/William_Lynch_speech. Regardless of the veracity of this speech, active and retired players remarked about the divide and conquer approach of the NFL.

3. Retired six-year NFL veteran Anthony Prior expresses a similar sentiment in his book *The Slave Side of Sunday* (Stone Hold Books, 2006).

4. The portion of the US population that identified as only African American in 2013 was 13.2%, with 48% male, 52% female. Centers for Disease Control and Prevention, "Black or African American Populations," 2015, retrieved May 15, 2015, from http://www.cdc.gov.ezproxy.gc.cuny.edu/minorityhealth/populations/REMP/black.html. BlackDemographics.com, "Black Male Statistics," 2015, retrieved May 15, 2015, from http://blackdemographics.com/black-male-statistics/.

5. J. Hoberman, "Crisis of Black Athletes on the Eve of the 21st Century," *Society* 37, no. 3 (1997): 9–13; J. Hoberman, Darwin's Athletes: How Sport Has Damaged Black America and Preserved the Myth of Race (New York: Mariner Books, 1997); K. C. Harrison, "Black Athletes at the Millennium," *Society* 37, no. 3 (2000): 35–39.

6. R. Lapchick, D. Beahm, G. Nunes, and S. Rivera-Casiano, *The 2013 Racial and Gender Report Card: National Football League* (Orlando, FL: Institute for Diversity and Ethics in Sport, 2013).

7. D. S. Looney, "Overpaid Athletes? It's Fans That Make Them So," *The Christian Science Monitor*, July 30, 1999, retrieved May 15, 2015, from http://www.csmonitor.com/1999/0730/p12s1.html; Bad Jocks, "BadJocks: Where COPS Meets SportsCenter," 2015, retrieved May 15, 2015, from badjocks.com.

8. Washingtonian, "Where the Redskins Hang Their Helmets," *Washingtonian*, December 8, 2010, retrieved January 27, 2014, from http://www.washingtonian.com/blogs/openhouse/where-the-redskins-hang-their-helmets.php.

9. H. Edwards, "Sports within the Veil: The Triumphs, Tragedies and Challenges of Afro-American Involvement," *Annals of the American Academy of Political and Social Sciences* 445 (September 1979): 116–127.

10. At the ceremony for the 200-meter dash at the 1968 Summer Olympics, American medal winners John Carlos and Tommie Smith wore black socks and no shoes in protest to symbolize African American poverty, and black gloves to express African American strength and unity. As the national anthem played Smith also wore a scarf, and Carlos beads as each man bowed his head and raised a fist as in memory of lynching victims. D. Davis, "Olympic Athletes Who Took a Stand," *Smithsonian Magazine*, August, 2008, retrieved March 3, 2018, from https://www.smithsonianmag.com/articles/olympic-athletes-who-took-a-stand-593920/.

11. D. Hartmann, *Race, Culture, and the Revolt of the Black Athlete: The 1968 Olympic Protests and Their Aftermaths* (Chicago: University of Chicago Press, 2003).

12. E. Smith, "There Was No Golden Age of Sport for African American Athletes," *Society* 37, no. 3 (2000): 45–48.

13. M. J. Cozzillio and R. L. Hayman, eds., *Sports and Inequality* (Durham, NC: Carolina Academic Press, 2005).

14. On February 20, 2014, President Barack Obama commented on the severe challenges faced by boys and young men of color in the 21st century. Barack Obama, in the White House, remarks by the President on "My Brother's Keeper" Initiative, Washington, DC, Office of the Press Secretary.

15. S. N. Brooks, *Black Men Can't Shoot* (Chicago: University of Chicago Press, 2009).

16. R. B. A. May, Living through the Hoop: High School Basketball, Race, and the American Dream (New York: New York University Press, 2007).

17. L. J. D. Wacquant, *Body and Soul: Notebooks of an Apprentice Boxer* (New York: Oxford University Press, 2004).

18. C. Shilling, "Physical Capital and Situated Action: A New Direction for Corporeal Sociology," *British Journal of Sociology of Education* 25, no. 4 (September 2004): 473–487.

19. Sociologist Stan D. Eitzen challenges this theoretical construct by arguing against the myth of sports as a way out of poverty for racial minorities. According to Eitzen, parents and athletes alike naively believe that sports will lead to a lifetime of fame, fortune, and a comfortable retirement. D. S. Eitzen, "Upward Mobility through

Sports? The Myths and Realities, in *Sport in Contemporary Society: An Anthology*, pp. 256–262 (New York: Oxford University Press, 2005).

20. A. Young, *The Minds of Marginalized Black Men: Making Sense of Mobility, Opportunity, and Future Life Changes* (Princeton, NJ: Princeton University Press, 2006).

21. D. Royster, *Race and the Invisible Hand: How White Networks Exclude Black Men from Blue-Collar Jobs* (Berkeley: University of California Press, 2003); J. Niemonen, "Race, Class, and the State in the Postindustrial Period," *Contemporary Sociology* 35, no. 1 (January 2006), 1–4; F. H. Wilson, "*Race, Class, and the Postindustrial City: William Julius Wilson and the Promise of Sociology* (New York: SUNY Press, 2012).

22. E. Anderson, "The Social Situation of the Black Executive: Black and White Identities in the Corporate World," in *The Cultural Territories of Race: Black and White Boundaries*, ed. M. Lamont, pp. 3–29 (New York: Russell Sage Foundation, 1999).

23. Anderson, "The Social Situation of the Black Executive"; E. Cose, *The Rage of a Privileged Class* (New York: HarperCollins, 1999).

24. C. Watkins, "Miami GM Sorry for Bryant Prostitute Query," *ESPN*, April 29, 2010, retrieved March 3, 2018, from http://www.espn.com/nfl/news/story?id=5140313.

25. V. McClure, "Falcons Coach Sorry for Asking Eli Apple about Sexual Orientation," *ESPN*, March 8, 2016, retrieved January 26, 2016, from http://www.espn.com/nfl/story/_/id/14921148/atlanta-falcons-coach-sorry-asking-eli-apple-sexual-orientation.

26. P. L. Cunningham, "'Please Don't Fine Me Again!!!!!' Black Athletic Defiance in the NBA and NFL," *Journal of Sports and Social Issues* 33, no. 1 (February 2009): 39–58.

27. V. Andrews, "African American Player Codes on Celebration, Taunting and Sportsmanlike Conduct," *Journal of African American Men* 2, no. 2–3 (Winter 1997): 57–92.

28. H. D. Simons, "Race and Penalized Sports Behaviors," *International Review for the Sociology of Sports* 38, no. 1 (March 2003): 5–22.

29. Simons, "Race and Penalized Sports Behaviors," 9.

30. R. Wilson, "Richard Sherman: 'Thug' Is Accepted Way of Calling Someone N-Word," *CBS Sports*, January 22, 2014, retrieved January 24, 2014, from http://www.cbssports.com/nfl/eye-on-football/24417234.

31. Associated Press, "Goodell Strengthens NFL Personal Conduct," *USA Today*, April 11, 2007, retrieved May 24, 2015, from http://usatoday30.usatoday.com/sports/football/nfl/2007-04-10-new-conduct-policy_N.htm.

32. Article 42: Section 1–9 of the 2011 Collective Bargaining Agreement outlines the maximum discipline that teams are allowed to fine players. The disproportionate allocation of fines reflects the feelings of many of the players that the NFL is more interested in the business of football than the personal welfare of individual players.

33. Upshaw died on August 20, 2008, and was replaced by attorney DeMaurice Smith on March 16, 2009.

34. Associated Press, "NFLPA Candidate Cornwell Challenging NFL's Discipline Policy," *NFL*, March 8, 2009, retrieved June 5, 2015, from http://www.nfl.com/news/story/09000d5d80f251b3/printable/nflpa-candidate-cornwell-challenging-nfls-discipline-policy.

35. Associated Press, "Goodell's Policy Gets Support from around the NFL," April 11, 2007, retrieved June 5, 2015, from http://sports.espn.go.com/espn/wire?section=nfl&id=2832917.

36. In 2014, former Carolina Panthers defensive end, Sean Gilbert announced his campaign to replace DeMaurice Smith as the NFL Players Association chief executive officer. The cornerstone of Gilbert's 22-point platform was "removing commissioner Roger Goodell from his role as 'judge, jury and executioner on matters of players' discipline.'" After receiving 17 votes on the first ballot, DeMaurice Smith gained all 32 votes in the second ballot to retain his position for a second term. E. Winston, "Gilbert Backs 18 Games as 'Carrot,'" *ESPN*, August 26, 2014, retrieved June 5, 2015, from http://espn.go.com/nfl/story/_/id/11411668/nflpa-chief-hopeful-sean-gilbert-wants-nix-cba-supports-18-game-season; M. Florio, "Unanimous Re-election of DeMaurice Smith Sends Right Message to NFL, Others," *NBC Sports*, March 16, 2015, retrieved June 5, 2015, from http://profootballtalk.nbcsports.com/2015/03/16/unanimous-re-election-of-demaurice-smith-sends-right-message-to-nfl-others/.

37. Social scientist Dr. Carla R. Monroe points out that teachers confine reprimands and punitive consequences to Black children even when youths of other races engage in the same unsanctioned behaviors. Monroe contends that teachers' actions are based on the perception that "popular views of African American life are connected to threatening images with predictable regularity. Both media and scholarly portrayals of contemporary Black life often highlight cultures of violence, drugs, anti-authoritarianism, and other social deficiencies." One result of the criminalization of Black males is that schools have increasingly begun implementing zero tolerance policies. Reportedly, 94% of public schools across the nation have adopted initiatives designed to curb behavior deemed inappropriate or criminal. C. R. Monroe, "Why Are "Bad Boys" Always Black? Causes of Disproportionality in School Discipline and Recommendations for Change," *Clearing House: A Journal of Educational Strategies, Issues and Ideas* 79, no. 1 (September–October 2005): 45–50; B. M. McCadden, "Why Is Michael Always Getting Timed Out? Race, Class, and the Disciplining of Other People's Children," in *Classroom Discipline in American Schools: Problems and Possibilities for Democratic Education*, ed. R. E. Butchart and B. McEwan, pp. 109–135 (Albany: Albany State University of New York Press, 1998); T. Johnson, J. E. Boyden, and W. J. Pittz, *Racial Profiling and Punishment in U.S. Public Schools* (Research No. 2010) (Oakland, CA: Applied Research Center 2001).

38. For a detailed examination of the Black Nationalist/Afrocentric philosophy, refer to the section "Black Political Responses to the New Racism" in the introduction to Patricia Hill Collins, *From Black Power to Hip Hop* (Philadelphia: Temple University Press, 2006).

39. As part of a speaker series entitled "Conversations with Cosby," comedian Bill Cosby gained national attention for expressing criticism of the African American community. Cosby was criticized by some in the media for pointing the finger at lower economic people, shoddy parenting, sexual promiscuity, and using poor English. J. Holt, "Conversations with Cosby," *Gateway Pundit*, June 21, 2005, retrieved March 3, 2018, from http://www.thegatewaypundit.com/2005/06/conversations-with-cosby/.

40. Sam Burris, former Washington State University wide receiver and rookie free agent with the Dallas Cowboys (from personal observations).

41. In 2007, in a federal conspiracy case, Michael Vick was sentenced to prison for running a dog fighting operation and for making "less than truthful" statements about killing pit bull dogs. ESPN, "Apologetic Vick Gets 23-Month Sentence on Dog Fighting Charges," *ESPN*, December 12, 2007, retrieved June 5, 2015, from http://sports.espn .go.com/nfl/news/story?id=3148549.

42. G. Garber, "Packman Jones Incidents," *ESPN*, April 10, 2007, retrieved June 5, 2015, from http://sports.espn.go.com/nfl/news/story?id=2790090.

43. G. W. Domhoff, *Who Rules America?*, 5th ed. (New York: McGraw-Hill, 2005); C. W. Mills, *The Power Elite* (New York: Oxford University Press, 1999).

44. A. Zimbalist and J. G. Long, "Facility Finance: Measurements, Trends, and Analysis," ch. 10, in *The Business of Sports* (Westport, CT: Praeger, 2008).

45. L. Munson, "Antitrust Case Could Be Armageddon," *ESPN*, 2009, retrieved March 3, 2018, from http://www.espn.com/espn/columns/story?columnist=munson_lester&id=4336261.

46. Scholar Michael Eric Dyson argues that it is not surprising that much of the ideological legitimation for the contemporary misery of African Americans in general, and Black men in particular, derives from the historical legacy of slavery, which continues to assert its brutal presence in the untold suffering of millions of everyday Black folk. M. Dyson, "Gender Views: The Plight of Black Men," in *The Michael Eric Dyson Reader*, pp. 137–146 (New York: Civitas Books, 2004). J. H. Lowe, An Analysis as I See It: The Forces Working against a Sitting President (Bloomington, IN: Xlibris, 2011), pp. 99–103.

47. W. E. William, *Race and Economics: How Much Can Be Blamed on Discrimination?* (Stanford, CA: Hoover Institution Press, 2001).

48. The study of retired NFL players conducted by the Institute for Social Research at the University of Michigan for the National Football League Player Care Foundation reports that NFL athletes disclose much higher rates of sleep apnea than the general population. The rate of arthritis among NFL retirees is also nearly five times higher among younger retirees than comparable men in the general population, and twice as high at older ages. D. R. Weir, J. S. Jackson, and A. Sonnega, *National Football League Player Care Foundation Study of Retired NFL Players* (Ann Arbor: University of Michigan Institute for Social Research, 2009). S. Reinberg, "Ex-Pro Football Players Struggle with Health Problems: Depression, Chronic Pain Can Contribute to Alcohol Abuse, Financial Difficulties, Study Finds," *HealthDay: News for Healthier Living*, April 11, 2007, retrieved June 6, 2015, from http://consumer.healthday.com/mental-health-information-25/depression-news-176/ex-pro-football-players-struggle-with-health-problems-604116.html.

49. Article 26: section 5 of the 2011 NFL Collective Bargaining Agreement stipulates that "unless agreed upon otherwise between the Club and the player, each player will be paid at the rate of 100% of his salary in equal weekly or bi-weekly installments over the course of the regular season commencing with the first regular season game."

50. Shortly after passing the personal-conduct policy, NFL clubs began unprecedented efforts to crack down on loutish behavior. Among the tactics implemented by teams include hiring former police officers and FBI agents as security chiefs, ordering up extensive background checks, installing video-surveillance systems in locker rooms, chasing down rumors, and sometimes forbidding players from talking to the press. H. Karp, "Why the NFL Spies on Its Players," *The Wall Street Journal*, November 7, 2008, retrieved February 6, 2014, from https://www.wsj.com/articles/SB122601853947707055.

51. Article 42 of the 2011 NFL Collective Bargaining Agreement contains eight sections of rules that outline how clubs can discipline athletes for unwarranted or inappropriate behavior that includes anything from failure to promptly report an injury to throwing a football in the stands.

52. G. Yancy, *Black Bodies, White Gazes: The Continuing Significance of Race* (Lanham, MD: Rowman & Littlefield, 2008).

53. National Football League/National Football League Players Association Collective Bargaining Agreement, 2011. Near the end of the 2014 season, NFL owners voted to strengthen the league's personal conduct policy to include a baseline suspension of six games without pay for a first violation in domestic abuse and sexual assault cases. Media outlets report the new policy could help dispel criticism directed at Goodell for the handling of high-profile domestic abuse cases such as the one involving Baltimore Raven's running back Ray Rice. B. Chappell, "The NFL's Owners Approve New Off-Field Conduct Policy," *The Two-way*, December 10, 2014, retrieved June 11, 2015, from http://www.npr.org/sections/thetwo-way/2014/12/10/369883551/the-nfls-owners-approve-new-off-field-conduct-policy. A. Wells, "Roger Goodell Confirms He Will Hear Tom Brady's Deflategate Suspension Appeal," June 3, 2015, retrieved June 9, 2015, from http://bleacherreport.com/articles/2484096-roger-goodell-confirms-he-will-hear-tom-bradys-deflategate-suspension-appeal.

54. League reports suggest that about 20 fines are assessed each week based on a review of approximately 2,300 plays conducted over a weekend. Though the NFL declines to release the amount of fines levied, at least one report claims that $3.3 million in player fines were collected in 2005. These are reportedly used to support retired player programs and charity causes agreed upon by the NFL and the NFL Players' Association. M. Maske, "NFL Players' Union Seeks New Process for Appealing Illegal Hits," *Washington Post*, November 7, 2008, retrieved from http://www.washingtonpost.com/wp-dyn/content/article/2008/11/06/AR2008110603453.html; J. Weinbach, "When Players Don't Pay," *Wall Street Journal*, June 18, 2005, retrieved from http://www.wsj.com/articles/SB111897034755762207; A. Stites, "NFL Fines Are Donated to Help Former Players," SBNation, October 28, 2015, retrieved March 3, 2018, from https://www.sbnation.com/nfl/2015/10/28/9628160/nfl-fines-explained-former-players-donate-charity.

55. J. Clayton, "Stagnant Salary Cap? Pretty Much," *ESPN*, March 28, 2012, retrieved February 6, 2014, from http://espn.go.com/nfl/story/_/id/7744901/nfl-soaring-revenues-coincide-salary-cap-growth.

56. Prior to the start of the 2011 season, the Minnesota Vikings announced that Adrian Peterson had agreed to a seven-year deal worth a maximum $100 million, which includes a guarantee of $36 million. The contract makes Peterson the highest paid tailback in league history. S. Smith, "Adrian Peterson: NFL Like "Modern-day Slavery," *CBS News*, March 15, 2011, retrieved March 3, 2018, from https://www.cbsnews.com/news/adrian-peterson-nfl-like-modern-day-slavery/.

CHAPTER 9

1. M. Burke, "Average Player Salaries in the Four Major American Sports Leagues," *Forbes Magazine*, 2012, retrieved February 20, 2014, from http://www.forbes.com/sites/monteburke/2012/12/07/average-player-salaries-in-the-four-major-american-sports-leagues/.

2. NBC Sports reported that Under Armor gave Cam Newton the biggest financial deal ever signed by an NFL rookie. http://profootballtalk.nbcsports.com/2011/02/14/under-armour-gives-cam-newton-biggest-deal-ever-for-nfl-rookie/.

3. B. G. Link, R. M. Carpiano, and M. M. Weden, "Can Honorific Awards Give Us Clues about the Connection between Socioeconomic Status and Mortality?" *American Sociological Review*, 78, no. 2 (Fenruary 2013): 192–212.

4. The United Way, "About the NFL and United Way Partnership," 2015, retrieved March 5, 2015, from https://www.unitedway.org/nfl/about-the-partnership.

5. R. W. Turner II, "NFL Means Not For Long: The Life and Career of the NFL Athlete" (PhD diss., City University of New York, 2010).

6. On November 29, 2011, Shahid Khan, a Pakistani American billionaire and business tycoon, agreed to purchase the Jacksonville Jaguars from Wayne Weaver and his ownership group subject to NFL approval. R. Sandomir, "Shahid Khan Buys Jacksonville Jaguars and Realizes Dream," *The New York Times*, November 30, 2011, retrieved from https://www.nytimes.com/2011/12/01/sports/football/shahid-khan-buys-jacksonville-jaguars-and-realizes-dream.html. J. B. Dworkin and R. A. Posthuma, "Professional Sports: Collective Bargaining in the Spotlight," in *Collective Bargaining in the Private Sector*, ed. Paul F. Clark, John T. Delaney, and Ann C. Frost, pp. 217–262, Industrial Relations Research Association Series (Ithaca, NY: Cornell University Press, 2002).

7. R. Horrow and K. Swantek, "So You Wanna Own a Sports Team?," in *Beyond the Box $core: An Insider's Guide to the $750 Billion Business of Sports*, p. 121 (Garden City, NY: Morgan James, 2010). Between February 2008 and January 2009 Stephen M. Ross agreed to purchase 95% of the Miami Dolphins franchise, Dolphin Stadium, and surrounding land for $1.1 billion.

8. S. Farmer, "Q&A: For Cowboys Owner Jerry Jones, Taking Risks Has Paid Off," *The Los Angeles Times*, 2011, retrieved August 15, 2012, from http://articles.latimes.com/print/2011/nov/06/sports/la-sp-jerry-jones-qa-20111107.

9. Aaron Hernandez, Ray Rice, and Adrian Peterson are several of the NFL athletes who have been arrested since 2012.

10. S. Grosshandler, "All-America Football Conference," *Coffin Corner* 3, no. 7 (1980), retrieved January 1, 2017, from http://www.profootballresearchers.org/

coffin-corner80s/02-07-035.pdf; R. Rothschild, "Birth of the National Football League," *Chicago Tribune*, 2010, retrieved from http://www.chicagotribune.com/news/nationworld/politics/chi-chicagodays-nationalfootball-story-story.html.

11. Article X of the NFL's bylaws prohibited the telecasting of any NFL games into the "home territory" (generally defined as a 75-mile zone) of a team playing a home game the same day. The league was concerned about the impact on live attendance that televising games could have. At the time, television rights fees were insignificant relative to ticket and other stadium revenue. Article X, however, also prohibited teams from broadcasting their games in another team's home territory, even if that team was playing an away game (unless permission was received from both teams playing that game).

12. G. Pelnar, *Antitrust Analysis of Sports Leagues* (Munich: Munich Personal RePEc Archives, 2007). Section 1. Trusts, etc., in restraint of trade illegal; penalty, of the Sherman Antitrust Act (1890) states: Every contract, combination in the form of trust or otherwise, or conspiracy, in restraint of trade or commerce among the several States, or with foreign nations, is declared to be illegal. Every person who shall make any contract or engage in any combination or conspiracy hereby declared to be illegal shall be deemed guilty of a felony, and, on conviction thereof, shall be punished by fine not exceeding $10,000,000 if a corporation, or, if any other person, $350,000, or by imprisonment not exceeding three years, or by both said punishments, in the discretion of the court.

13. *United States v. National Football League*, No. 12808 (United States District Court, 1953).

14. M. Leeds, "The Economics of Professional Sports and Leagues: American Football," in *Handbook on the Economics of Sports*, ed. W. Andreff and S. Szymanski, pp. 514–523 (Cheltenham, UK: Edward Elgar, 2006).

15. Pelnar, *Antitrust Analysis of Sports Leagues*.

16. On Writ of Certiorari to the United States Court of Appeals for the Seventh Circuit: Brief Amici Curiae for the National Football League Players Association, Major League Baseball Players Association, National Basketball Players Association, and National Hockey League Players' Association. In Support of Petitioner, No. 08-661 1-57 (Court of Appeals for the Seventh Circuit 2009).

17. M. Yost, *Tailgating, Sacks, and Salary Caps: How the NFL Became the Most Successful Sports League in History* (Chicago: Kaplan, 2006).

18. Leeds, "The Economics of Professional Sports and Leagues."

19. On Writ of Certiorari to the United States Court of Appeals for the Seventh Circuit: Brief Amici Curiae for the National Football League Players Association, Major League Baseball Players Association, National Basketball Players Association, and National Hockey League Players' Association. In Support of Petitioner, No. 08-661 1-57 (Court of Appeals for the Seventh Circuit 2009).

20. T. Slack, ed., *The Commercialization of Sport* (New York: Routledge, 2004).

21. A May 10, 1999, *Brandweek* magazine article states that the most reliable way to reach the 18- to 49-year-old male demographic is through televised sports. T. Lefton, "18–49 MEN Ups and Downs (Demographic Group)," *Highbeam Business*, May 10, 1999,

retrieved March 5, 2015, from http://business.highbeam.com/137330/article-1G1-54616755/1849-men-ups-and-downs.

22. Yost, *Tailgating, Sacks, and Salary Caps.*

23. NFL H.O.F. "Pete Rozelle's Legacy," *Pro Football Hall of Fame*, 2012, retrieved August 7, 2012, from http://www.profootballhof.com/hof/release.aspx?release_id=1864.

24. See, e.g., *United States Football League v. NFL*, 634 F. Supp. 1155, 1170-71 (S.D.N.Y. 1986), Mid-South Grizzlies, 720 F. 2d at 784-85 & n.7. Part C of Chapter 14 discusses the Noerr immunity. J. M. Jacobson, *Antitrust Law Developments*, 6th ed. (New York: American Bar Association, 2007).

25. Department of Justice, A. D, *Public Documents Antitrust Division Manual*, 2009, retrieved June 7, 2010, from http://www.justice.gov.ezproxy.gc.cuny.edu/atr/public/divisionmanual/index.htm.

26. The USFL claimed that the NFL conspired to retain trade and did in fact monopolize the market for professional football by, among other things, jeopardizing the USFL's broadcasting contract with the major television networks. Within legal circles the *USFL v. NFL* case is often described as the television case because the central issue of the case revolved around whether the more established league prevented its competitor from obtaining a television contract thereby limiting their ability to remain competitive in the professional football market.

27. Bloomberg Business: Media. *Company overview of NFL properties, LLC*, 2015, retrieved December 22, 2015, from http://www.bloomberg.com/research/stocks/private/snapshot.asp?privcapId=4640494.

28. Yost, *Tailgating, Sacks, and Salary Caps.*

29. Associated Press, "NFL Loses on Vending," *New York Times*, January 28, 1983.

30. D. Kaplan, "NFL Halfway to 25B Goal," *Sports Business Journal*, February 29, 2016, retrieved March, 2018, from https://www.sportsbusinessdaily.com/Journal/Issues/2016/02/29/Leagues-and-Governing-Bodies/NFL-revenue.aspx.

31. Kaplan, "NFL Halfway to 25B Goal."

32. W. Gregory, "Nike Wins Deal for NFL Merchandise," *Memphis Business Journal*, June 13, 2011, retrieved August 9, 2012, from http://www.bizjournals.com/memphis/news/2011/06/13/nike-wins-deal-for-nfl-merchandise.html.

33. D. Kaplan, "Roger Goodell's NFL Compensation Exceeds $44M in 12-month Period," *Sports Business Daily*, 2014, retrieved March 4, 2015, from http://www.sportsbusinessdaily.com/Daily/Closing-Bell/2014/02/14/Goodell.aspx.

34. K. Belson, "Goodell's Pay of $44.2 Million in 2012 Puts Him in the Big Leagues," *New York Times*, 2014, retrieved March 4, 2015, from https://www.nytimes.com/2014/02/15/sports/football/goodell-nfl-commissioner-earned-44-2-million-in-2012.html.

35. R. Nader, *Cutting Corporate Welfare* (New York: Seven Stories Press, 2000).

36. Walter Adams and James W. Brock, "Monopoly, Monopsony, and Vertical Collusion: Antitrust Policy and Professional Sports," *Antitrust Bulletin* 42 (Fall 1997): 721–747.

37. W. Adams and J. W. Brock, "The 'Sports-Industrial' Complex," in *The Bigness Complex*, pp. 284–298 (Stanford, CA: Stanford University Press, 2004).

38. A. Shipley, "NFL Executives Lobbying Blitz on Capitol Hill," *The Washington Post*, 2011, retrieved August 11, 2012, from http://www.washingtonpost.com/wp-dyn/content/article/2011/01/30/AR2011013004545.html.

39. K. Reich, "Settlement Research in Raiders' Antitrust Suit against NFL," *Los Angeles Times*, 1989, retrieved December 22, 2015, from http://articles.latimes.com/1989-03-05/local/me-394_1_antitrust-suit.

40. Associated Press, "NFL Owners, Players Ratify Cap Deal That Punishes Redskins," *The Washington Times*, 2012, retrieved August 4, 2012, from http://www.washingtontimes.com/news/2012/mar/27/nfl-owners-players-ratify-cap-deal-that-punishes-r/?page=all.

41. USFL.info, "A Brief History of the USFL," 2007, retrieved August 2, 2012, from http://www.usflsite.com/.

42. D. Meggyesy, "The National Football League Monopoly," *Society* 23, no. 4 (May 1986): 16–22.

43. Adams and Brock, "Monopoly, Monopsony, and Vertical Collusion."

44. A. Zimbalist and R. G. Noll, "Sports, Jobs, and Taxes: Are New Stadiums Worth the Cost?," *Brookings*, 1997, retrieved March 27, 2009, from https://www.brookings.edu/articles/sports-jobs-taxes-are-new-stadiums-worth-the-cost/.

45. J. Siegfried and A. Zimbalist, "The Economics of Sports Facilities and Their Communities," *Journal of Economic Perspectives* 14, no. 3 (2000): 76–95.

46. Zimbalist and Noll, "Sports, Jobs, and Taxes."

47. Zimbalist and Noll, "Sports, Jobs, and Taxes."

48. N. DeMause, "Why Do Mayors Love Sports Stadiums? Numerous Cities Are Littered with 'Downtown Catalysts' That Failed to Catalyze," *The Nation*, 2011, retrieved March 5, 2015, from http://www.thenation.com/article/162400/why-do-mayors-love-sports-stadiums#.

49. Yost, *Tailgating, Sacks, and Salary Caps.*

50. The NFL salary cap agreement has been in place since 1994. The agreement puts a limit on the amount of money teams can spend on player salaries. As a result of this setup, NFL contracts almost always include the right to cut a player. If a player is cut, his salary for the remainder of his contract is neither paid nor counted against the salary cap. One consequence of the salary cap was the release of many higher-salaried veterans once their production started to decline. In an attempt to counter this practice, which tends to push out veteran players, the NFL Players Association accepted an arrangement whereby a veteran player who receives no bonuses in his contract and signs for the veteran minimum only accounts for $425,000 against the salary cap.

51. E. Frenz, "Les Brown: Chronicling the Journey of Dolphins' Hard Knock's Star," *Bleacher Report*, 2012, retrieved March 5, 2015, from http://bleacherreport.com/articles/1290952-les-brown-chronicling-the-journey-of-dolphins-hard-knocks-star.

52. espn.com, "Warrick, Klingler Fell Way Short in Ciny," *ESPN*, 2008 retrieved March 15, 2013, from http://sports.espn.go.com/nfl/draft08/news/story?id=3326109.

53. D. Maley, "Peter Warrick: Remember, the NFL Is a Business," *The Bradenton Times*, 2012, retrieved March 6, 2015, from http://thebradentontimes.com/ports-peter-warrick-remember-the-nfl-is-a-business-p10306-158.htm.

54. Reuters, "Plus: Pro Football—Cincinnati: Warrick Signs 7-Year Contract," *The New York Times*, 2000, retrieved March 6, 2015, from http://www.nytimes.com/2000/06/05/sports/plus-pro-football-cincinatti-warrick-signs-7-year-contract .html?ref=peterwarrick.

55. National Football League, Compliance Plan [Statement of Policy], New York, National Football League, 2014.

56. 2016 NFL Compliance Plan, Respect – Integrity – Responsibility to Team – Resiliency, https://secure.ethicspoint.com/lrn/media/en/gui/19375/NFLCompliancePlan .pdf.

CHAPTER 10

1. R. O Crockett, "Business: NFL Players Chief Shares Realities of Pro Football," *Roger Crockett, Business. Leadership. Diversity*, October 22, 2013, retrieved April 24, 2015, from http://rocrockett.com/2013/10/business-nfl-players-chief-shares-realities-of-pro football/. Commissioner Roger Goodell argues that statistics indicate athletes play an average of 6.1 seasons; and those players on a roster on the first day of the season average a total of almost 10 seasons. NFL Communications, "What Is the Average NFL Player's Career Length? Longer Than You Might Think, Commissioner Goodell Says," *NFL Communications*, April 18, 2011, retrieved April 24, 2015, from https://nfllabor.wordpress.com/2011/04/18/what-is-average-nfl-player%E2%80%99s-career-length-longer-than-you-might-think-commissioner-goodell-says/.

2. E. R. Garvey, "From Chattel to Employee: The Athlete's Quest for Freedom and Dignity," *Annals of the American Academy of Political and Social Science* 445 (September 1979): 91–101.

3. National Football League; National Football League Players Association Collective Bargaining Agreement, 2011.

4. E. Lock, "The Scope of the Labor Exemption in Professional Sports: A Perspective on Collective Bargaining in the NFL," *Duke Law Journal* (April 1989): 328–338.

5. See *Brady v. National Football League* (Brady II), 644 F. 3d 661 (8th Cir. 2011); R. T. Gorkin, "Sports-League Player Restraints, Section 1 of the Sherman Act, and Federal Labor Law in the Context of the National Football League," *Harvard Journal of Sports and Entertainment Law* 5, no. 1 (2014).

6. National Football League; National Football League Players Association Collective Bargaining Agreement, 2011.

7. CBS Sports NFL Insider Jason La Confora wrote, "Contracts are not guaranteed, and even many guarantees aren't really guaranteed. Teams demand rolling guarantees with a period of time each year in which a player they just signed can be released after any given season with almost no cash or cap consequences." J. La Confora, "Reality of Free-Agent Contracts Means That Most Teams Have an Out," *CBS Sports*, March 14, 2014, retrieved May 4, 2015, from http://www.cbssports.com/nfl/writer/jason-la-canfora/24482973/reality-of-free-agent-contracts-means-that-most-teams-have-an-out.

8. Article I, Section 3 (at) " 'Salary Cap' means the absolute maximum amount of salary that each Club may pay or be obligated to pay or provide to players or Player Affiliates,

or may pay or be obligated to pay to third parties at the request of and for the benefit of Players or Player Affiliates, at any time during a particular League Year, in accordance with the rules set forth in Article XXIV (Guaranteed League-wide Salary, Salary Cap and Minimum Team Salary), if applicable.

9. A. W. Heller, "Creating a Win-Win Situation through Collective Bargaining: The NFL Salary Cap," *Sports Lawyers Journal* 7 (2000): 375–409.

10. M. Mondello and J. Maxcy, "The Impact of Salary Dispersion and Performance Bonuses in NFL Organizations," *Management Decisions* 47, no. 1 (2009): 110–123.

11. L. Mullen, D. Broughton, and Staff Writers, "Has MLB Overrun NBA's Star-Salary System?," *Sports Business Journal*, January 13, 2014, retrieved August 24, 2015, from http://www.sportsbusinessdaily.com/Journal/Issues/2014/01/13/Labor-and-Agents/Player-salaries.aspx.

12. M. Burawoy, *Manufacturing Consent* (Chicago: University of Chicago Press, 1979).

13. Burawoy, *Manufacturing Consent*, pp. 81–82.

14. Donald R. Latham and David W. Stewart. "Organizational Objectives and Winning: An Examination of the NFL," *Academy of Management Journal* 24, no. 2 (June 1981): 403–408.

15. N. Grow, "There's No 'I' in 'League:' Professional Sports Leagues and the Single Entity Defense," *Michigan Law Review* 105, no. 1 (2006): 183–208.

16. US Supreme Court, *National Football League v. North American Soccer League*, 459 U.S. 1074 (1982) 74 L.Ed.2d 639 459 U.S. 1074.

17. M. L. Devault and Liza McCoy, "Institutional Ethnography: Using Interviews to Investigate Ruling Relations," in *Institutional Ethnography as a Practice*, ed. D. E. Smith, pp. 15–45 (Lanham, MD: Rowman & Littlefield, 2006).

18. 519 F. Supp. 581 (C.D. Cal 1981), appeal docketed, No. 82-5572 (9th Cir., June 14, 1982).

19. 670 F. 2d 1249 (2d Cir.), cert denied, 103 S. Ct. 499 (1982).

20. Section I of the Sherman Antitrust Act provides a pertinent part: "Every contract, combination in the form of trust or otherwise, or conspiracy, in restraint of trade or commerce among the several States, or with foreign nations, is declared to be illegal." 15 U.S.C. § I (1982).

21. M. C. Grauer, "Recognition of the National Football League as a Single Entity under Section 1 of the Sherman Act: Implications of the Consumer Welfare Model," *Michigan Law Review* 82, no. 1 (October 1983): 71–116.

22. Player restraints include, for example, the NFL draft.

23. *Northern Pac. Ry. Co. v. United States*, 356 U.S 1, 4-5 (1958).

24. R. E. Bartok, "NFL Free Agency Restrictions under Antitrust Attack," *Duke Law Journal* 1991, no. 2 (April 1991): 503–559.

25. Bartok, "NFL Free Agency Restrictions under Antitrust Attack."

26. R. Beamish, "The Political Economy of Professional Sports," in *Sport: Issues in the Sociology of Sport*, ed. Eric Dunning and Dominic Malcolm, pp. 135–149 (New York: Routledge, 2003).

27. The NFL Collective Bargaining Agreement, 1963.

28. 543 F.2d. 606, 609 (8th Cir. 1976).

29. Bartok, "NFL Free Agency Restrictions under Antitrust Attack."

30. *Alexander v. NFL*, 1977-2 Trade Case. (CCH), 61,730, at 72,998 (D. Minn. 1977), *aff'd sub nom. Reynolds v. NFL*, 584 F.2d 280 (8th Cir. 1978).

31. Bartok, "NFL Free Agency Restrictions under Antitrust Attack."

32. A player had to complete at least three years of NFL service to be eligible for free agency. His team was required to respond within seven days of receiving the offer sheet; otherwise the player was free to sign with the offering team.

33. R. H. Boyle, "The 55% Solution: This Is the Controversial Proposal of Ed Garvey and the NFL Players' Union as Contract Talks Approach," *Sports Illustrated: Vault*, February 1, 1982, retrieved from http://www.si.com/vault/1982/02/01/540950/the-55-solution.

34. Garvey, "Foreword to the Scope of the Labor Exemption in Professional Sports."

35. Garvey, "Foreword to the Scope of the Labor Exemption in Professional Sports."

36. D. Schaal, "Mike Ditka Flags NFL on Its CR Gameday: League, Union Slow to Take Decisive Steps for Retired Players," *Corporate Responsibility Magazine*, December 13, 2007, retrieved February 26, 2018, from http://thecro.com/topics/business-ethics/mike-ditka-flags-nfl-on-its-cr-gameday/.

37. T. Baugh, "John Mackey Fund and the 88 Plan for Dementia," *NFL Retired*, 2010, retrieved January 5, 2015, from http://nflretired.baughweb.com/NFLMackey%2088%20Plan.htm.

38. Associated Press. "Union, Retired Players Agree to $26.25 Million Settlement of Lawsuit," *NFL News*, July 26, 2012, retrieved January 5, 2015, from http://www.nfl.com/news/story/09000d5d810aa9df/article/union-retired-players-agree-to-2625-million-settlement-of-lawsuit.

39. J. Nixon, "The NFLPA Is Losing the 'Trust' of Legacy Players," *The Nixon Report*, November 27, 2013, retrieved January 5, 2015, from https://jeffnixonreport.wordpress.com/2013/11/27/the-nflpa-is-losing-the-trust-of-legacy-players/.

40. A perspective rooted in political sociology considers a generational group as a cohort of individuals that experiences a particular event, such as organizational entry, within a specific interval. A. Joshi, J. C. Dencker, G. Franz, and J. J. Martocchio, "Unpacking Generational Identities in Organizations," *Academy of Management Review* 35, no. 3 (July 2010): 392–414.

41. Replacement players hired during the 1987 strike were often called scabs. E. Merrill, "NFL Replacements Part of History, *ESPN*, June 9, 2011, retrieved February 26, 2018, from http://www.espn.com/nfl/news/story?id=6642330.

42. The National Football League Players Association, "About the NFLPA: History," nflpa.com, 2014, retrieved from https://www.nflpa.com/about/history.

43. *Powell v. NFL*, 930 F.2d 1293, 1303-04, 930 1293 (8th Cir. 1989).

44. B. Murphy, "Minnesota's Doty Has Dominated Football's Contract Bargaining for 20 Years," *Twin Cities Pioneer Press*, May 4, 2008, retrieved February 26, 2018, from https://www.twincities.com/2008/05/04/minnesotas-doty-has-dominated-footballs-contract-bargaining-for-20-years/.

45. T. George, "Football: N.F.L.'s Free-Agency System Is Found Unfair by U.S. Jury," *New York Times*, September 11, 1992, retrieved from http://www.nytimes.com/1992/09/11/sports/football-nfl-s-free-agency-system-is-found-unfair-by-us-jury.html.

46. Between February 1 and April 1, 229 of the 619 unconditional free agents changed teams in 1989.

47. *Powell v. NFL*, 930 F.2d 1293, 1303–04, 930 1293 (8th Cir. 1989).

48. *McNeil v. National Football League*, 1992-2 Trade Case.(CCH), 69,982 (D. Minn. 1992); *Jackson* v. *National Football League*, 802 F. Supp. 226 (D. Minn. 1992); *White v. National Football League*, 822 F. Supp. 1389 (D. Minn. 1993).

49. J. S. Shapiro, "Warming the Bench: The Nonstatutory Labor Exemption in the National Football League," *Fordham Law Review* 61, no. 5 (1993): 1203–1234.

50. 790 F. Supp. 871—Dist. Court, Minnesota 1992.

51. The National Football League Players Association, "About the NFLPA: History."

52. The National Football League Players Association, "About the NFLPA: History."

53. A. N. Wise and B. S. Meyer, eds., *International Sports Law and Business*, vol. 1 (The Hague: Kluwer Law International, 1997).

54. C. F. George, V. Kab, P. Kab, J. J. Villa, and A. M. Levy, "Sleep and Breathing in Professional Football Players," *Sleep Medicine* 4, no. 4 (July 2003): 317–325.

55. The NFL Players Association also won verdicts in *Jackson v. NFL* and *Brown v. NFL*.

56. D. M. H. Lewis, "Analysis of Brown v. National Football League," *Villanova Sports and Entertainment Law Journal* 9 (2002): 263.

57. *White v. National Football League*, 822 F. Supp. 1389 (D. Minn. 1993).

58. G. Macnow, "NFL Loses to Players in Court; a Federal Jury Ruled the League's Restrictive Free-Agency Setup Illegal. The Consequences of the Decision Could Be Huge," *philly.com*, 1992, retrieved February 5, 2015, from http://articles.philly.com/1992-09-11/news/26021498_1_restrictions-on-player-movement-limited-free-agency-ruling.

59. M. Tanier, "Too Deep Zone: The First Franchise Player," *Football Outsiders*, February 19, 2007, retrieved from http://www.footballoutsiders.com/walkthrough/2007/too-deep-zone-first-franchise-player.

60. The National Football League Players Association, "About the NFLPA: History."

61. The National Football League Players Association, "About the NFLPA: History."

62. The National Football League Players Association, "About the NFLPA: History."

63. The National Football League Players Association, "About the NFLPA: History."

64. R. D. Forbes, "Call on the Field Reversed: How the NFL Players Association Won Big on Salary Forfeiture at the Bargaining Table," *Virginia Sports and Entertainment Law Journal* 6 (October 2007): 333.

65. J. Clayton, "NFL Owners Opt Out of Labor Agreement," *ESPN*, May 21, 2008, retrieved April 24, 2015, from http://www.espn.com/nfl/news/story?id=3404596.

66. Wire Reports, "NFL Owners Opt Out of Labor Agreement," *Herald-Tribune*, May 21, 2008, retrieved April 24, 2015, from http://www.heraldtribune.com/article/20080521/SPORTS/805210474.

67. M. Maske, "NFL Owners Want New Deal," *The Washington Post*, May 21, 2008, retrieved April 24, 2015, from http://www.washingtonpost.com/wp-dyn/content/article/2008/05/20/AR2008052001693.html; M. Yost, *Tailgating, Sacks, and Salary Caps: How the NFL Became the Most Successful Sports League in History* (Chicago: Kaplan, 2006).

68. L. Peek, "Forget Deflategate. Here's the Real NFL Scandal," *The Fiscal Times*, January 29, 2015, retrieved May 1, 2015, from http://www.thefiscaltimes.com/Columns/2015/01/29/Forget-Deflategate-Here-s-Real-NFL-Scandal.

69. A. Marvez, "Lockout Lifted for Now, but What's Next?," *foxsports.com*, April 25, 2011, retrieved May 25, 2011, from http://msn.foxsports.com/nfl/story/Judge-lifts-NFL-lockout-injunction-owners-appealing-analysis-042511?gt1=39002.

70. B. Volin, "Now More Than Ever, We Realize N.F.L. Owners Won," *Boston Globe*, July 21, 2013, retrieved from https://www.bostonglobe.com/sports/2013/07/20/nfl-owners-destroyed-players-cba-negotiations/ia3c1ydpS16H5FhFEiviHP/story.html.

71. The NFL's salary cap is called a "hard cap" (which no team can exceed for any reason under penalty from the league), and a hard salary floor (a minimum team payroll that no team can drop beneath for any reason). Both the cap and the floor are adjusted annually based on the change in the league's revenues. The cap is based on income that the teams earn during a league year. Originally that "pot" was limited to what was known as defined gross revenues (DGR), which consisted of the money earned from the national television contract, ticket sales, and NFL merchandise sales. Under the current agreement the "pot" has been expanded to include total revenue. Thus, other sources of revenue, including such other items as naming rights and local advertising, have been added. As was the case with the original DGR, the expanded revenue is divided equally among all 32 teams for purposes of calculating the salary cap.

   During the 2007 season, the NFL CBA set the minimum salary for a rookie as $285,000. The minimum salary increases according to the number of years the player has been in the league. The highest minimum salary is $820,000 for players who have been in the league 11 years or more.

72. For a comprehensive explanation of the rookie salary cap, consult J. Fitzgerald, "Explaining the NFL Rookie Pool and Its Impact on the Salary Cap," *Over the Cap*, March 7, 2013, retrieved from https://overthecap.com/explaining-the-nfl-rookie-pool-and-its-impact-on-the-salary-cap/; M. Maske, "NFL Rookies Signing New Contracts Rapidly under New Salary System," *The Washington Post*, May 16, 2012, retrieved December 21, 2013, from http://www.washingtonpost.com/blogs/football-insider/post/rookies-signing-contracts-rapidly-under-new-salary-cap-system/2012/05/16/gIQAfSQMUU_blog.html.

73. T. Van Riper, "Top Ten NFL Draft Picks Will Make Two-Thirds Less Than Class of 2010," *forbes.com*, April 26, 2012, retrieved from http://www.forbes.com/sites/tomvanriper/2012/04/26/top-ten-nfl-draft-picks-will-make-two-thirds-less-than-class-of-2010/.

74. Volin, "Now More Than Ever."

75. A. Fox, "More Than They Bargained For," *ESPN*, June 3, 2013, retrieved December 21, 2013, from http://espn.go.com/nfl/story/_/id/9337079/reality-hits-veteran-free-agents.

76. K. Garriott, "The Economic Truth behind the NFL CBA," *Pro Player Insiders*, May 22, 2012, retrieved December 21, 2013, from http://proplayerinsiders.com/nflpa-foxworth-the-economic-truth-behind-cba/.

77. For a detailed explanation of player benefits, see articles 8; 26; 27; 29; 30; 39; 41; and 52 through 67 of the 2011–2020 NFL, NFLPA Collective Bargaining Agreement.

78. Article 8: Section 1. of the 2011 NFL CBA states that for the purpose of calculating accrued seasons, a player shall receive credit for one accrued season for each season during which he was on, or should have been on, full pay status for a total of six or more regular season games.

79. W. Rhoden, *Forty Million Dollar Slaves: The Rise, Fall, and Redemption of the Black Athlete*, 5th ed. (New York: Crown, 2006).

80. D. J. Leonard, "Golden Shackles: A Veteran Journalist Finds Little Racial Progress in the World of Sports," *Washington Post*, August 13, 2006, retrieved from http://www .washingtonpost.com/wp-dyn/content/article/2006/08/10/AR2006081001366 .html.

81. Rhoden's work points to the absence of Black ownership and the institutionalization of rules to regulate Black athletic style as evidence of Black athletes' subservience to White interest. For Rhoden, this absence of power leaves Black athletes in a continuously precarious position of being kept out, persecuted, and eased out when White owners and management decide they are no longer needed or wanted (Leonard, "Golden Shackles"). I have no intention of minimizing the influence that race has on the observations made by Rhoden; however, one must question how much power any athlete wields in the NFL.

82. A. Barra, "How Curt Flood Changed Baseball and Killed His Career in the Process," *The Atlantic*, July 12, 2011, retrieved from https://www.theatlantic.com/entertainment /archive/2011/07/how-curt-flood-changed-baseball-and-killed-his-career-in-the-process/241783/.

83. E. Adelson, ". . . Listens to His Head . . . Follows His Heart," *ESPN*, April 10, 2008, retrieved April 9, 2008, from http://sports.espn.go.com/espnmag/story?id=3336339.

84. S. J. Dubner, "N.F.L. vs. M.L.B. as a Labor Market: A Freakonomics Quorum," *New York Times*, November 28, 2007, retrieved from http://freakonomics.com/2007/ 11/28/nfl-vs-mlb-as-a-labor-market-a-freakonomics-quorum/.

85. K. Marx, "Part I, Chapter I: The Circulation of Money-Capital," in *Capital: A Critique of Political Economy*. Volume 2, *The Process of Circulation of Capital*, ed. F. Engels; trans. E. Untermann, 2nd German ed. (Chicago: Charles H. Kerr, 1910).

86. R. J. Hill and E. Taylor, "Do Professional Sports Unions Fit the Standard Model of Traditional Unionism?," *Journal of Labor Research* 29, no. 1 (March 2008): 56–67.

87. Hill and Taylor, "Do Professional Sports Unions Fit the Standard Model of Traditional Unionism?"

88. Crockett, "Business."

89. Sports economist John Vrooman argues, "It is common for veteran players to coalesce with management to bargain away the rights of future generations of disenfranchised rookies and forgotten former players. This creates a twisted bilateral monopoly where veteran players are often overpaid because of upper-tier monopoly power, while rookies are exploited because of owners' lower-tier monopsony power. The solidarity of the NFL Players Association (NFLPA) is especially fragmented because of the relatively short careers of NFL players. The unrestricted NFL free-agent eligibility requirement of four years exceeds the average NFL experience of 3.8 years. NFL players are now split into a dual labor market where horizontal bargaining coalitions

cut across vertical labor-management lines. As a result, CBA outcomes usually reflect the coalition of upper-tier owners and veteran players." J. Vrooman, "The Economics Structure of the NFL," in *The Economics of the National Football League: The State of the Art*, ed. K. G. Quinn, 3rd ed., pp. 7–31 (New York: Springer + Business Media, LLC, 2012).

CHAPTER 11

1. Lefton Report, "Tiki Barber Adding Cadillac to Endorsements, Sources Say," *Sports Business Journal*, September 11, 2006, retrieved July 29, 2013, from http://www.sportsbusinessdaily.com/Journal/Issues/2006/09/20060911/Marketingsponsorship/Tiki-Barber-Adding-Cadillac-To-Endorsements-Sources-Say.aspx; S. Goodyear, "Ad Nauseam: Tiki Barber and His Cadillac Escalade," March 28, 2007, retrieved June 15, 2015, from http://www.streetsblog.org/2007/03/28/dont-drive-what-tiki-drives/.

2. A. E. Housman, "To an Athlete Dying Young," in *The Norton Anthology of Poetry*, ed. E. A. A. Alexander, 3rd ed. (New York: W. W. Norton, 1983).

3. J. Corbette, "With Retirement Looming, Tiki Balances NFL with His Next Career in the Media," *USA Today*, 2006, retrieved July 27, 2013, from http://usatoday30.usatoday.com/sports/football/nfl/giants/2006-12-06-tiki-barber-cover_x.htm.

4. ESPN.com News Services, "Tiki Torches 'Idiots' for Criticizing Retirement Decision," *ESPN*, October 29, 2006, retrieved July 28, 2013, from http://sports.espn.go.com/nfl/news/story?id=2639376.

5. *Sports Business Daily*, "Tiki Barber Formally Introduced as New NBC Personality," February 14, 2007, retrieved July 28, 2013, from http://www.sportsbusinessdaily.com/Daily/Issues/2007/02/Issue-101/Sports-Media/Tiki-Barber-Formally-Introduced-As-New-NBC-Personality.aspx.

6. Fox News/NewsCore, " 'Broke' Tiki Barber Can't Afford Divorce Settlement after Alleged Affair with NBC Intern," *Fox News Entertainment*, June 23, 2010, retrieved February 8, 2013, from http://www.foxnews.com/entertainment/2010/06/23/broke-tiki-barber-afford-divorce-settlement-alleged-affair-nbc-intern/.

7. ESPN New York, "Tiki Barber Coming Out of Retirement," *ESPN*, May 27, 2011, retrieved July 29, 2013, from http://sports.espn.go.com/new-york/nfl/news/story?id=6193850.

8. NFL.com Wire Reports, "Tiki Barber Plans Comeback, but It Won't Be with Giants," *NFL News*, August 31, 2012, retrieved February 8, 2013, from http://www.nfl.com/news/story/09000d5d81ea9545/article/tiki-barber-plans-comeback-but-it-wont-be-with-giants.

9. *Sport Illustrated* reports that many NFL, NBA, and MLB players lose most or all of their money in retirement regardless of how much they make. P. S. Torre, "How (and Why) Athletes Go Broke," *Vault*, March 23, 2009, retrieved June 16, 2015, from http://www.si.com/vault/2009/03/23/105789480/how-and-why-athletes-go-broke. J. Chadiha, "Life after the NFL Is a Struggle for Many Former Players," *ESPN*, May 31, 2012, retrieved June 16, 2015, from http://espn.go.com/nfl/story/_/id/7983790/life-nfl-struggle-many-former-players.

10. T. L. Schwenk, D. W. Gorenflo, R. R. Dopp, and E. Hipple, "Depression and Pain in Retired Professional Football Players," *Medicine and Science in Sports and Exercise* 39, no. 4 (April 2007): 599–605.

11. E. Frenz, "Les Brown: Chronicling the Journey of Dolphins' Hard Knock's Star," *The Bleacher Report,* August 10, 2012, retrieved March 5, 2015, from http://bleacherreport.com/articles/1290952-les-brown-chronicling-the-journey-of-dolphins-hard-knocks-star.

12. W. Rhoden, *Forty Million Dollar Slaves: The Rise, Fall, and Redemption of the Black Athlete* (New York: Crown, 2006).

13. B. Volin, "Now More Than Ever, We Realize N.F.L. Owners Won," *Boston Globe,* July 21, 2013, retrieved from https://www.bostonglobe.com/sports/2013/07/20/nfl-owners-destroyed-players-cba-negotiations/ia3c1ydpS16H5FhFEiviHP/story.html; M. Florio, "Minimum Salaries Shoot Up under New Deal," *NBC Sports,* July 25, 2011, retrieved June 15, 2015, from http://profootballtalk.nbcsports.com/2011/07/25/minimum-salaries-shoot-up-under-new-deal/.

14. My approach to examining "identity" derives from *identity theory,* which in its simplest form emphasizes the social structural sources of identity and the relationship among differing identities. For my purposes, an important aspect of this theory is that it focuses on the internal cognitive processes of identity. Essentially, identity theory reasons that people are typically enmeshed in multiple role relationships in multiple groups while holding onto multiple identities. According to scholars such as Stryker and Burke, and Ogilvie and Howe, people possess as many selves as groups of persons with whom they interact. In other words, people have as many identities as the distinct networks of relationships in which they occupy positions and play roles. S. Stryker and P. J. Burke, "The Past, Present, and Future of an Identity Theory," *Social Psychology Quarterly* 63, no. 4 (December 2000): 284–297; S. Stryker, "Traditional Symbolic Interactionism, Role Theory, and Structural Symbolic Interactionism: The Road to Identity Theory," in *Handbook of Sociological Theory,* ed. J. H. Turner, pp. 211–232 (Dordrecht, the Netherlands: Kluwer, 2001); B. C. Ogilvie and M. Howe, "Career Crisis in Sport," *Proceedings of the Fifth World Congress of Sport Psychology,* ed. T. Orlick, J. T. Partington, and J. H. Salmela, pp. 176–183 (Ottawa, Canada: Coaching Association of Canada, 1982).

15. L. A. Killeya-Jones, "Identity Structure, Role Discrepancy and Psychological Adjustment in Male College Student-Athletes," *Journal of Sport Behavior* 28 (June 2005): 165–185; J. Taylor and B. C. Ogilvie, "Career Transitions among Elite Athletes: Is There Life after Sports?," in *Applied Sport Psychology: Personal Growth to Peak Performance,* ed. J. M. Williams, pp. 429–444 (Mountain View, CA: Mayfield, 2001).

16. Taylor and Ogilvie, "Career Transitions among Elite Athlete"; S. H. Lerch, "The Adjustment to Retirement of Professional Baseball Players," in *Sociology of Sport: Diverse Perspectives,* ed. S. L. Greendorfer and A. Yiannakis, pp. 138–148 (West Point, NY: Leisure Press, 1981); E. M. Blinde and T. M. Stratta, "The 'Sport Career Death' of College Athletes: Involuntary and Unanticipated Sport Exits," *Journal of Sport Behavior* 15 (March 1992): 3–20.

17. B. Svoboda and N. Vanek, "Retirement from High Level Competition," in *The Fifth World Congress of Sport Psychology*, ed. T. Orlick, J. T. Partington, and J. H. Salmela, pp. 166–175 (Ottawa, Canada: Coaching Association of Canada, 1982).

18. B. P. McPherson, "Retirement from Professional Sport: The Process and Problems of Occupational and Psychological Adjustment," *Sociological Symposium* 30 (1980): 126–143.

19. Sociologist Helen Ebaugh argues that the role exit is sociologically and psychologically intriguing since it implies that interaction is based not only on current definitions but, more important, on past identities that somehow linger on and define how people see and present themselves in their present identities. Role exit is "the process of disengagement from a role that is central to one's self-identity, and the reestablishment of an identity in a new role that takes into account one's ex role" (p. 1). The process of exiting a role comprises three primary characteristics: disengagement, dis-identification, and re-socialization. Disengagement encompasses withdrawing from the type of behavior associated with a former role. Dis-identification refers to the time when self-identification is no longer associated with the exited role. The re-socialization process is completed once an individual learns to incorporate his or her former self into a new role. H. R. F. Ebaugh, *Becoming an Ex: The Process of Role Exit* (Chicago: University of Chicago Press, 1988). Drahota and Eitzen broaden the scope of the role exit theory by incorporating characteristics unique to athletes, especially the involuntary nature of most exits. Interviews conducted with former professional athletes from various sports led the researchers to add four unique characteristics: (1) a stage of original doubts that precedes becoming a professional athlete; (2) the difference by the era in which the athlete played; (3) the "withdrawal" behavior associated with leaving the sport; and (4) the significance of the type of involuntary exit. J. T. Drahota and S. D. Eitzen, "The Role Exit of Professional Athletes," *Sociology of Sports Journal* 15 (September 1998): 263–278; Allison and Meyer extended the focus of role exit by introducing gender and participation in an individual sport as key variables affecting how tennis athletes experience the retirement process. M. T. Allison and C. Meyer, "Career Problems and Retirement among Elite Athletes: The Female Tennis Professional," *Sociology of Sport Journal* 5, no. 3 (September 1988): 212–222.

20. Status inconsistency and role conflict are other complications that may result from an unexpected NFL retirement. According to Stryker and Macke, the principle of expectancy congruence suggests that people require a consistent set of expectations with which to meet their experiences; however, the disjunction between expectations and status inconsistency can often result in stress. When the loss of a valued social identity leads to status inconsistency for the athlete it can also cause a conflict for those who benefit from his role as an NFL athlete. Parents, a spouse, girlfriends, extended family, childhood friends, and other associates often rely on congruence as a condition of their relationship with the athlete. S. Stryker and A. Macke, "Status Inconsistency and Role Conflict," *Annual Review of Sociology* 4 (1978): 57–90.

21. J. J. Coakley, "Leaving Competitive Sport: Retirement or Rebirth?," *Quest* 35, no. 1 (1983): 1–11.

22. A second major theoretical strand I draw from is self-concept theory, which sees role-identity salience and psychological centrality as closely linked. The self-concept theory has a long theoretical history as the conceptual link between the individual and larger society. Sociologically, self-concept is based on the notion that the self is fundamentally social in nature rather than being an isolated psychological unit. Similar to identity theory or identity salience, role-identity salience suggests that some role identities are more a part of the self than others and consequently have a variable effect on the self-concept. For example, Callera claims that for one person the occupational role identity may be the dominant aspect of the self, taking precedence over other role identities and affecting general self-perceptions and actions. Similarly, Stryker and Burke believe that when multiple roles do not reinforce one another they introduce identity competition or conflicts that complicate the reciprocal relationships between commitments, identity salience, identity standards, and self-relevant perceptions. P. L. Callera, "Role-Identity Salience," *Social Psychology Quarterly* 48 (1985): 203–214; Stryker and Burke, "The Past, Present, and Future of an Identity Theory."

23. NFL Europa began in 1991 as the World League of American Football, with 10 teams competing in the United States and Europe. National Football League, "News: NFL Europa Closes," *NFL News*, August 3, 2007, retrieved December 23, 2015, from http://www.nfl.com/news/story/09000d5d801308ec/article/nfl-europa-closes.

24. Ethnographer Jooyoung Lee writes about a similar social phenomenon between rappers and gang members in South Central Los Angeles. J. Lee, *Blowin' Up: Rap Dreams in South Central* (Chicago: University of Chicago Press, 2016).

25. Taylor and Ogilvie, "Career Transitions among Elite Athletes."

26. Killeya-Jones, "Identity Structure, Role Discrepancy and Psychological Adjustment in Male College Student-Athletes."

27. There is a discrepancy between published reports of his draft ranking and BK's claim of being selected in the second-round selection. In the recorded conversation BK states that he was drafted in the second round; however, the NFL draft records list BK as a third-round selection, the 84th player selected that year.

28. According to the 2006 NFL record and fact book, the waiver system is a procedure by which a player's contract is made available to other clubs in the league. During the procedure, the 31 other clubs either file claims to obtain the player or waive the opportunity to do so.

29. Upon conducting in-depth interviews and personal conversations along with quantitative analysis of dozens of current and former NFL players, based on Emile Durkheim's theoretical conception of anomie (a social phenomenon that represents the impact of rapid change on human beings), E. M. Carter and M. V. Carter discovered that rapid change occurring in the lives of NFL players potentially causes anomic characteristics that can lead to deviant/unnormative behavior. E. M. Carter and M. V. Carter, "Fame, Fortune, and Anomie: A Social Psychological Analysis of Deviance in the NFL," *Campbellsville Review* 2, no. 59 (2003): 83.

According to Bush and Simmons, the assumption underlying the anticipatory socialization concept is that if the individual is prepared ahead of time for the new role, in the sense of understanding the norms associated with that role, having the necessary skills to carry out that role, and becoming aware of expectations and rewards attached to the role, he or she will move into the new role easily and effectively. These scholars further argue that the one situation that seems to be an exception to this notion of role transition is the case in which role transition involves a loss in status. D. M. Bush and R. G. Simmons, "Socialization Process over the Life Course," in *Social Psychology: Sociological Perspective,* ed. M. Rosenberg and R. H. Turner, pp. 13–150 (New York: Basic Books, 1990).

30. I. Rosow, "The Transition to Old Age," in *Socialization to Old Age,* ed. I. Rosow, pp. 22–27 (Berkeley: University of California Press, 1974). Sociologist Ashley Mears discovered that in the fashion industry the careers of most models are over when they reach 26. A. Mears, *Pricing Beauty: The Making of a Fashion Model* (Oakland: University of California Press, 2011).

31. Neuropathologist Bennet Omalu determined that Waters's brain tissue had degenerated to that of an 85-year-old man with characteristics similar to those of early stage Alzheimer's victims, most likely from playing football. A. Schwarz, "Expert Ties Ex-Player's Suicide to Brain Damage," *The New York Times,* January 18, 2007, retrieved June 22, 2015, from http://www.nytimes.com/2007/01/18/sports/football/18waters .html?pagewanted=all&_r=0.

32. P. Sheridan, "Suicide of Ex-Eagle Andre Waters Hits Hard," *Free Republic,* November 22, 2006, retrieved June 21, 2015, from http://www.freerepublic.com/focus/f-news/ 1742477/posts.

33. Soon after signing his $68 million contract, Arrington filed a grievance with the NFL Players Association claiming the Redskins lied to him and wanted to cheat him out of $6.5 million in bonus money that he and his agent negotiated in good faith. T. Boswell, "The 6.5 Million Dollar Man," *The Washington Post,* March 25, 2004, retrieved June 22, 2015, from http://www.washingtonpost.com/archive/sports/ 2004/03/25/the-65-million-dollar-man/33d3067b-c1a0-489f-8dab-32c008bc1119/.

34. Paul Berrettini graduated from Notre Dame University in 1996, serves on the board of directors for the South Bend Center for the Homeless, and is a partner with Derrick Mayes in a safety and technology consulting corporate enterprise. A. Montoya, "Adventures Being Alex: My Adventures, Thoughts, and Observations as I Swing through Life," December 4, 2011, retrieved March 7, 2015, from http://alexmontoya619 .blogspot.com/2011/12/golden-memories-yes-you-can-go-home.html.

35. The sentiments expressed by Glen seem to align with views espoused by the Notre Dame football program, "serving as a captain of the Notre Dame football team is a privilege reserved for a select group of individuals. Often times, the title will supercede the glory of individual honors and accomplishments and can even transcend some of the social boundries of the time. C. Masters, "Notre Dame Remembering Its Past On Captains' Weekend," *Notre Dame Football,* 2018, retrieved March 5, 2018, from http:// www.und.com/sports/m-footbl/spec-rel/091103aaa.html.

36. T. Thompson, "GQ Coolest Athletes of All Time: Which Pick Are Genius and Which Are Jokes?," *Bleacher Report,* January 26, 2011, retrieved March 7, 2015, from http://bleacherreport.com/articles/584439-gq-coolest-athletes-of-all-time-which-picks-are-genius-and-which-are-jokes.

37. For an extensive investigation of the hidden costs of upward mobility and the Black community, see E. R. Cole and S. R. Omari, "Race, Class and the Dilemmas of Upward Mobility for African Americans," *Journal of Social Issues* 59 (November 2003): 785–802.

CHAPTER 12

1. F. Darabont, director and producer, *The Shawshank Redemption*, Video/DVD, 1994, Castle Rock Entertainment.

2. H. Edwards, "The Nation's Largest African American Video Oral History Collection," 2011, retrieved March 1, 2018, from http://www.thehistorymakers.org/biography/harry-edwards-41.

3. H. Edwards, "Sports within the Veil: The Triumphs, Tragedies and Challenges of Afro-American Involvement," *Annals of the American Academy of Political and Social Sciences* 445 (September 1979): 116–127.

4. H. Edwards, "The Olympic Project for Human Rights: An Assessment Ten Years Later," *Black Scholar* 10 (March–April 1979): 2–8.

5. Edwards, "The Olympic Project for Human Rights."

6. H. Edwards, "The Exploitation of Black Athletes," *AGB Reports* 25, no. 6 (November–December 1983): 37–46; H. Edwards, "The Single-Minded Pursuit of Sports Fame and Fortune Is Approaching an Institutional Triple Tragedy in Black Society," *Ebony* 43, no. 10 (1988): 138–140; Janet C. Harris, *Athletes and the American Hero Dilemma*, vol. 4 (Champaign, IL: Human Kinetics, 1994); M. Oliver, "Race, Class, and the Family's Orientation to Mobility through Sports," *Sociological Symposium* 30 (1980): 62–86.

7. Edwards, "The Single-Minded Pursuit of Sports Fame and Fortune Is Approaching an Institutional Triple Tragedy in Black Society."

8. Professor Krystal K. Beamon argues that "the consequences of overemphasizing athletic participation that have been identified in the literature are lower levels of academic achievement, higher expectations for professional sports careers as a means to upward mobility and economic viability, highly salient athletic identities, and lower levels of career maturity." K. K. Beamon, "Are Sports Overemphasized in the Socialization Process of African American Males? A Qualitative Analysis of Former Collegiate Athletes' Perception of Sport Socialization," *Journal of Black Studies* 41, no. 2 (August 2009), 281–300.

9. Edwards, "The Olympic Project for Human Rights."

10. Edwards, "The Exploitation of Black Athletes"; H. Edwards, "Crisis of Black Athletes on the Eve of the 21st Century," *Society* 37, no. 3 (March 2000): 9–13.

11. M. Koba, "Spending Big on Kids' Sports? You're Not Alone," CNBC, January 13, 2014, retrieved March 1, 2018, from https://www.cnbc.com/2014/01/13/youth-sports-is-a-7-billion-industryand-growing.html.

12. H. Kantor and B. Brenzel, "Urban Education and the 'Truly Disadvantaged': The Historical Roots of the Contemporary Crisis, 1945–1990," *Teachers College Record* 94, no. 2 (Winter 1992): 278–314; P. A. Noguera, "The Trouble with Black Boys: The Role and Influence of Environmental and Cultural Factors on the Academic Performance of African American Males," *Urban Education* 38, no. 4 (July 2003): 431–459.

13. H. Edwards, "Black Athletes: Minority Access to Sports Programs," *Current* 413 (1999): 15–21.
14. P. Ward and M. O'Sullivan, "Chapter 1: The Contexts of Urban Settings," *Journal of Teaching in Physical Education* 25 (October 2006): 348–362.
15. G. D. Borman and L. T. Overman, "Academic Resilience in Mathematics among Poor and Minority Students," *Elementary School Journal* 104, no. 3 (January 2004): 177–195; A. Livingston and J. Wirt, *The Condition of Education in Brief* (Washington, DC: National Center for Education Statistics, US Department of Education, 2004).
16. G. Toppo, "Integrated Schools Still a Dream 50 Years Later. Decades after 'Brown,' Income, Not the Law, Separates the Races," *USA Today*, March 1, 2008, pp. 1A–2A.
17. RFC Case Number: T-014-3709N, Court Case Number: 0:14-cv-03709; Plaintiff Counsel: Jason E. Luckasevic, Jason T. Shipp, David B. Rodes of Goldberg Perskey & White, PC.
18. P. D. Anderson, "NFL Concussion Litigation: Plaintiffs/Former Players," 2015, retrieved June 29, 2015, from http://nflconcussionlitigation.com/?page_id=274. In December 2016 the US Supreme Court denied petitions from two groups of retired NFL players to review the class action settlement between more than 20,000 retired NFL athletes and the NFL. The denial cleared the way for the settlement to go into effect sometime in early 2017. M. McCann, "As Expected, the Supreme Court Denies Review of NFL Concussion Settlement," *Sports Illustrated*, December 12, 2016, retrieved January 13, 2017, from http://www.si.com/nfl/2016/12/12/supreme-court-nfl-concussion-settlement-retired-players.
19. The Boston University CTE Center defines chronic traumatic encephalopathy as a progressive degenerative disease of the brain found in athletes (and others) with a history of repetitive brain trauma, including symptomatic concussion as well as asymptomatic subconcussive hits to the head. Boston University CTE Center, "What Is CTE?," 2009, retrieved June 29, 2015, from http://www.bu.edu/cte/about/what-is-cte/.
20. With the advent of the NFL concussion lawsuit, this question has taken on an additional significance. Former quarterbacks Bret Favre and Curt Warner are among a small but growing number of NFL athletes to publicly voice concerns about allowing their sons to play the sport. Conversely, Ed Riley, professor of anesthesiology at Stanford University, suggests that parents should let their children play. Riley argues that kids are "just as safe on the football field as they are in most of the other sports and activities we regard as a necessary part of a healthy adolescence." E. Riley, "G&T Guest Column: Research Suggests Parents Should Allow Kids to Play Football," *The Spokesman-Review*, February 8, 2015, retrieved June 29, 2015, from http://www.spokesman.com/stories/2015/feb/08/gt-guest-column-research-suggests-parents-should/.
21. While football has been the subject of numerous scientific studies and news reports, research presented at the annual meeting of the American Academy of Orthopedic Surgeons found that high school female soccer athletes suffer concussions at a significantly higher rate than athletes who play football, boys' soccer, basketball, baseball, softball, volleyball, and wrestling. B. Raven, "High School Girls Soccer Had Highest Concussion Rate for Decade," March 25, 2017, retrieved October 23, 2017, from http://www.mlive.com/news/us-world/index.ssf/2017/03/concussions.html.

INDEX